Leveraging Japan

George Fields
Fields Associates
Japan

Hotaka Katahira
University of Tokyo

Jerry Wind
The Wharton School

with
Robert E. Gunther

Leveraging Japan

Marketing to the New Asia

Jossey-Bass Publishers
San Francisco

Jossey-Bass books and products are available through most bookstores. To contact Jossey-Bass directly, call (888) 378-2537, fax to (800) 605-2665, or visit our website at www.josseybass.com.

Substantial discounts on bulk quantities of Jossey-Bass books are available to corporations, professional associations, and other organizations. For details and discount information, contact the special sales department at Jossey-Bass.

 Manufactured in the United States of America on Lyons Falls Pathfinder Tradebook. This paper is acid free and 100 percent totally chlorine free.

Library of Congress Cataloging-in-Publication Data

Fields, George.
   Leveraging Japan : marketing to the new Asia / George Fields, Hotaka Katahira, Jerry Wind with Robert E. Gunther.—1st ed.
      p.   cm.—(The Jossey-Bass business & management series)
   Includes bibliographical references and index.
   ISBN 0-7879-4663-X (acid-free paper)
   1. Marketing—Japan.   2. Marketing—Asia.   3.
Consumers—Japan—Attitudes.   4. Consumers—Asia—Attitudes.   I.
Katahira, Hotaka, date   II. Wind, Jerry.   III. Title.   IV. Series.
HF5415.12.J3F54 1999
658.8'0095—dc21

99-6831

The Jossey-Bass
Business & Management Series

Contents

Preface

The Japanese market is an enigma to outside observers. After World War II, the world counted Japan out, and then it was surprised when the Japanese economy surged forward to become one of the most powerful on the globe. The view shifted to Japan as an unstoppable juggernaut. When its economy faltered, jaws dropped again. As with most puzzling pictures, the true explanations are only found by probing beneath the surface.

Beneath all the visible changes that have dominated the media, there have been fundamental transformations in the Japanese consumer and market. A rise in single working women, a shift from a producer-driven to a consumer-driven market, innovations in distribution, and a relaxation of regulations are just a few of the pounding waves of change that are reshaping the coastline of the Japanese market. All of these changes have created new opportunities for the companies that have the marketing savvy to take advantage of them. These changes have meant that the insulated Japanese market has become more open than ever to new ideas and new entrants.

There may be no better time to enter Japan. As radical as this idea may seem, given the nation's recent economic instability, many companies obviously share this view, as evidenced by an upsurge in foreign investment. Japan continues to be the second-largest market in the world and a very important gateway to the rest of Asia.

The current economic turmoil creates opportunities, such as falling real-estate prices and the restructuring of financial services, that have attracted new investments by Western firms.

Marketing skill will be one of the key factors that separates winners and losers in this new consumer-driven market. Large corporations can no longer throw their weight around like sumo wrestlers. Customers will no longer "drink in" the latest products at high prices. This has tremendous implications for companies in Japan, as well as for those considering entering the Japanese market:

• Companies in Japan (both foreign and domestic) need to develop more sophisticated marketing, yet with an understanding that it will never be "Western." The culture and structure of the Japanese market—and its past evolution—continue to give a distinctive character to Japanese marketing, which we will explore in this book.
• Companies considering entering Japan may be able to leverage their marketing strengths in new ways if they understand these changes. Any companies engaged in marketing to emerging Asian markets can benefit from our insights on Japanese marketing and its implications for Asia.

These insights are drawn from decades of experience in Japan. George Fields was vice chairman of the largest research company in Asia, with direct responsibility in Japan and other parts of Asia. He is in great demand as a consultant and speaker on Japanese and Asian trends. Hotaka Katahira, as the first marketing professor at the University of Tokyo, is a pioneer in the formal study of marketing in Japan and around the world. Jerry Wind, marketing professor at the Wharton School, is an authority on global marketing strategy and a frequent lecturer and consultant in Japan and other Asian countries. In this book, we summarize some of the key insights into the Japanese market that we have developed in cooperation with major foreign and domestic corporations in Japan and Asia.

These insights can give you an advantage in entering Japan and using it as a gateway to Asia. For foreign managers, the book offers an examination of effective marketing strategies and how the knowledge of marketing changes can be used to enter and thrive in Japan. For domestic managers, it offers fresh insight into a market that you may not know as well as you think you do. (Japanese managers are as guilty as foreigners in holding onto outdated wisdom, attributing to culture the distinctive characteristics that actually are the result of market structure.) For students and scholars, the book offers one of the first comprehensive examinations of successful marketing in Japan and Asia.

The forces of change have led to new opportunities in Japan and Asia, and transformed the role and practice of marketing. The exhibit below illustrates these relationships and summarizes the key issues covered in the book.

We open the book with an examination of the current increase in foreign investment in Japan and a discussion of opportunities, myths, and realities about the market. Sometimes we need to relearn our hard-earned lessons about Japan because what we think we

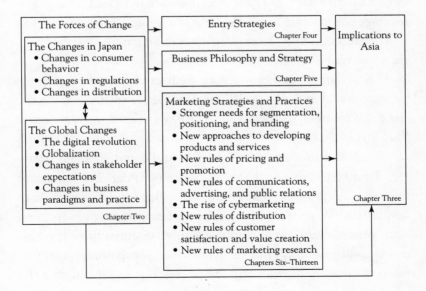

know just isn't true anymore. The second chapter examines some of the forces transforming the Japanese market, including the emergence of a new consumer, shifts in regulations, and restructuring of distribution channels, as well as global changes such as the growth of the Internet. The third chapter explores how Japan serves as a gateway to Asia, followed by an examination of strategies for market entry in Japan in Chapter Four. Finally, in Chapter Five, we look at the increasing importance of marketing as a corporate philosophy.

Beginning in Chapter Six, we turn to a more detailed discussion of specific aspects of marketing in Japan. We explore segmentation, branding and positioning, new product development, pricing and promotion, advertising and public relations, cybermarketing, distribution, customer satisfaction, and marketing research. We examine the traditional approaches in each area of marketing, the emerging changes, and how they create opportunities. Some of these changes and opportunities are summarized in the table on the next page.

This book is written not only for passive reading but as a way to stimulate your thinking and the creation of your own strategies in Japan. To help in this process, we offer "Points of Leverage" at the close of each chapter. These questions are designed to help you leverage the insights in your specific situation. We encourage you to work through these to explore what the changes described here mean for your own strategies.

U.S. dollar/yen exchange rates have fluctuated wildly during the period covered in the book. Where possible, we use the rates at the time the number is cited. Otherwise, we used a conversion of ¥120/per U.S. dollar.

We should also note that the successful companies and strategies described in this book should not be considered *representative* examples of Japanese marketing or a "Japanese" approach to marketing. We are focusing on the best practices of exceptional firms that are looking toward the future (in contrast to the best practices of yesterday's market). These are, for the most part, pioneering firms that are among the pacesetters in recognizing the

Forces of Change	Possible Opportunities for Leverage
Japan's central role in the rest of Asia	Using Japan as a gateway to Asia (Chapter Three)
New consumer, relaxing regulations, and shifting distribution	New opportunities for market entry (Chapter Four)
Shift from producer-driven to consumer-driven market	The rising importance of marketing expertise (Chapter Five)
Increasing heterogeneity of Japanese customers	Importance of segmentation, positioning, and branding (Chapter Six)
More demanding and individual customers	More customer-focused approaches to developing products and services (Chapter Seven)
Greater competition on value	Increased attention to pricing and promotion (Chapter Eight)
Changing relationships between customers and large corporations	More emphasis on creative messages in advertising (Chapter Nine)
Spread of Internet technology	Opportunities for cybermarketing (Chapter Ten)
Shifts in regulations, mobility, and consumer demands	Emergence of new distribution channels (Chapter Eleven)
Demand for more professional rather than personal relationships	Rising interest in value and customer service (Chapter Twelve)
More diverse and fast-changing markets	Increased advantage from marketing research (Chapter Thirteen)
Overall changes in the Japanese market and changes in the global digital environment	Greater opportunities for success for companies who understand the changing marketing paradigm (Chapters One through Thirteen)

power of marketing in Japan. While their examples do not offer recipes for success, they do provide insight into new opportunities in the Japanese market and suggest ways companies can build the marketing strength to capitalize on these opportunities.

If there is one thing we have learned from Japan's post-war experience, it is never to underestimate their resourcefulness. As Minoru Makihara, chairman of Mitsubishi Corporation, commented, Japan must take advantage of its economic challenges "to redefine soci-

[1]*International Herald Tribune*, April 12, 1999.

ety."[1] This redefinition will create new opportunities. As Japan moves through this phase, the nation will probably be more open and interesting than in the past. It will continue to be a vital market in any global strategy. Although Asia presents a very complex fabric of different cultures and markets, Japan can serve as an introductory course—just as you might go to London, Brussels, or Amsterdam if you were thinking of European entry.

You may be puzzled by the Japanese market. You may be frustrated by it. But if you ignore Japan, you are missing out on tremendous opportunities there and in the rest of Asia for years to come.

Acknowledgments

W e are very grateful for the insight, formally and informally, from a wide range of executives with experience in Japan and Asia. Although not an exhaustive list, we would like to acknowledge the perspectives contributed by Chris Walker of HMV Japan; Hajime Saburi, general manager of the corporate office of Mercedes-Benz Japan Co. Ltd.; Robert Simon, president of Estée Lauder K.K.; Sue Brockman of REI; and Evan Denhardt of Hanna Andersson.

The book was originally planned as a collection of readings, and a number of authors willingly contributed their papers to us. Because of the many changes in the Japanese market, we decided to write a book on our own rather than edit the book of readings. We tried to reflect their inputs as much as possible in the present book. We owe much of the content of the present book to the original contributions. We would like to express the foremost thanks to the following authors:

Masatoshi Ito (Ajinomoto, Co., Ltd.)
Akira Sakaida (Hakuhodo, Ltd.)
Tadashi Kuga (Hosei University)
Ichiro Furukawa (Hitotsubashi University)
Hiroshige Hayashi (Novaction Japan, Inc.)
Hiroshi Tanaka (Hosei University)
Masahiko Yamanaka (Ajinomoto, Co., Ltd.)

This book also would not have come together without the assistance of Abigail Radice and Karen Sherry in Jerry Wind's office, who managed an endless stream of conference calls, notes, manuscripts, and permissions that were shuttled from one side of the world to the other—helping to keep these far-flung authors on the same page. We are grateful for the graphic genius of John Carstens in the Wharton Marketing Department, who was able to transform the most obtuse transnational scribbles into the polished figures you see here. We would like to thank Tom Parker and Masaki Yano for their research contributions in their respective parts of the globe. They substantially enhanced the content, particularly in exploring advances in electronic commerce. Finally, we would like to thank our wives for their patience and support through the late night and early morning phone calls, long travel hours, and incessant work on this manuscript.

We are grateful to our editor Cedric Crocker for his patient persistence and skilled hand in bringing this project to fruition. The manuscript also benefitted greatly from the attention of Cheryl Greenway, Stephanie Kang, and Kathe Sweeney at Jossey-Bass, as well as Brittney Corrigan-McElroy and Kerry Conroy at Interactive Composition Corporation.

The full list of people who contributed to making this project a success—and to the lifetime of study that is reflected in the broader insights contained herein—would be impossible to enumerate.

About the Authors

George Fields

George Fields is one of the most sought-after authorities on Japanese markets and marketing. He was involved in market-entry projects for such firms as American Express, Avon, BMW, Estée Lauder, Levi Strauss, Johnson & Johnson, Kentucky Fried Chicken, Nestlé, Procter & Gamble, and Unilever. He was nominated by *Fortune* in 1989 as one of the "25 People You Ought To Know in Asia." In addition to his work in Japan, he has also been responsible for operations in South Korea, Hong Kong, Singapore, and Malaysia. He was vice chairman of AGB Pacific, the largest research company in Asia, which was later acquired by A.C. Nielsen. He is the author of twelve books, including the popular *From Bonsai to Levis* (1983), *Gucci on the Ginza* (1989), and *Japanese Market Culture* (1991), which introduced many managers to the intricacies of the Japanese market. *The* Japanese version of *From Bonsai to Levis* sold 80,000 copies before it was rewritten by the author for an English-speaking audience. It became the best seller of the month for Macmillan when it was published in 1983. Fields is a regular contributor to various print media and is well-known in Japan for anchoring the top-rated weekly news program, "Broadcaster," with more than ten million viewers, and for his regular radio program, "George Fields's Business File." He serves as councilor for various committees, including the Japan Productivity Center for Socio-Economic Development.

Hotaka Katahira

Hotaka Katahira, professor of marketing science at the University of Tokyo, is a leader in research on marketing in Japan. He has consulted on brand management and other marketing issues for major Japanese firms, including Toyota, NEC, Ajinomoto, and Hakuhodo. Katahira is the director of the Japan Institute of Marketing Science and editor of the *Journal of Marketing Science*. He is the author of several books in Japanese, including *Marketing Science* (1987) and *A New Approach to Consumer Choice* (1991). He is also coauthor of *Marketing Information Revolution* (1991).

Jerry Wind

Jerry Wind, the Lauder Professor and a professor of marketing at the Wharton School, is one of the most cited authors in the field of marketing and a leader and pioneer in marketing research. He has consulted with many Fortune 500 firms and non-U.S. multinationals on globalization and business strategy, as well as marketing strategy. As the founding director of the Lauder Institute of Management and International Studies, Wind has been active in international research and education, particularly in Japan. He is now founding director of the SEI Center for Advanced Studies in Management, the first "think tank" on management education for the twenty-first century. His contributions to the field have been recognized with some of the most prestigious awards in marketing, including the Parlin Award and the American Marketing Association's Distinguished Educator Award. He is author or editor of more than a dozen books on marketing and related topics, including *Driving Change* (1998), coauthored with former *Fortune* editor Jeremy Main.

Robert Gunther

Robert Gunther is founder of Robert Gunther Communications and former director of publications in the executive education division of the Wharton School. He is coauthor of *Reinventing Fatherhood*

(1993), *I'd Rather Die Than Give a Speech* (1994; paperback—1995), *Hypercompetition* (1994; reissued in paperback as *Hypercompetitive Rivalries*, 1995), *The Wealthy 100* (1996), and *Wharton on Dynamic Competitive Strategy* (1997).

Leveraging Japan

1

The Fourth Rush

A large orange Hermes box in the middle of Tokyo's posh Ginza shopping district seemed strangely out of place, given the gloomy economic picture in Japan. Was this bold promotion a sign that the company was out of step with the times? Was it wishful thinking? Not at all. The success of Hermes, Tiffany's, Mercedes-Benz, and other luxury marketers, the rise of category killers and outlet malls, and the continued success of long-standing brands such as Coca-Cola and McDonald's are all indications that there is more to the Japanese market than its economic crisis. Tiffany & Company continued to grow its jewelry business at 13 percent per year from 1996 to 1998, despite the lackluster overall economy in Japan.[1] Tiffany's sales rose 21 percent year-to-year in the first half of 1998, even while sales fell by 16 percent in the rest of Asia.[2] Gucci is expanding its presence in Japan, opening several large stores in rapid succession, and it has a three-year backlog of orders from Japan for its version of the popular Hermes "Kelly" bag (named for Grace Kelly). Hermes, with sales up 30 percent in the first half of 1998, plans to open a flagship store in the Mercedes's Ginza in 2000. Mercedes's new "A Class" model reached its first-year target of selling 7,000 cars well before the end of 1998.[3] There is a wait of five to twenty-four months for some Mercedes- Benz models. At the other end of the market, McDonald's Japan posted a 13.4-percent increase in sales in 1998 (and nearly an equal increase in profits) driven by skillful pricing strategies and the opening of 459 new stores.[4]

What is going on here? Against the apparent economic stagnation, there is another cycle moving. There have been tremendous shifts in the Japanese market, a rise of new consumers, relaxation of regulations, and fundamental shifts in marketing. Sales of luxury goods are fueled by young women in their twenties, working women with few responsibilities, and the over-sixty "silver" generation who have already paid off their homes and are sitting on the largest savings hoard in the world. Other shifts, such as discounting and value consciousness, were underway when the recession hit and they have been accelerated by the economic crisis and increasing globalization—again creating new opportunities.

Companies who are able to discern these changes and capitalize on them are finding that this may be the best time to enter Japan. The Japanese market is essential in capitalizing on the opportunities across Asia. An October 1998 survey of foreign companies in Japan found that nearly three-quarters of participants cited the market's size and growth potential as key reasons for the market's attractiveness.[5]

Although some companies have cut back on their Japanese investments, others are moving in agressively. Companies such as Starbucks, the Gap, and Merrill Lynch are expanding operations. Given the recent headlines about Japan, are all these new entrants crazy? They are not. These new entrants recognize that despite the turbulent restructuring of the Japanese economy—and in some cases because of it—there are tremendous opportunities due to changes in the Japanese market and its consumers.

The economic recession does create challenges, but it also creates favorable circumstances. Plummeting real-estate prices and high unemployment are making it easy to set up shop and find workers in Japan, both of which have been challenges for foreign entrants in the past. As shown in Exhibit 1.1, Tokyo's astronomical real-estate prices are now almost in line with those of New York City.

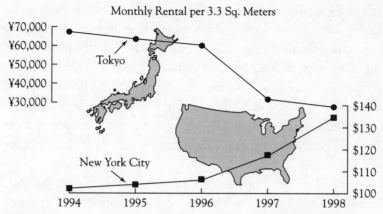

Monthly Rental per 3.3 Sq. Meters

Note: Bases: Tokyo—Central Maruno-Uchi/Otemarhi Arm; NYC—Mid-Town Averages

Exhibit 1.1. Office Rentals in Tokyo and New York City
Source: Nihon Keizai Shinbun, January 1, 1999.

Foreign companies also have a productivity advantage, particularly in the service sector. A September 1997 Ministry of International Trade and Industry (MITI) survey found that productivity per employee was 1.7 times higher for foreign companies in Japan than for Japanese companies and 1.9 times higher for non-manufacturing companies.[6]

What are the insights of creative domestic firms that are taking advantage of the market shifts to build their positions in Japan and Asia? How can you find the opportunities in these changes?

The Fourth Wave of Investment

Despite the turbulence of Japanese markets, foreign investors continue to swim like salmon against the current into Japan. A 1999 Japanese External Trade Organization (JETRO) Investment White Paper found that foreign direct investment in Japan from April through September 1998 was more than double that of the previous year. (It had tapered off slightly in 1997 after a tremendous surge in 1996.) Stock and ownership acquisitions reached an all-time high of $4.9 billion (¥593 billion) in 1997. Although manufacturing investments were up slightly, most of the new investment was from non manufacturing sectors, particularly financial institutions and insurance, driven by the financial Big Bang. United States financial services firms, for example, invested $1.3 billion (¥171 billion) in Japan in the first half of 1998. There were also increases in foreign investments in areas such as computer software and networks, advertising, cinema complexes, and satellite digital broadcasting.

Many of these companies were finding profit in Japan. A December 1998 survey of more than 3,000 foreign-capitalized firms found that more than half had increased profits over the year before, and that a third expected continued growth in 1999.[7] Investments by foreign capital companies in Japan increased threefold between 1991 and 1995.[8]

The influx of foreign investment into Japan has been so great that it has led to speculation that a "fourth rush" into Japan is underway, as illustrated in Exhibit 1.2. The first was just after World War II, the second in the late 1960s and early 1970s when the West began to pressure Japan to open its markets, and the third came with the Plaza Accord of 1985, which brought in finance and brokerage entries in particular.[9] The fourth is now driven by changes in consumer attitude and demographics that are

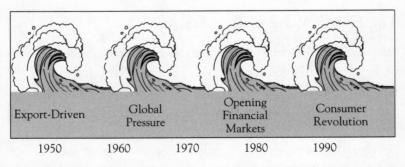

| Export-Driven | Global Pressure | Opening Financial Markets | Consumer Revolution |

| 1950 | 1960 | 1970 | 1980 | 1990 |

Exhibit 1.2. Four Waves of Opening Japanese Markets

creating new opportunities for foreign entrants to enter the Japanese market.

There is increasing acceptance of foreign firms. A 1998 survey by Nikkei Research of 4,000 men and women in Japan found that a significant portion of the population had no aversion to dealing with a foreign capital financial services firm (see Exhibit 1.3). They also showed a high awareness of foreign banking, brokerage, and insurance companies, as shown in Exhibit 1.4. (It should be noted that, with a 35.7-percent response rate, these awareness levels may be inflated.)

This may be a trying time for the Japanese economy, but it could be a key opportunity for companies entering or expanding their position in Japan to create a foundation for future growth in Asia.

Changing Consumers

Beneath the shifts in the economy, there are more fundamental changes taking place among Japanese consumers. Changes in demographics—in particular, a rise in unmarried working women—and

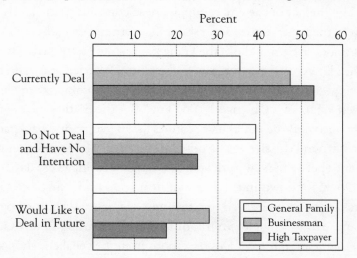

Exhibit 1.3. Dealings with Foreign Capital Financial Services
Source: Nikkei Research, 1998.

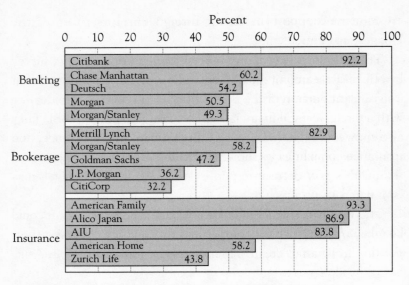

Exhibit 1.4. Awareness Rankings for Foreign Firms
Source: Nikkei Research, 1998.

changes in consumer behavior and attitudes are reshaping the post-war economy and mentality.

The impact of the emerging Japanese consumer can clearly be seen in the heart of the Ginza shopping district. A weathered sign-post stands in the middle of the Eddie Bauer store on the second floor of the Hankyu department store in the Ginza. Wooden arrows on the old rural sign point to: "New York 10,807 km., Hamburg 8,985 km., Aspen 9,470 km., Chicago 10,067 km." But the Eddie Bauer flying goose logo and the duffel bags, canvas fishing vests, and backpacks that surround the sign give a different reading. They show that the distance between New York and Tokyo is decreasing every day.

One floor down in the Hankyu store, one of the first two Gap stores in Japan is engaged in a thriving business. A smiling young Japanese father juggles an infant as he walks through Baby Gap. As American soul artist Des'ree croons from the speakers, shoppers browse through racks of "Madison Avenue" pants. Striped Oxfords and jeans are on sale at prices comparable to Western stores in a nation where the cost of a shirt had typically been greatly inflated by a long chain of middlemen. Opening-day sales at this particular Gap topped ¥10 million ($100,000), and the sales figures of the new stores quickly became among the highest of the retailer's 1,600 worldwide stores. The company has since opened more than thirty stores in Japan.

On the fourth floor, past the Timberland store, the escalator glides up into the sprawling HMV music store, where Japanese youth move through aisles of thousands of CDs. The latest albums of popular Japanese rock groups like Mr. Children and Ulfuls and Tomomi Kahara sit side by side with albums by global pop stars such as Eric Clapton, George Michael, and Bon Jovi. Along one wall, a magazine rack displays Cosmopolitan, Vogue, Elle, GQ, and Esquire. Teenagers pick up headphones to sample music from all parts of the world. Seven years after entering Japan in 1989, British-based HMV had opened eighteen stores, generating more than $200 million (¥21 trillion) in sales. Its nine stores in Tokyo outsell the chain's ninety stores in Canada.

In April 1998, the American president of Eddie Bauer traveled to Tokyo to celebrate the opening of the company's twenty-ninth store. The Shinjuku Southern Terrace Store attracted the president's attention because it had set a world record for daily sales, with approximately ¥14 billion ($106,000) in daily sales. This occurred during one of the most turbulent economic periods in Japan's recent history. The company continues to experience dramatic growth in both stores and sales since its arrival in Japan, as shown in Exhibit 1.5.

Following the flight path of the Eddie Bauer goose are a host of other firms. In 1998, two years after Starbucks entered Japan, it had opened more than twenty-six stores and increased the pace of its expansion, announcing plans to build 250 Japanese stores by 2004.[10] It has outpaced entrenched competitors and lower-priced rivals. Starbucks sees Japan as a key beachhead for Asian expansion. One of its biggest problems: The long lines of consumers snaking

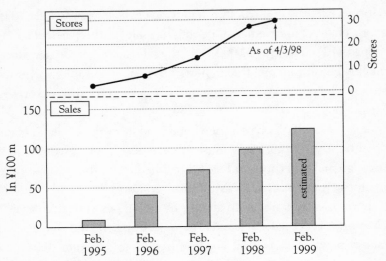

Note: February 1995 period shows store performance over six months.

Exhibit 1.5. Eddie Bauer Japan: Performance and Stores
Source: Nikkei Ryutsu Shinbun, April 7, 1998.

out of Starbucks coffee shops could alienate some consumers. For the company, it is a nice problem to have.

L.L. Bean had opened sixteen stores in Japan by early 1999. Sports Authority shook up sports specialty retailing when it opened its first store in Nagoya in the summer of 1996, and it continued to expand. Foot Locker soon joined in. By 1999, Office Depot and OfficeMax had each opened three stores, placing pressure on Japanese office supply firms. Saturn shipped its first cars over to new dealerships in Japan in 1997. Drug store Walgreen, furniture retailer Crate and Barrel, French supermarket Carrefour, copy store Kinko's, Electrolux, and discounter Price CostCo are just a few of the other recent arrivals.[11] Toys "R" Us, one of the pioneering foreign retailers to enter Japan, estimated that its seventy Japanese stores would generate sales of ¥100 billion ($840 million) in the first quarter of 1999.[12] These companies are not simply transplanting Western businesses to Japan— they are using their global brands to develop distinctly Japanese businesses.

Leveraging the World's Second-Largest Market

The Japan visible in this rising consumer market is not the wounded samurai of the news headlines. Nor is it the impenetrable walled market discussed in the boardrooms of Detroit's auto companies. While the Japanese economy is facing unprecedented struggles and changes, the emerging nation is very much alive. This vibrant consumer market—the second largest in the world—is unlike anything Japan has seen in the past. A transformation is taking place, creating new opportunities for those companies that haven't passed by Japan on their way to other parts of Asia. "If you are not in Japan, you are missing out on a big opportunity for a number of years," says Robert Simon, former chairman of Estée Lauder K.K., one of the most successful foreign cosmetic firms in Japan. "No matter how big the potential is in most of Asia, it will take time to develop."

Asian markets may be the future, but Japan is the present. While Vietnamese consumers are buying Honda Cub motorbikes, Japanese consumers are buying BMWs and Mercedes. More than 21 percent of Gucci's worldwide sales come from Japan, and an estimated 70 percent of sales are to Japanese buyers (including visitors to Milan, Hawaii, and so on).[13] As shown in Exhibit 1.6, Japan's gross domestic product (GDP) per capita overshadows almost every other country.[14] Japan's per capita GDP is 3.4 times that of South Korea, 8.7 times that of Malaysia, 54.6 times that of China, and 30 percent more than that of the United States. Even after real estate and financial shocks, Japan still boasted a hefty $10.3 trillion (¥1,195 trillion) in household savings in early 1997.[15]

Even with recent declines, the Japanese GDP per capita exceeds $30,000, ahead of most advanced nations and at least parallel with the United States. It was only in 1980 that the Japanese GDP rose above the $10,000 mark usually associated with developed nations. By 1995, Japan had more than tripled its GDP per capita.

In sheer size, the Japanese economy accounts for more of the world GDP than any other nation besides the United States, as

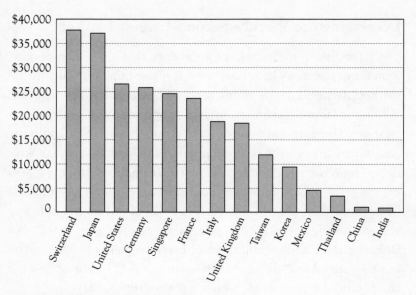

Exhibit 1.6. GDP per Capita
Source: Comparative International Statistics, 1995, BOJ, Economic Planning Agency, in *Japan 1996: An International Comparison* (Keizai Koho Center, 1996).

shown in Exhibit 1.7. Japan's contribution to the world GDP outranks those of Oceana, China, and the rest of Asia combined.

Some companies and trade negotiators, particularly from the United States, were already suffering from "Japan fatigue," bypassing Japan for other parts of Asia. But as Asian economies have stumbled, many have realized that in the short term, the money is in Japan. In the long term, the Japanese market and economy provides one of the best platforms for success in Asia.

Many companies have recognized the importance of this market. Equitable Life Insurance was inspired to make a serious commitment to Japan after it realized that capturing just 1 percent of the Japanese life insurance market would result in insurance business equivalent to the fifteenth-largest American life insurer. In some markets, Japanese unit volume is as great as it is in the United States even though there are only half as many people.[16]

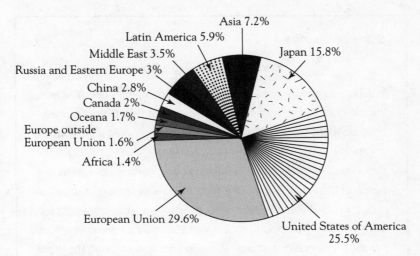

Exhibit 1.7. The World According to GDP (%)
Source: Economic Planning Agency, 1996.

Open for Business

This large market, once locked behind regulations, complex distribution systems, and loyal and enigmatic consumers, is now open for business. The changes in the Japanese market are a sign of a fundamental revolution: the emergence of a true consumer market. Japan's move to a consumer market can not only offer insight into the development of other Asian economies, but observe key Japanese players in their development as well.

Post-war Japan was dominated by large corporations churning out a steady stream of products that were snatched up by willing customers. Customers liked newness and change, but also tended to be more averse to risk and more quality-conscious than their Western counterparts. A new product from a respected corporation had nearly universal appeal, reducing the need for positioning and segmentation. Pricing and promotion played a minor role. Advertising focused on mood rather than benefits. Market research focused on quantitative measures such as market share and brand awareness rather than qualitative input such as communication

---

Signs of Change

Showing Their True Colors

In Japan, a nation that values harmony and conformity above all else, the idea of sporting a hairstyle that stood out was almost unthinkable. Up to the early 1990s, hair coloring was unheard of, except for the middle-aged with graying temples. In fact, a best-selling novel described the trials of a girl whose hair was naturally brownish in a nation of black hair. Today, one has only to walk through the sea of brown-headed youth in the streets of Harajuku—the center of teen fashion—on a weekend to realize that young Japanese consumers have few reservations about "showing their true colors." The word *chapatsu* (brown hair) entered the Japanese vocabulary in the mid-1990s—and not as a derogatory term. A survey of 1,000 Tokyo youths (between the ages of 19 and 22) found that 20 percent of females either bleach or dye their hair. Even more surprising, 16 percent of males in this age group sport *chapatsu*. A 1996 survey of single women between the ages of 20 and 35 found that 52 percent have dyed their hair and 32 percent were planning to do it within the next year. A market research organization estimated the size of the market for hair coloring in 1994 to be ¥53 billion (approximately $530 million), up 12 percent from just one year before.

---

effectiveness and persuasion. In a market in which there were numerous competitive entries due to rapid growth, the focus was on product quality and on being the first to fill the shelf space or showrooms. Developing channels of distribution and a corporate identity as a reliable supplier were the priorities, rather than creating differentiation through brand personalities. In a market in which the manufacturer dominated, there was no need to understand the customer.

This parallels the development of U.S. and European markets, but on an accelerated scale. To speed up the process of development, Japan relied much more heavily on scaffolding regulations and economic controls than the United States did. Now that the Japanese economy has emerged as one of the most powerful in the world, these "training wheels" are no longer an advantage; in fact, they threaten to slow it down and trip it up if Japan cannot dismantle them and create a more open economy. This is a central focus of Japanese government policy today. But the government and companies are still changing far more slowly than consumers. This gap creates opportunities for foreign entrants and creative domestic competitors.

Now, a market that was once treated as homogenous—where even experienced marketers spoke of "we Japanese"—has proven to have distinctive tastes. Skill in marketing has become a crucial factor for success. But companies cannot merely transplant their successful Western strategies into the Japanese market. They have to understand the complex mix of tradition and innovation that characterizes today's Japanese market.

While the overall growth of the Japanese economy is slow, market changes are creating pockets of new opportunities. Department store sales are declining, but convenience store sales and frozen food sales are increasing as more women enter the workforce. While the overall car market may be decreasing, there has been an increase in luxury car purchases. Sales of flat-screen televisions, cell phones, and personal computers are also on the rise.

Myths and Realities of the Japanese Market

Several interrelated forces have conspired to transform the Japanese market. There have been fundamental shifts in the nature of the Japanese consumer and the emergence of creative entrepreneurs to meet these new consumer needs. Consumer shifts have been precipitated by an increase in working women and a steadily rising

Signs of Change

Humble Weddings

Major Tokyo hotels once did a considerable business in lavish wedding ceremonies. More than half of couples had such traditional weddings, often with price tags in the millions of yen. Now, more value-conscious young couples are opting for *jimi-jon*, or "humble weddings," a troubling trend for the hotels. Couples are marrying in small ceremonies in Japan or even Hawaii or Switzerland. A few years ago, to have such a small wedding would have meant losing face. By 1996, however, only 12 percent of single women between the ages of 20 and 35 said they would choose a traditional hotel wedding. For these young consumers, even tradition has its price. Some of those who are having formal weddings are importing Western traditions— and even whole churches (brought from Europe and reconstructed), priests, and choirs—showing the fascination with the West and the secularization of the marriage ceremony.

marriage age. Changes have been encouraged by the slow, steady loosening of the stranglehold of regulations. And they have been driven forward by a typhoon of technology and innovation sweeping through distribution channels.

Changes in Japanese consumers, regulation, and distribution have turned traditional marketing wisdom about Japan on its head. In the old market, Japanese corporate leaders encouraged the myth that because of its traditional values, the Japanese social infrastructure was unique and immutable. According to this view, the *keiretsu* (networks of Japanese firms), the byzantine distribution systems, and the trading customs were all an intrinsic part of these values. Thus, they were difficult, if not impossible, to change. But recent transformations in the Japanese market are exposing these views as myths.

Consider a few of the "myths" about the Japanese market that have been contradicted by recent experience:

Myth: Japanese customers make purchases based on relationships with retailers and manufacturers, so they rarely shop around.

Reality: Japanese customers shop around for value. Young consumers, in particular, do as much comparison shopping as their Western peers—and perhaps even more. Consider a study by MITI that asked consumers in New York, Tokyo, and London: "Do you shop around for a better deal in making a purchase?" Among older consumers, New Yorkers and Londoners were far more likely to shop around than their Japanese peers. The surprising result was for the under-twenty-nine group. In this age group, 75 percent of New York youth and 64 percent of Londoners shopped around for better deals. But in Tokyo, 78 percent of all young people would shop around for a better deal. This is nearly double the percentage of Tokyo consumers over fifty years of age.

The Japanese market, which once was differentiated based on social status (for example, from employment in a large corporation or seniority in a given career), is now being differentiated based on age, gender, and psychosocial criteria. There is no longer a coherent national system of values, and a new emphasis on individuality is expressing itself in a greater independence in all decisions, including purchases.

Myth: Japanese consumers equate price with quality.

Reality: Japanese consumers are now intensely concerned with price. In some cases, they are more price sensitive than their Western counterparts. Whereas the traditional Japanese customer demanded quality at any price, today's customers are seeking value. While more than 70 percent of retailers sold products at manufacturer's suggested price in 1998, only 29.4 percent were still following that practice five price-busting years later. The rest had cut prices.[17] At the height of discounting in 1993, one out of every two suits was bought from a discounter. In general, Japanese customers are less willing to compromise quality for price than their Western peers.

(Many discounters failed to see this, offering shoddy products at reduced prices, and they quickly lost their newfound markets to major brands, which had lowered their prices in response but maintained high quality.) Price is now a key competitive weapon.

Myth: Japanese customers are fiercely nationalistic, making it hard for foreign companies to enter the market.

Reality: If Japanese customers scorn foreign products, they don't show it. Japan is far more open to foreign products than some of its neighbors. Ninety-two percent of Japanese consumers said they prefer a superior product regardless of its nation of origin, compared to just 59 percent of respondents in South Korea and 68 percent in China.[18] Products no longer have to be produced by Japanese workers to be accepted. McDonald's dominates fast food, Coca-Cola in soft drinks, Schick in razors, and Mars in pet foods. Japanese customers increasingly look for the best value, wherever it is produced. Japanese brands are still strong, but customers have accepted a dramatic rise in imports produced by offshore and foreign manufacturers (usually sold under Japanese brands). Even sales of import cars (including, for example, Hondas made in the United States) doubled between 1991 and 1995, and foreign cars rose from 4 percent to 11 percent of all new car registrations between 1991 and 1996.

Myth: Japanese consumers are conservative and will buy only well-known brands.

Reality: Consumers are willing to experiment with new tastes and brands, as shown in the rise of Asahi dry beer discussed later on. The initial rise of private brands in the late 1980s indicated the willingness of customers to trade a brand image for lower price. (A November 1998 survey of distribution companies found that the number handling private brands had increased to 56 percent, although the rate of increase had tapered off, perhaps because of concerns about quality.[19]) The experience of the 1980s and 1990s shows that customers are not wedded to traditional brands.

Myth: Japanese customers like face-to-face shopping and will not buy a product sight unseen.

Reality: Working women have less time to shop, so convenience has become more important. Direct-mail sales have grown from virtually nothing in the 1970s to more than one-fifth of the sales of large department stores today.[20] While retail sales fell during the recession, direct marketing sales continued to grow at a rate of 5 to 7 percent each year.[21] Internet sales also continue to grow, both from domestic and foreign companies, showing that Japanese customers don't necessarily prefer shopping face to face, as long as value and selection are high enough.

Myth: Japanese distribution channels are impossible to enter.

Reality: Direct marketers and mail order companies are bypassing the distribution channels altogether. The rise of parallel imports is breaking through the expensive multilevel wholesale channels. Manufacturers are relying less on their traditional networks of *keiretsu* stores, and regulators are beginning to relax the large-scale retail law.[22]

Myth: Japanese firms place long-term, stable relationships with other firms above all other considerations.

Reality: Today, the value-added of the relationship is most important. Every expenditure is carefully evaluated, and relationships between firms are far more expendable. For example, under pressure from clients, top advertising agencies are restructuring, focusing more on their creative contributions than merely on their access to media and to major firms. Tokyo Electric Power set aside its long-term relationship with equipment supplier Statchi to invite global contracts. *Keiretsu* relationships are disintegrating. In business-to-business sales, relationship-based marketing is losing power to benefits-based marketing

Opportunities in Change

These changing realities create opportunities. In addition to the many foreign entrants moving into Japan, other foreign and domestic firms have taken advantage of the nation's new realities to find opportunities in this $4.6 trillion (approximately ¥552 trillion) market. Companies are creating unique selling propositions in a land where "big and ambiguous" used to be a marketing virtue. A few examples:

• Procter & Gamble didn't sell dish detergent in Japan until 1995. By the end of 1997, its Joy brand had captured one-fifth of the $400 million (¥51 billion) market to become the best-selling detergent in the nation. This was in a mature market that was dominated by powerful Japanese competitors such as Kao and Lion. But consumers proved they were willing to set aside respected Japanese brands for a product that better met their needs.

P&G had given up selling dish soap in Japan after the failure of Orange Joy in the 1970s, but times had changed. By studying Japanese consumers, P&G researchers found a need for a more concentrated detergent developed specifically for Japan. Shifting dietary patterns (such as increasing consumption of meat and fried foods) increased the need for a grease-fighting soap. P&G's advertising stressed Joy's concentrated power in cutting grease as well as its gentleness on hands. P&G used a documentary format featuring interviews of homemakers by a famous comedian. Customers proved very willing to shift to a new brand that offered a better value proposition. P&G also used clever incentives in the distribution channel to encourage retailers to promote the brand. The company gave retailers higher margins and redesigned its bottles to save shelf space, improving the efficiency of transporting and selling the soap.[23] P&G's experience in cleaning up the detergent market also shows how a success in Japan can be leveraged in other Asian markets. P&G has taken the formula for Joy developed for Japan and has begun selling it in the Philippines and other Asian markets.[24]

• Asahi Beer's careful positioning and segmentation allowed it to rise from a marginal role in the Japanese beer market to establish itself as the leader in a fast-growing niche for dry beer. The industry had long been dominated by Kirin, whose strong corporate image and monotonic offering of lager beer had earned it a fairly stable 60-percent share. But in 1987, Asahi launched Asahi Super Dry, a new beer with a fresh, sharp taste that helped to establish the dry beer market in Japan. By its third year, the Asahi name had become virtually synonymous with dry beer and it had captured 90 percent of the dry beer market. Its share of the overall beer market continued to grow until, in the spring of 1998, it was neck-and-neck with Kirin. Asahi's share was 39 percent, compared to 41 percent for its rival (although Kirin regained some strength by developing the market for a new low-priced beverage with reduced malt content called *happoshu*).[25]

Asahi exploded the myth that all beers taste the same and that Japanese consumers would accept anything served up by a dominant firm. To Kirin's surprise, it turned out that Japanese consumers did have taste buds and minds of their own. (Kirin also lost ground to Asahi in distribution. Reluctant to antagonize its networks of small liquor stores, Kirin was slow to move to discount and convenience stores, which have become key outlets in distributing alcoholic beverages.)

• MosBurger, a Japanese hamburger restaurant, has found success in differentiating itself against McDonald's and other large rivals. It has nearly as many stores as McDonald's and has posted remarkable growth despite a sluggish economy. Although McDonald's still dominates the market (with a 51.6-percent share compared to Mos's

25.5 percent), MosBurger has built and sustained a strong position by focusing on a niche. Even when McDonald's ran a ¥100 (under a dollar) burger campaign next door, MosBurger sales were virtually unaffected (although an ¥80-campaign helped drive McDonald's sales up 18 percent in 1996, while MosBurger remained static.)[26] Nonetheless, MosBurger has held a solid number two position in Japanese burgers through its distinctive strategy. MosBurger left prime locations and speedy service to its fast-food rivals. It instead relies upon off-beat locations, small stores, and customers willing to withstand long waits for flavorful, cooked-to-order burgers. For a growing group of loyal fans, the inconveniences and inaccessibility only add to MosBurger's attractiveness.

• The Body Shop, a U.K.-based firm that entered Japan in 1991, has experienced soaring growth in sales and new stores. By 1995, sales had multiplied by ten and the number of shops had quadrupled without any advertising, instead relying on word of mouth and store displays. The company's environmentally friendly products appeal to young Japanese women concerned about value, distinctive style, and ecological issues.

• Convenience stores became the most profitable retail category in the late 1980s, led by Itoh-Yokado's 7-Eleven. These small stores offered the efficiency of a retail chain without invoking the restrictions that tied the hands of large stores in Japan. But the convenience stores' most powerful source of success was their effective use of information about product sales and customer needs. By developing highly sophisticated point-of-sale (POS) information systems, they aggressively tracked sales and replaced slow-moving items on their shelves. The market was shocked when Itoh-Yokado, then only the third-largest retailer as measured by stores and sales volume, posted higher profits than first-ranked Daiei. The logic of the producer-driven market—in which more shelf space devoted to a manufacturer meant higher profits—had been inverted. Instead of the manufacturer being able to push its product by having larger shelf space, manufacturers had to earn shelf space by generating consumer pull. The Japanese franchise was so successful, it ended up buying U.S.-based parent Southland Corporation.

• Using round-the-clock 800 numbers and specially designed catalogs for the Japanese market, U.S. retailers such as Lands' End and L.L. Bean are bypassing Japanese distribution channels to reach customers directly. Foreign direct-mail sales grew to an estimated ¥200 billion ($1.8 billion) in 1996, accounting for about 10 percent of total direct-mail sales. A survey of 149 overseas catalog marketers found that 14.8 percent of the firms mailed Japanese-language catalogs and others were preparing to offer translated catalogs.[27] Japanese sales accounted for 60 percent of total sales of the British-based Cashmere Store and nearly a quarter of foreign companies surveyed reported that Japanese sales exceeded 10 percent of total sales. In 1998, American insurance company AIG announced plans for one of the first Japanese campaigns to sell auto insurance by mail.[28]

• Luis Vuitton, Hermes, Gucci, and other fashion leaders are undergoing rapid expansion. They are taking advantage of the new tastes and disposable income of unmarried working women and the increasing expression of individuality.

• Financial services firms such as Merrill Lynch and Citibank have taken advantage of the big bang in financial markets, weakened banking institutions, and increased consumer acceptance to rapidly develop their positions in Japan.

• Major world advertising agencies, which have made limited progress due to the differences in the culture and structure of the Japanese advertising industry, are now moving steadily into Japan through acquisitions and alliances. WPP and Omnicom, for example, have stepped up their investments. As success in advertising depends increasingly on creative strengths as opposed to media access, the opportunities are increasing for companies that have or can develop these strengths.

To take advantage of the wealth of new opportunities, these companies understood and used the changes in Japanese markets. It was not structural advantages, distribution relationships, regulatory favors, or strong corporate names that were the primary reasons for their success. In fact, many were tiny upstarts or players with small positions in Japan. Instead, it was savvy, entrepreneurial courage and sophisticated marketing, which had rarely been as effective in Japan before. Now, these market-driven approaches had dramatic results. The smart companies rethought their strategies for branding and positioning. They used pricing and promotions as marketing tools. They reshaped their distribution channels. They gathered and used market information. They discovered and met the needs of an emerging Japanese and Asian consumer market, the likes of which had never before been seen. We will examine these changes in more detail in Chapter Two.

Opening the Gateway to Asia

The value of understanding changes in Japanese markets is not limited to Japan. Japanese companies are among the most important players in all emerging Asian markets. The nation still accounts for nearly two-thirds of the entire East Asian economy, and it would be hard to develop a coherent strategy for the region while ignoring this part of the market.[29] A 1998 JETRO survey of 705 foreign companies found an increasing interest in Japan as a base for future Asian operations. While only 10 percent considered Japan as their current base for Asian operations, some 24 percent said they considered Japan to be "the base in the future."[30]

How does success in the Japanese market contribute to success in other parts of Asia? As we will consider in more detail in Chapter Three, there are a variety of ways Japan serves as a "gateway" to Asia.

A Window on Asian Culture

Although there are great cultural gulfs separating Japan from other Asian countries, the leap from Japan to the rest of Asia is in many

ways not as great at the step from the West to Japan. Recent studies have shown significant similarities among young Asian consumers and important differences from their Western peers.[31]
Awareness of some similarities, such as a rice culture, similar hair
and skin needs, and other characteristics often give companies
with an experience in Japan an edge over rivals without that experience. For example, P&G's Whisper, a sanitary napkin tailored to
the needs of Japanese women, is the leading brand in its category
in Japan and has been very successful in other parts of Asia.
Unilever's dishwashing products designed for Japan have also been
successful in Asia. (It should be stressed, however, that Asian markets are no more Japanese than Japan is Western, and they are as
heterogeneous as most Western markets.)

Blueprint

Japan is one of the best case studies for the rapid emergence of a
modern economy—from its post-war start to a fully developed modern economy. Japan's experience in shifting from a producer-driven
economy to a consumer-driven market, its shift from a closed to an
open society, its move from a homogeneous market to a heterogeneous market, the power of institutions such as MITI in shaping the
economy, the rise of entrepreneurship, and the changing role of
women are all trends that can be or are being repeated in various
parts of Asia. Emerging Asian economies won't be identical to
Japan's, but by examining how these changes play out in Japanese
markets, companies can gain experience in handling these changes
in other Asian markets.

Trendsetter

Asia looks to Japan for fashion and products in much the same way as
Japan looks to the West. While Japanese tourists head to Disneyland
in California, Asian travelers pour into Tokyo Disneyland. They read
Japanese *manga* comics, use Japanese appliances, drive Japanese vehicles, and play Japanese computer games. Tokyo is the financial and

cultural "capital" of Asia in the way that New York City is the "capital" of North America.

Collaborator

In addition to offering perspectives on Asian markets, Japan also offers experience and insight into working with Japanese partners. Japan is the most powerful player in the development of Asia. There are few parts of Asia in which new entrants will not find themselves working with Japanese suppliers, retailers, or other firms. Japanese companies are huge investors in Asia. They have also been involved in Asia for far longer than most Western firms.

Competitor

Just as Japanese firms are very often the most powerful partners in entering Asia, they are also the most significant competitors. For companies facing off against Japanese firms in Asia, the home market offers insight into their strategies and corporate approach.

Cash Generator

Because of the size and spending power of the Japanese market, companies can build capital and a base of operations for other parts of Asia. While other Asian markets are still developing, firms can actually make money in Japan in the short term.

Japan's Emerging Marketing Age

The overriding impact of the transformation of the Japanese market is that marketing has become more important than ever to success in Japan. The market has transformed from a "push" economy based on what companies produced to a "pull" economy based on what consumers demand. Whereas they once were an afterthought, marketing issues now make or break a company's position in Japan. The winners in the new Japanese market will be the companies with the most creativity and skill in marketing. Japan has entered its Marketing Age and it is very likely many other Asian countries will follow suit as their economies develop.

The changes in Japan are not "Westernization," but "modernization." It is not the creation of a Westernized Japanese market, but rather the emergence of a distinctly Japanese consumer market. Although global music predominates, a full 40 percent of popular music sales in Japan are by Japanese groups. Citizens live in contemporary apartments, but they still take their shoes off when they enter. Companies such as Snapple, which failed to adjust its pulpy products for the Japanese market, or car companies that have neglected to shift steering wheels or worry about scratches or other cosmetic problems, have learned that they ignore these differences at their peril.

Soccer Among the Sumos

In the old market, large corporations threw their weight around like massive sumo wrestlers as the customers looked on. The matches were fierce but also ceremonial, aggressive yet civil. These were highly stylized matches. Like sumos, the most successful new products came from the large and established stables. The customer was on the sidelines.

The new market is much more like soccer. Small, nimble players move the ball down the field. There is no long staring match or clash of titans, just a rapid-fire drive for the goal. It is probably no coincidence that the first professional soccer league in Japan was created in 1993, and the team made it to the World Cup in Paris in 1998.

It is important to note that soccer has not displaced the sumos. Soccer and sumos exist in nearby arenas, a few channel clicks apart on Japanese television. In the same way, the traditional Japanese market with all its idiosyncrasies is still very much a part of Japanese business, even as the new one emerges. The old system remains like the closed walls of the emperor's palace that rise in the heart of modern Tokyo. While a new consumer, new distribution, and new advertising approaches are transforming the landscape of the Japanese market, the old consumer and the old market remain.

This is the delicate balance of Japanese marketing today. To ignore the developments at the Hankyu department store, discussed in the opening of the chapter, is to miss a tremendous opportunity in one of the world's most lucrative markets. It would also mean missing important lessons for the rest of Asia. To ignore the Imperial Palace is to risk assuming that the Japanese market has been remade in the image of the West. Tokyo is not New York. It is still a uniquely Japanese model, in which sumo wrestling and soccer exist side by side.

Points of Leverage

- Given these changes, what are the implications for your strategy in Japan?

- What are the assumptions on which you are basing your Japan strategy? In light of the discussions of myth and reality, how much of your strategy is based on myth or the new realities?

- What are the marketing strategies that might be possible for you to use now?

- Is this a time for increasing your investment and involvement in Japan? In what areas? Why or why not? As you continue to read through the book, you may want to consider whether the changes described here warrant a change in your initial strategy for investment and involvement in Japan.

Signs of Change

A New Ballgame

Baseball has been played in Japan since 1873 and professional leagues were set up in 1935, but, as *Newsweek* writer Jeffrey Bartholet points out, "they [Japanese] viewed baseball not as a mere sport but as a Zen-like test of character." Now, dynamic young ballplayers such as Ichiro Suzuki are defying their managers and tradition, much to the delight of young fans. Ichiro has even created a new fashion trend called *Ichi-caz*, or Ichiro Casual. It consists of a t-shirt, baggy jeans, and a baseball cap. Free agency made its first small inroads into Japan in 1993, as players began to value their independence above harmony. Defectors such as Hideo Nomo have left for the United States, but have found themselves even more popular at home by a generation that values independence above conformity.[32] While the game has been around for a long time, the rules have clearly changed.

2

From Shoji Screen to Sheet Glass—
Forces Shaping the Japanese Market

*"I thought someone was pulling a big joke on me. . . .
Frankly, I thought it was a very, very improbable
objective."*

Paolo Fresco, General Electric vice chairman, recalling his
reaction to the assertion by Japanese discounter Kojima that
it could sell 100,000 full-size GE refrigerators in Japan.[1]

*"At half the price of a Japanese model, how could we
pass it up?"*

Yukie Tanaka, a Japanese consumer[2]

How should a U.S. company sell refrigerators to the Japanese
market? General Electric had learned the rules of the old
Japanese market well. It found a Japanese partner, Toshiba, to provide access to the complicated Japanese distribution system to sell
its product through low-volume specialty stores. Consumers paid
much more for the products because they passed through so many
middlemen, but this was how business was conducted in Japan.

GE also couldn't expect Japanese customers to buy a standard
American-size refrigerator. Japanese consumers have small homes
and tend to shop frequently. So the company had to design a smaller
refrigerator, tailored to the needs and tastes of the Japanese

customer. The company was an excellent student of the rules of Japanese marketing.

But the rules changed. In 1995, Japanese discounter Kojima Company started importing General Electric refrigerators directly from the manufacturer, bypassing GE's Japanese partner to offer the product for about half the price of an average, smaller Japanese model. The refrigerators were massive, unaltered U.S. models, but customers, tired of high prices and needing more space as working women shopped less frequently, snatched them up. The same refrigerator the GE–Toshiba partnership offered for $2,400 (¥225,000) sold for just $800 (¥75,000) at Kojima. Kojima, a 126-store retailer, sold 120,000 models between May 1995 and April 1996, boosting GE's share of the Japanese market from less than 1 percent to 3 percent.

The hardest part of making the arrangements for Kojima was not Japanese regulations, but the inability of the American manufacturer to see the new marketing opportunity. Kojima cut out layers of middlemen, streamlining the distribution process and passing the savings along to customers.[3]

It was not General Electric who recognized this change, even though it knows well how to sell through discounters in the United States and other countries. General Electric understood the old Japanese market well, but not the current one. Ironically, it was a Japanese discounter who taught GE the lesson about the new reality of marketing in Japan. Imagine how much more effective they might have been if GE had actually tailored its product to the market, rather than forcing consumers to accept a compromise for a lower cost.

Kojima recognized not only changing attitudes, but also changing living conditions. The average size of the Japanese home, while still small by U.S. standards, was getting larger. At the same time, the average number of occupants in each home was decreasing and more women were working. This created additional space and an increased need for food storage space for families who had less time for shopping.

Fluctuations in exchange rates ultimately killed sales of GE refrigerators by Kojima. Even without GE's refrigerators, Kojima continued to increase its sales to more than ¥300 billion ($2.5 billion) by 1997, three times its 1994 level. Its sales were driven by air conditioners, flat-screen televisions, and notebook computers. The discounter's responsiveness continued to allow it to build its business in Japan. As company founder Akitoshi Kojima told one of the authors in 1998, "There is no reason why we should suffer from a stagnant economy, if we can convince people that the new products are so much better. Recent product improvements in appliances and PCs are unbelievable. We just achieved 30 percent sales growth over the previous year."[4]

From Shoji Screen to Sheet Glass

The traditional Japanese market was as clouded as a *shoji* screen, the thin white paper walls that are a fixture of Japanese homes and buildings. In a market in which the manufacturer dominated, there was no need to understand the customer. Behind this *shoji* screen, the Japanese consumer was an enigma. While trade negotiators were complaining about the impenetrability of this *shoji* screen market, Japanese consumers themselves were changing it. The new consumers are more transparent, making their demands and tastes known. As the *Wall Street Journal* noted, "If the 1980s were the Factory Era in Japan, this decade is ushering in the Shopping Mall Age."[5]

Three primary forces of change are responsible for this transformation:

1. *The New Japanese Consumer.* There have been fundamental shifts in customer demographics and behavior, led by a growing group of unmarried working women.

2. *Breaking the Stranglehold of Regulations.* Under pressure from these new consumers and foreign governments, there have been sweeping and fundamental reforms loosening the tight regulations of many areas of Japanese business.

3. *The Distribution Revolution*. These shifts in customers and
   regulations are creating opportunities to break through the
   labyrinthine Japanese distribution system, cutting out layers
   of middlemen, and reducing costs to the end consumers. New
   entrepreneurial players are emerging who are willing to use
   discounting, direct mail, and electronic commerce to reshape
   Japanese distribution.

These changes are further accelerated by an influx of new entrants,
both from rising foreign investments and through new domestic
competitors. As these new players operate by new rules, they continue to accelerate the market transformation.

These social and market shifts are overlaid on the general financial crisis in Japan. In some cases, the financial crisis has accelerated
and reinforced these changes. For example, the recession reinforced
a growing concern of Japanese consumers with value. Plummeting
real-estate values and increased mobility of Japanese shoppers made
it easier to establish large stores and malls outside the city centers
or expand retail presence in the city. In other cases, however, the
economic crisis has dampened the change. For example, shifting
exchange rates have made investments in Japan more affordable but
have decreased opportunities for low-priced imports, as in GE's case.

To understand the changes in Japan and how they create opportunities—as well as their implications for other Asian markets—we
need to understand some of the dimensions of these three shifts in
the Japanese market.

The New Japanese Consumer

The emergence of the more transparent "sheet glass" market has
been driven first by the rise of a new consumer. This new consumer
is a result of demographic shifts—most notably the dominance of
the post-war generations (75 percent were born after 1945) and a
sharp increase in unmarried women—greater global travel, an

awareness of global pricing, and an increasing emphasis on value. The new consumer has been both a driving force of changes in regulation and distribution as well as a product of these changes.

The traditional pre-war values held by Japanese born before 1940 were changed first by the pre-war generation. This serious minded "catch-up" generation, born between 1941 and 1975, ushered in an era of mass consumption and the creation of large specialty stores. The next generation, born after 1975 and coming of age in the 1980s, represented such a sharp break with the past that they were dubbed the *shinjinrui*, meaning "a new species of human." This is not merely a "new generation," as in the U.S. Pepsi ads, but actually a *new species*. The term is applied not to a small subculture of the new generation but to anyone who came into adulthood in this period. The concept of a new species recognizes that this is not a small transition or generational divide. This is a fundamental shift in the nature of Japanese consumers.

These changes were further strengthened by the 1985 Plaza Accord, which propped up the dollar and sent the yen soaring. This gave the average Japanese citizen the buying power to travel and shop abroad. Consumers had the money to buy more and were also increasingly aware of the price they were paying in this top-down market compared to other parts of the world.

As the consumer population began to be dominated by people with post-war values, there was increasing tension from the pre-war values maintained by the government and corporations. This gap reached a critical point between 1992–1995, resulting in a number of small explosions—price busting, deregulatory movement, active foreign entry, and so on. The companies and the government are still slow to adapt to markets that are typically a mixture of post-war and modern values. This creates opportunities for foreign entrants both for selling their products and services and for recruiting talented employees.

The *shinjinrui* lived through the burst of the bubble economy that plunged Japan into a recession, leading the way into an era of discounting and deregulation—dismantling many of the traditions and structures of the post-war generation. This new generation began to marry (later than their parents) and became the "new family" (smaller than their parents' families).

The evolution of values from the pre-war to post-war to new consumer is illustrated in Exhibit 2.1. These are generalizations and perhaps exaggerations of the prevailing values in each period, but they help to highlight the dramatic shift in the Japanese consumer.

We might find similar trends in other Asian countries, but to a lesser extent, due to strong cultural and religious heritages and to an economy that has not grown as rapidly as in Japan. The rise of the middle class is uniformly observed in most of the other Asian countries. The differences between other Asian countries as compared to Japan might be pointed out as follows:

- stronger family ties
- intrinsically capitalistic (particularly Chinese)
- more disciplined and diligent
- less hedonistic

Old and New Consumers

Given these changes, how does the emerging consumer differ from the traditional one? Consider how two female consumers might approach the purchase of a new car. (We focus on female consumers because it is predominantly young women who are instigating many of the changes among Japanese consumers.)

The traditional consumer is a housewife in her sixties. Having paid for their home long before the burst of the bubble economy eroded real-estate values, she and her husband are quite comfortable. They have more than $100,000 (¥12million) in savings. She shops for food every day and prepares her meals from scratch, although she has begun to introduce some of the convenience foods that are popular in the supermarkets.

Pre-war Values (Born before 1940)	Post-war Values (Born 1941–1975)	Modern Values (Born after 1975)
Pre-war education	Full post-war education	Parents had full post-war education
Harmony is everything	Harmony is desirable	Harmony is nothing
Money is nothing	Money is desirable	Money is everything
Seniority is everything	Seniority is desirable	Seniority is nothing
Foreigners are enemies	Foreigners are friends	Foreigners are nothing
Discipline without reason	Discipline with reason	No discipline
Arranged marriage	Marriage for love	No marriage
Large family hierarchy	Nuclear family	Single life
Hide sex	OK to enjoy sex	OK to sell sex
We are unequal	We should be equal	We are equal
We live in a "village"	We live in Tokyo	We live on Earth

Exhibit 2.1. Values Shifts Among Japanese Consumers

She has a long-standing relationship with a sales representative at the local Toyota dealership. He recommends a new model and prepares the complete deal, including an offer for her trade-in (which he also sold her). He handles registration and other paperwork and takes care of everything associated with the car after the sale. If she has problems with the car, she will call him first. She did not shop around on high-ticket items, although she is always frugal on daily goods. She believes that relying on her relationship with the sales person is the best strategy in the long run. She has never had any reason to be dissatisfied with him or the cars he sold her in the past. She doesn't have a strong preference for a specific car, as long as it provides reliable transportation.

The typical new consumer is in her late twenties or thirties and she is unmarried (or married without children). She works and has more money to spend. She lives with her parents (although an increasing number are living on their own). She has traveled widely and frequently. When she purchases a car, she knows what she wants. She collects as much information as possible and shops around for the best deal. She is concerned about safety and environmental impact. She is less concerned about her relationship with the salesperson than she is about saving yen and finding a model she likes. She will take her car to an independent repair shop for maintenance. She doesn't let the manufacturer make her decisions. She is capable of judging quality on her own and she is prepared to work to find it.

Most consumers are a complex combination of these two extremes. There is a mix of old rules and new rules operating at the same time in the market. The new and old consumers do not always break neatly along age lines, although many signs of new behaviors are most pronounced in younger consumers. But some older consumers are also changing how they approach purchases.

This is similar to the heterogeneous markets of Europe and the United States, where companies need to focus on specific segments. For example, in U.S. financial markets, there are the traditional brokerage customers who delegate their investments to a money manager, the "do-it-yourself" electronic traders, and those who mix self-serve and professional management through a trusted advisor. The old and new customers exist side by side and define valuable segments to pursue.

Characteristics of the New Consumer

How is this new consumer different from the old one? Among the differences, the new consumer is:

- More willing to shop around for a better deal

- Not afraid to be different

- More likely to choose family over the corporation

- Increasingly loyal to brands instead of corporations

- Interested in benefits beyond newness

- Willing to experiment

More Willing to Shop Around

Younger Japanese consumers are far more likely to shop around for a better deal than their older compatriots. For consumers under the age of twenty-nine, nearly four out of five will do some comparison shopping. This is nearly double the rate for Japanese consumers over fifty, as shown in Exhibit 2.2. Clearly, younger Japanese consumers have a very different attitude toward their purchases. In fact, an international study found that Tokyo residents under twenty-nine are even more likely to shop around than their peers in New York or London, as shown in Exhibit 2.3. In this sense they are even more modern than American and European youth.

This increased willingness to shop has also driven a variety of other changes, including price busting, the rise of "small and smart" brands, and the increasing popularity of overseas mail-ordering.

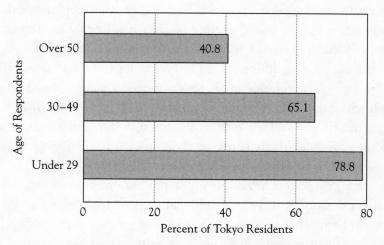

Exhibit 2.2. Do You Shop Around for a Better Deal?
Source: The Report of Home-Abroad Price Differentials Survey 1995, Research Institute for International Price Mechanism, MITI, March 1996.

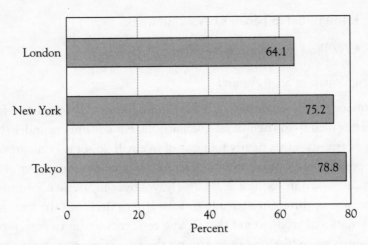

Exhibit 2.3. Do You Shop Around for a Better Deal? Tokyo Youth (under 29 years old) Are More "Modern" than New Yorkers
Source: The Report of Home-Abroad Price Differentials Survey 1995, Research Institute for International Price Mechanism, MITI, March 1996.

Not Afraid to Be Different

In a television advertisement for Toyota Celica, an English-speaking actor says, "So, being different bothers you. I never let it worry me. Go ahead, go for it. When you're out in front, there's nobody to imitate." Being different used to bother Japanese consumers in a land where conformity and harmony were key values. Now being different is a virtue. When Japanese consumers were asked in 1990 whether they would act boldly or cautiously in making a change in their lifestyles, the majority said "cautiously." Just five years later, the bold movers outnumbered their cautious peers.[6]

Today's Japanese are less likely to put harmony above individual expression. A survey by the Japanese Life Insurance Culture Center found that Japanese respondents of all ages were less likely to respect harmony and more likely to insist on their own views. As shown in Exhibit 2.4, the value of harmony went down across age groups between 1985 and 1996. The drop was most extreme among the young. For example, women aged sixteen to nineteen were half

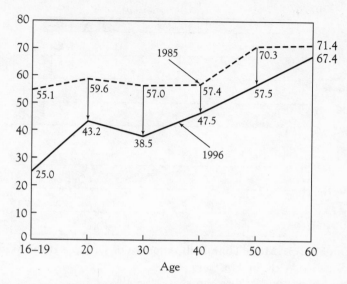

Exhibit 2.4. "Rather than insisting on my own views, I would like to respect harmonious relationships with others"
Source: Japanese Life Insurance Culture Center Study, 1996.

as likely to respect harmony in 1996 as this age group was in 1985. There was also an increase in respondents who preferred to act without being bound by convention.[7]

The signs of individualism and rebellion are particularly strong among young Japanese. One of the most popular shows in Japan in the mid-1990s was *Long Vacation*. It was a story about rebels, not like James Dean, but young Japanese men who had scrapped the traditional salaryman work ethic in favor of a life of leisure and fun.

Another sign of individualism is the rising acceptance of divorce and declining emphasis that women marry, as shown in Exhibit 2.5. From 1992 to 1997, the percentage that agreed it was acceptable to divorce if not satisfied with your partner rose from 44 percent to 56 percent. In the same period, those who felt women should be married fell from nearly 80 percent to just over 70 percent. (This was from a survey of 5,000 Japanese by the Prime Minister's Office, and there was little difference between responses from men and women.)

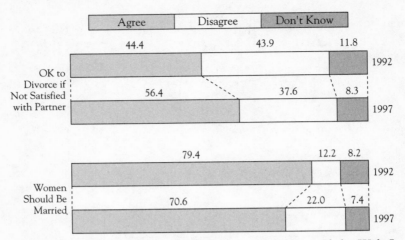

Exhibit 2.5. More Than Half Approve of Divorce If the Wife Is Not Satisfied With the Husband
Source: Survey by the Prime Minister's Office, 1997.

The increasing importance of individuality can also be seen in the movement away from seniority pay, as shown in Exhibit 2.6. While 56.7 percent of respondents in a 1998 survey felt seniority was currently important or somewhat important, just 8.2 percent expected it to be important in the future.[8]

More Likely to Choose Family Over the Corporation

Large corporations once dominated every aspect of Japanese life. Parents wanted their children to work for large companies and they trusted products from those companies. But now, Japanese consumers and employees are setting other priorities. This was graphically illustrated in a McDonald's ad, in which a young father playing baseball on a corporate team is faced with a difficult challenge. As he waits on third base, his daughter approaches with a McDonald's french fry. The father puts aside his corporate loyalty, takes the fry, and is promptly tagged out. The ad is part of a popular campaign showing young, involved fathers, in sharp contrast to the distant, corporate salarymen of the past who rarely saw their children.[9] In a survey by Tokyo Kikaku, one of the McDonald's ads was ranked

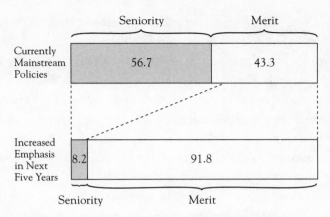

Exhibit 2.6. Systems of Employment: Present and Future
Source: Survey by Economic Planning Agency of 2000 Publicly Registered Firms (excluding financial institutions), March 1998.

first among commercials that give viewers a "heartwarming" feeling. Although the reality has yet to catch up to the image, their popularity marks a shift in the relative value of the corporation in Japanese life.

An attitudes survey conducted by the Japanese Ministry of Education found a tremendous increase in respondents who consider family "the most important consideration in life." The affirmative answers to this question increased from 11 percent to 42 percent between 1958 and 1993.[10] Younger Japanese workers are particularly less likely to sacrifice family for work. For example, a survey by the Japanese Life Insurance Culture Center found that just 17.5 percent of men aged sixteen to nineteen felt family had to be sacrificed for work, while 37 percent of men over fifty agreed.[11]

Similar increased participation by men in households is seen in other parts of Asia. In 1998, Procter & Gamble launched detergent advertisements in India playfully portraying a man doing the laundry. (While the man does his laundry, a woman's voice asks, "Where's your wife?" and "Are you actually going to do them?")

As more Asian women work outside the household (with 47 percent of Malaysian women working, for example), these types of role reversals in advertising and in life are more common. Similar ads include one for a South Korean vacuum cleaner showing a husband vacuuming around his wife, and an ad for a Hong Kong bank depicts a husband bringing tea to his wife as she works on a computer, and then he drives her to the airport. Fathers caring for children are also more common, including a Malaysian ad showing a father giving a bottle to a newborn. While some advertising experts questioned the effectiveness of the role reversal ads, advertisers claimed they had a positive impact.[12]

Government advertising, reflecting both changing values and concerns about declining birthrates, actively encourages fathers to play a more active role in the family. One series of advertisements by the Ministry of Health and Welfare said, in effect, that a man who does not look after his children does not deserve to be called "father."

These shifts in family values not only require new approaches to advertising and other marketing communications, but also create new opportunities for products and services directed toward families (for example, Baby Gap). This shift also means that by offering better worklife balance, companies entering Japan have an advantage in attracting new employees.

Increasingly Loyal to Brands Instead of Corporations

The motto of the old consumer was: "You can't go wrong with . . . ." She finishes the sentence with a large and established name such as Toyota, Ajinomoto, the Liberal Democratic Party, or the University of Tokyo. She is risk-adverse and her "choice set" includes few brands, only a stable group of large and established companies. This choice set never changes unless she becomes extremely dissatisfied with one of the members.

This loyalty to a company rather than brands is shown in a survey on toothpaste purchases of 717 households by Video Research. Of the respondents, 51 percent were loyal to the top three companies, 32 percent were loyal to a single company, and just 17 percent were loyal to a brand. This brand loyalty was even weaker over a two-year period, dropping to just 7 percent for this period.[13]

This is changing. A recent University of Tokyo survey of Japanese women found that 28 percent of married women over fifty would look for a specific manufacturer when purchasing a new appliance, compared with just 7 percent of single women. A second study found that 60 percent of companies in Japan feel they have already started brand-building activities.[14]

Younger Japanese are more likely to consider changing jobs. A study by Recruit Research found that while about 60 percent of workers from forty-five to forty-nine had no intention of changing their jobs or going independent, only about 30 percent of workers in their twenties felt the same way.[15]

This decline in the blind loyalty to established Japanese firms is also seen in the rising popularity of foreign companies, among both male and female graduates of Japanese universities. A survey of approximately 13,000 graduates by Recruit Research found that one in four University of Tokyo graduates was applying for employment at foreign capital firms in 1998, up from just 4 percent the year before.[16] Japanese graduates also ranked the companies they would most like to work for—IBM moved from number 58 in 1997 to twenty-fifth place in 1998, Merrill Lynch moved from 239 to 71, and Procter & Gamble Far East moved from 287 to 105.[17] The decreasing job security of Japanese firms and increasing perceived opportunities at foreign companies contributed to the shift in view of foreign companies. This is a very positive development for foreign entrants, which traditionally have had a hard time attracting talented Japanese staff.

Interested in Benefits Beyond Freshness

The old consumer was a "freshaholic." She wanted things to be new and fresh, yet still familiar. To keep Mrs. Old loyal, a company such as Toyota must: 1) regularly say hello to her; 2) tell her the company completely changed the model; but 3) tell her it has not made any drastic physical changes to the product. One such advertisement in the late-1980s for Toyota's Mark II reads, "Everything but the name is completely new!" The advertisement gives almost no information about the actual changes that were or were not made, but it gives the customer the sense of freshness as well as an air of stability. This emphasis on freshness is seen in Japanese *sashimi* (sliced raw fish), which is considered to be better the fresher it is. The ultimate is *ikizukuri* (live fish).

Another example of the extreme nature of this desire for freshness is a variety of automatic teller machines (ATMs) that could not have succeeded anywhere but in Japan. This machine, developed by Hitachi, irons and sanitizes the bills it dispenses. There are also germ-free pens, stationery, and bicycle handles (impregnated with an antiseptic chemical). Sanitary coatings are applied to fax machines, telephones, and dishwashers.[18]

The new consumer is not only concerned about freshness or newness but also about other product benefits. She expects the company to give her information rather than greetings. She is constantly looking for more information and she expects the advertiser to supply it. The car makers are describing the features of their cars in their advertisements. Consumers are weighing benefits and costs to find the best value.

Willing to Experiment

Consumers are also showing an increasing willingness to try new products and practices. A University of Tokyo study of Japanese women found that more than 40 percent of the entire sample had used a department store discount card or credit card. A study of 300 teenagers found that more than half of urban youth owned beepers. This is not merely product innovation, but a change in buying behavior, willingness to experiment, a desire to try products and services from relatively unknown companies, and an interest in new tastes (such as bagels and expresso coffee). This overall willingness to experiment creates opportunities for new and different products to enter the country.

Overall, Japanese customers still are less willing to take risks in the financial arena than their Western peers and Asians in Hong

> **Signs of Change**
>
> **A New Year Dawning**
>
> The streets of Tokyo used to be virtually deserted on New Year's Day, as residents left to pay visits to their ancestral homes. But as January 1997 dawned, the traffic in Tokyo was heavier than ever. Tokyo citizens bypassed their traditional family celebrations. Supermarkets and department stores that normally didn't reopen until January 4, were running normal hours. It was yet another visible sign that the power of the individual—and commerce—had overtaken the power of tradition.

Kong and Singapore. This risk aversion has serious implications for how financial services are presented in Japan. The promise of windfall profits or get-rich-quick proposals are much more likely to fall upon deaf ears than more conservative propositions.

Consumers in Transition

The new consumer is not always the most youthful consumer. A University of Tokyo study of 500 Japanese women ranging from their twenties to their fifties found that sometimes older customers are more price sensitive, particularly for everyday purchases. (The generation in their fifties was the hardest hit by the economic recession and corporate restructuring, so it may not be so much a change in consumer attitudes as a result of belt-tightening.) If the unmarried women aged twenty to thirty-five knew a dress was going on sale next week, the survey found that more than a third of them would buy it right away rather than wait, compared with just 14 percent of married women in their fifties.

Surprisingly, when asked if they were loyal to large brands, half of the married women in their fifties said they were not, compared with about a third of younger married and unmarried women. These older women are more likely to use self-service cosmetics counters to save money. They are also more likely to complain about poor food in a restaurant. Married women tend to check newspaper advertising and sale prices in supermarkets more often than single women.

Young single women are more likely to make impulse purchases and shop at convenience stores rather than the mom-and-pop stores favored by their elders. The exception is with big-ticket items such as appliances, for which younger customers are more likely to shop around for a better deal. Half of singles from twenty to thirty-five said they would go to three or more stores compared with just 31 percent of the women over fifty. Married women in their twenties were more likely than any other group to shop around for the purchase of an automobile. Older customers are more like to stay with the local appliance retailer they have known.

While the younger unmarried women don't like to spend time waiting to purchase an item such as a dress, they are more willing to spend time to tailor products and services to their own tastes. When asked if they would prefer a prearranged tour when traveling abroad or plan their own itinerary, only 11 percent of the unmarried women opted for the planned tour, compared with 53 percent of the married women in their fifties.

Given their penchant for innovation, unmarried women aged twenty to thirty-five were significantly more likely to make purchases by direct mail or over the Internet, with 28 percent of the unmarried women and 27 percent of the married women in their twenties stating that they had used these channels. Yet it is still significant that a full 9 percent of women in their fifties were also willing to make such purchases.

Differences Remain

Although Japanese consumers may look more like their Western peers than ever before, there are still important differences that businesses need to understand to succeed in the market. For example:

Assumption of Homogeneity

Although the Japanese market is increasingly heterogeneous, we should not forget that Japanese consumers are less diverse than their Western peers. Japanese consumers have similar ways of thinking and styles of living, and they speak the same language, are educated in more or less the same way, and are exposed to similar media. They also consider themselves to be homogeneous, and so they expect that others understand their situation, desires, and problems—even when meeting for the first time. Communication that exchanges the minimum of explicit information is therefore highly admired.

A Few Outliers Lead the Way

Few Japanese are brave enough to be lone wolves. Hair coloring, piercing, humble weddings, bargain hunting, and other activities are pioneered by a few brave outliers, who then attract a wider following. Often this following is within a specific subculture. Once a sufficient number of followers adopt the fad, it then explodes.

Quality Perfectionists

While Japanese consumers are more price sensitive, they still maintain a higher standard for quality. They are less willing to trade low price for low quality.

Frugality and Extravagance

Extreme combinations of price sensitivity and conspicuous consumption are not uncommon. New consumers who search for lower prices for household items or buy generic food spare no expense on their Luis Vuitton bags or Tiffany jewelry. They drive their new Mercedes to an inexpensive apartment. The combination is not predictable and not accounted for by demographics, income, or social class.

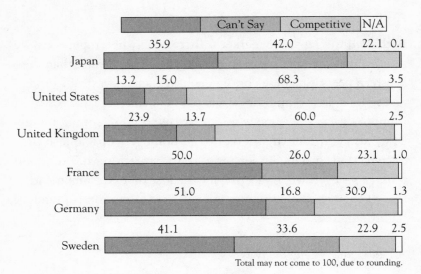

Exhibit 2.7. Image of an Ideal Society
Source: 2801 Male/Female respondents aged 18–69, Dentsu Soken, 1987.

Mix of Egalitarian and Competitive Values

As shown in Exhibit 2.7, Japan has a unique mix of egalitarian and competitive values. While it is far less egalitarian than European countries, it is also less competitively focused. Japan is far less competitively focused than the United States. What is telling in this survey is that the majority of Japanese respondents found themselves in the middle—between the extremes of collective egalitarianism and individual competitiveness. This is a distinctive balance, or conflict, in the Japanese market that affects the progress of business and the activities of the market. Companies need to walk this fine line between these two poles to succeed.

Drivers of Change

Where are these changes coming from? There are a variety of forces that are driving these shifts, including:

The New Female Consumer

Perhaps the most striking demographic change is the increase in single women. The percentage of unmarried females between twenty-five and twenty-nine has climbed from just 24 percent in 1980 to nearly 50 percent in 1995, as shown in Exhibit 2.8. This dramatic increase has created a group of consumers with sharply defined tastes and interests in style. Because many of these women still live with their parents or grandparents, they have disposable income to act on these tastes. However, an increasing number are setting up on their own, this no longer considered to be a social stigma. Unbelievable as it may seem, young women living alone used to be suspected of having loose morals. They are a significant segment in and of themselves, as well as a change agent for the broader market.

Women have led the way in emphasizing the individual over the group. They have indulged their interests in travel, cultural activities, sports and health clubs, cosmetics, and fashion. Females between twenty-five and thirty-five, virtually all working women, are viewed as trendsetters by both older and younger Japanese women.

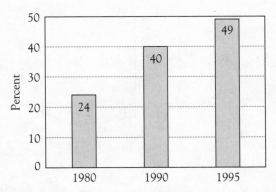

Exhibit 2.8. Rise in Unmarried Women (Age 25 to 29)
Source: National Census

Men and women of all ages are less likely to feel that married women should concentrate on keeping the home, as shown in Exhibit 2.9. Women were also less likely to feel they should sacrifice for the family.[19]

More of these women are working. About half of all women sixteen years old or over held jobs in 1988, roughly comparable to the percentage in the United States. In 1996, more than 20 million Japanese women were working, although one in three were part-time employees. In a recent poll of Tokyo office workers, only one in four female employees said they would retire completely from the workplace after marriage.

This group is also a formidable source of spending. The average monthly discretionary funds of females twenty-seven to thirty-five working in Tokyo for companies of more than one hundred employees is $940 (¥112,000), and nearly half spend more than $2,500 (¥300,000) on clothing every year. (This compares with the average household clothing expenditures of just $700.) These women are voracious travelers, averaging 4.6 trips abroad per year.[20]

In addition, many of these women receive financial assistance from their parents, who have substantial assets and savings. Young

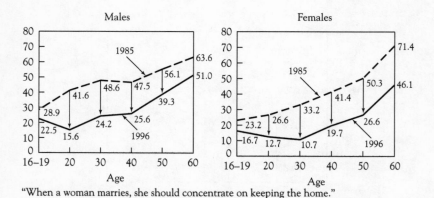

"When a woman marries, she should concentrate on keeping the home."

Exhibit 2.9. The Perception of Gender Roles Has Weakened Among All Ages

Source: Japanese Life Insurance Culture Center, 1996.

people usually are subsidized by their parents even after they obtain full-time jobs and sometimes even after they are married, making them relatively immune to fluctuations in the business cycle.

Teenagers also have more money to spend. A survey by *Nikkei Newspaper* of 300 teenagers found that 45 percent had part-time jobs. Between their earnings and their allowances, they had a monthly disposable income of about $600 (¥72,000). This is more than the $540 (¥64,800) of the average salaried worker's monthly disposable income.

The Rise of Childless Families and Singles

Later marriages and an increase in working women are reshaping the Japanese family. Although the 1990 census found that 60 percent of Japanese families were traditional nuclear families (parents and unmarried children), there has been a rise in childless families and singles. The proportion of single households is expected to rise from 23 percent in 1990 to 28 percent in 2010. The average household size dropped from four members in 1960 to three in 1990.

There also has been a rise in divorce to an all-time high of 225,000 in 1997, or 1.8 divorces per thousand marriages. Mature divorces, among people married more than twenty years, were also on the increase. Attitudes toward divorce have shifted significantly. In 1988, respondents were evenly divided on the issue of whether it is acceptable to obtain a divorce from a spouse with whom you don't get along. By 1997, twice as many respondents condoned divorce as those who didn't.[21] Couples value their freedom more. Japanese spouses who felt husband and wife should act as *isshin dotai* (one mind, one body) fell from 36 percent to 29 percent between 1988 and 1997.

The average number of children per household had fallen to 1.46 by 1993 and the trend promises to continue. Sumito Life Insurance Research Institute predicts that the number of newborns will drop from 130,000 in 1991 to just 77,000 by 2025. The percentage of the population under fourteen dropped from 35 percent in 1950 to just 16 percent in 1995.

Increase in Travel

In 1964, when Japan emerged from isolation by hosting the Tokyo Olympics, there were only 128,000 Japanese overseas travelers, most of them on socially approved errands which ostensibly contributed to the advancement of the country. In the decade between 1986 and 1996, overseas travel increased by threefold, from 5.5 million to 16.7 million.[22] This dramatic increase in travel is shown in Exhibit 2.10. Japanese tourists spent $4.8 billion (¥1 trillion) during all of 1985, but were spending the same amount every six weeks a decade later.[23]

These travelers often combined shopping with sightseeing, offsetting part of the cost of the trip by purchasing products at prices far below those at home. This global comparison shopping became so widespread that Japanese consumers coined a term for it, *naigai kakakusa*, meaning the differential between domestic and overseas prices. This awareness created new opportunities for imports and discounting.

The forces that are reshaping consumer behavior in Japan, along with other pressures, are helping to transform Japanese regulations and distribution systems. These more lenient regulations and dis-

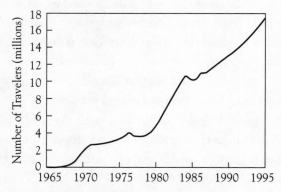

Exhibit 2.10. Overseas Travel by Japanese
Source: The Ministry of Justice.

tribution networks, in turn, are encouraging the further spread of new consumer attitudes in a reinforcing cycle.

Forget What You Learned About Japanese Marketing Before 1985

Overall, these many changes are part of a broader shift in the direction of information flow and power in Japanese society. Where it was once a top-down society, it is now much more of a bottom-up society.

As late as the 1980s, one of the authors, in a joint effort with the Naisbitt Group, tried to analyze reports in the Japanese media to predict national market trends. These experiments found that the techniques used to successfully analyze trends in John Naisbitt's *Megatrends* didn't work in Japan. It soon became apparent that Japan's trends weren't reflected in media reports. They didn't percolate up from the bottom, but instead reflected decisions from the top. Official documents or edicts were disseminated by the media, and popular reaction followed.

Throughout the post-war period, Japanese leaders had pursued a policy of "economic progress without societal change." Changes were initiated from the top down through regulation and less formal "administrative guidance." Before 1985, government and the traditional values of Japanese culture shaped the market, as shown in Exhibit 2.11. These values were strengthened and enforced by the social and corporate infrastructures that were consistent with them.

Under this model, the consumer was the recipient of change, not the initiator of it. Changes in the social and corporate infrastructures did not come from consumer pressure. Instead, they came at the instigation of foreign sources, or *gaiatsu*, which tended to reshape the environment. The most important of these traditional values at the top left-hand side of Exhibit 2.11 is *wa* (harmony or stability). Japanese regulators and companies were reluctant to rock

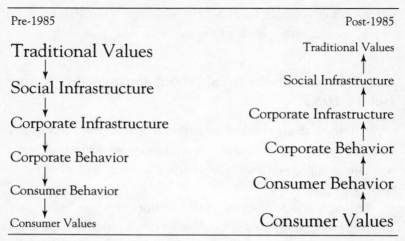

The forces of changed are ranked (by size) according to their relative importance and affect on the market.

Exhibit 2.11. Parameters Affecting the Japanese Market

the boat, and top-down changes were implemented slowly so as not to disturb the balance set by traditional values.

Turning the Top-Down Society On Its Head

The top-down society that dominated until the 1980s has been turned on its head, as shown in the right-hand side of Exhibit 2.11. The policy of "economic progress without societal change" has become a victim of its own success, as progress inevitably changed the society. By the 1990s, even the Japanese government was forced to acknowledge this shift in emphasis from national economic development to personal quality of life. A 1992 government white paper titled "Seikatsu Hakusho" (White Paper on Daily Life Style) declares a fundamental shift from a policy of economic growth to a diversion of resources for the enhancement of domestic well-being. The consumer has gone from being a cog in the wheel of the national economy to a driving force reshaping the Japanese market and society.

Breaking the Stranglehold of Regulation

At the same time consumers are changing, the regulations that once circumscribed virtually every aspect of Japanese business and society are beginning to loosen. A combination of pressure from foreign interests and internal demands by consumers and businesses in Japan is slowly but surely reducing the constrictions of central control. The bureaucracy that had driven Japan to become an industrial power is increasingly becoming a burden not just on businesses but on worldly wise consumers who have had to struggle with the inefficiencies of Japanese regulations.

For a long time, the government pursued a policy of "protecting the consumers from their own ignorance." This resulted in myriad regulations that didn't protect consumers so much as they protected producers. And consumers paid the price.

Japanese consumers clearly paid a price for regulations. In the 1990s, it cost 60 percent more to live in Tokyo than in New York (although this gap has narrowed considerably, as noted in the Introduction).[24] In 1996, the average Japanese airline traveler paid more than three times as much public levee and tax per kilometer than travelers on U.S. airlines.[25] A bottle of aspirin that sold for a few dollars in the United States retailed for $20 (¥2,000) in Japan. It cost more to send a domestic letter in Japan (80 cents) than an international letter from New York to Tokyo (50 cents). It cost more to fly round-trip from Tokyo to Okinawa than between Tokyo and Chicago.[26] "It is the piling up of thousands of such petty, price-raising rules that makes the Japanese that tenth poorer than they ought to be," read an article in a July 1996 edition of *The Economist*.[27]

Consumer advocates were not much help. One of the authors recalls testifying before the Japanese Fair Trade Commission in the 1980s in favor of relaxing local regulations restricting premiums on foreign confectioneries. A consumer-group representative at the meeting, speaking in favor of the regulations, complained that premiums would entice children to buy things they didn't really need and that restrictions should be placed on advertising confectioneries. The author pointed out that the manufacturer takes all the risk in offering the premium. Consumers do not have to repeat the purchase if the product is not of high quality. He further suggested, to the audience's shocked surprise, that the consumer representative might enjoy shopping in Moscow, which was practically devoid of advertising at the time.[28]

Slowly, the government began to recognize that it needed to respect the sovereignty of the consumer. It became apparent that just as Japan's post-war recovery depended on a tightly controlled economy, its future growth depended upon its willingness to relax these same regulations and allow the market to flourish.

The need for regulatory and financial reform has emerged as the central issue in Japanese politics and is seen as a key factor in the economic stability of the region. There is new pressure for deregulation, which was already underway. The government is instituting far-reaching reforms in financial services, insurance, oil imports, airlines, telecommunications, retailing, and many other areas. Restrictions have been relaxed on large retail stores, parallel imports, and a host of other activities. It is like London's "Big Bang," the AT&T break-up, and the U.S. deregulation of electric utilities—all at once.

These types of reforms, dramatic in any nation, are particularly noteworthy in Japan because of the extent of the regulations that are being dismantled. Economist Rudiger Dornbusch once quipped that the invisible hand is at work in Japan, but it's not 18th-century economist Adam Smith's theory of the invisible hand. It's the invisible hand of the government working with Japanese industry. Japan's tangle of regulations and protectionist practices, holding more than 40 percent of the economy in its grip, is a "Dickensian mixture of fusspottery and favouritism," read a July 1996 *Economist* article.[29]

A study by the General Agreement on Tariffs and Trade (GATT) found that Japan has relatively low tariffs and import quotas in comparison with most other countries. The majority of overt trade barriers in nonagricultural trade were eliminated by the end of the 1970s. "Most of the impediments of the Japanese market are structural—a result of the unique character of Japanese business organizations and their distinctive relationships with one another and with the Japanese government."[30]

Consider a few of the more dysfunctional examples:

• Until March 1995, Japanese regulations required that the care instructions on clothing (washing and ironing) be printed in red, rather than the simple black letters used in other parts of the world. The explanation for this rule was that the consumer needed to be able to see the instructions quickly. The annual cost of providing colorfast red tags for all clothing in Japan came to ¥500 million (approximately $5.5 million).

• Pharmaceutical testing in the United States or other parts of the world had to be repeated in Japan. Apparently Japanese rabbits and guinea pigs were considered to be different from those in other parts of the world. (The Ministry of Health eventually allowed data from "foreign" animals to be used.)

• There was a ban on foreign skis for a national sports event because the quality of Japanese snow was deemed to be different than that of overseas nations.

• Farmers' refusal to give up land near Tokyo's Narita Airport left a second runway unfinished for eighteen years after the airport was built.[31] The lack of runway space made it difficult for new airlines to gain access to Japan.

• Japan is the only country in the United Nations that has not approved the birth control pill. It was first deemed to promote bad morals. Then, with the rise of AIDS, there were concerns that it might decrease condom use. The emergence of the Internet and

Viagra broke thirty years of deadlock on the issue. Because Viagra is available to consumers online, Japanese regulators had no choice but to approve it for sale. Approval of the sale of birth control pills quickly followed.

Regulations created obstacles for entrant to Japan by using standards, testing and licensing, delays, lack of open bidding, and price ceilings. These regulations helped to protect industries from foreign and domestic competition, but at the same time they dampened the competition that could make companies more responsive to the needs of consumers.

The remnants of Japan's overbearing regulations continue to present challenges to marketers in Japan. To the extent that the market is controlled centrally, it will not respond to nor reflect the needs of customers. But to the extent that Japanese regulations prevent the market from responding to customers directly, these regulations face mounting pressures for change. Already the chinks that have appeared in the armor of Japanese regulations offer openings for companies to use their marketing skills more effectively.

The Distribution Revolution

One area in which regulatory changes and consumer pressures have transformed the Japanese market is in distribution. The changes can clearly be seen on Route 16, the beltway that encircles Tokyo, which is beginning to look like Los Angeles. Route 16 is lined with shopping malls, large apparel discounters, category killers, shoe discounters, car dealers, and McDonald's and KFC restaurants. Japanese consumers are increasingly willing to drive a few extra miles to save money. They will also head out of the city to seek parking spaces and the convenience of a wide range of products and services under one roof in a shopping mall. Similar shopping areas are springing up around other Japanese cities.

The new retailers that line the highway are only the tip of the iceberg of changes in Japanese retailing and distribution. As Japan is increasingly wired to the world, distribution through the Internet, telemarketing, and catalog sales are growing at a rapid clip.

All these changes have accelerated the growth of convenience stores, specialized superstores, and other retailers, while eroding the position of the department stores and small mom-and-pop stores.

The traditional Japanese distribution system is notorious for its complexity. Layers of middlemen carried products out to armies of small independent retailers. In 1994, there were approximately 1.5 million retailers and about 430,000 wholesalers, roughly a ratio of 3.5 retailers for every wholesaler. A 1989 study found that the number of wholesalers and retailers per capita in Japan was more than twice that of the United States.[32] The path from manufacturer to consumer was a third longer in Japan than in the United States.

The emergence of many small retailers is a natural outgrowth of the *Daiten-ho*, or Large-Scale Retail Store law. This law made it very difficult to construct large stores, giving local retailers and officials virtual veto power over a new large store. The law, which helped to sustain the relatively inefficient small stores, also restricted locations, operating hours, and other activities of the large stores. As a result of the large-scale retail store law, supermarkets took an average of six years to build from time of application. Given this system of many independent small stores, the proliferation of wholesalers and other middlemen became a necessity.

Japan's distribution system was also based upon long-term organizational transactions, relationships that make it harder for new companies, both domestic and foreign, to enter. This is in contrast to the traditional U.S. system driven largely by market transactions, which are completed on a one-time basis without a personal relationship between the buyer and seller.

But this system is very inefficient. The relative productivity of the Japanese distribution system in 1985 was only 59.4 percent as high as manufacturing productivity. In the United States, it was

67.8 percent; in France, 71.1 percent; and in West Germany, 78.4 percent.[33]

Now, the system is changing as layers of middlemen are being stripped out of the distribution networks. Sales handled by intermediate wholesalers declined by 41 percent between 1994 and 1997, and Japan lost more than 400,000 jobs in its wholesale networks in the same period.[34]

While sales directly from manufacturers to retailers increased by only 2 percent in that period, whole forests of middlemen were cut down, streamlining the distribution chains and reducing costs. The ratio of retail to wholesale sales dropped to 1.54, the lowest ratio in more than twenty-five years.

There has been a related decline of small mom-and-pop retailers. In 1982, over 84 percent of all retailers employed four or fewer people. Between 1994 and 1997, the number of stores with nine or fewer employees decreased while those with fifty or more employees grew by more than 10 percent.[35] Shopping center openings in Japan rose from eighty in 1991 to more than 150 in 1993. American Malls International (AMI) announced plans for the largest retail establishment in the nation opening in Kobe in 1999. AMI is planning to open eight large, American-style malls in Japan over a ten-year period. Hong Kong's Dairy Farm International, in partnership with Japan's Seiyu department stores, is planning to open a chain of seventy Wellsave discount food stores by the end of 2000.

Distribution has been transformed by discounters such as Kawachiya and Yamaya in liquor, cosmetics, and other staples; category killers such as Toys "R" Us, convenience stores such as 7-Eleven, parallel imports, direct mail operations such L.L. Bean and Lands' End, and even electronic commerce. These more powerful discounters are driving prices down and streamlining distribution processes, passing savings along to consumers. Some of the implications of and opportunities from these changes are explored in Chapter Eleven.

Signs of Change

A Market for Astros

As General Motors struggles to make headway in Japan, the company sold an estimated 14,000 of its boxy Astro minivan in 1996, which made the model the hottest American car in Japan. This puts it ahead of Chevy Cavalier and Jeep Cherokee. But Astro's success was not as a result of GM's own strategy. More than 80 percent of the Astros sold in Japan in 1996 were through unauthorized dealers. These retailers do what GM doesn't—they customize the vans for camping and outfit them with fancy paint, running boards, and fog lights. Prices from these dealers start around $35,000 compared with $41,000 from authorized dealers.[36] This leads to the question of whether GM's greatest barrier in Japan may be its own approach to the market.

Implications for Success in Japan and Asia

These changes in the Japanese market have tremendous implications for entering and succeeding in Japan. Among the important insights for managers:

The Japanese Market Is Increasingly Heterogeneous

The Japanese market can no longer be considered monolithic. Companies have to develop strategies that recognize the increasing segmentation of the Japanese market and position their products and services for specific parts of the market. Given these differences across segments, managers cannot assume that Japanese consumers will have the same values, so companies need to establish benefits for different sets of customers. The market is changing rapidly, creating opportunities for companies that can recognize and quickly respond to the needs of emerging segments.

Demographics Are Not Enough

In segmenting the Japanese market, managers need to look beyond demographics. While gender and age are important in distinguishing different segments of the market, and the new consumer behaviors are driven by younger women, changes in attitudes, and behavior across demographic lines. For example, in Japan, price-conscious older consumers have taken up day-to-day comparison-shopping but remain more loyal to small stores for their large purchases. Younger customers shop around extensively for large items such as appliances, but buy daily items at higher-priced convenience stores. They are willing to pay a premium to express their individuality. Many older, salaried males are taking an increasing interest in family along with their younger counterparts. By looking at these consumer shifts, companies can better understand ways to segment the market that go beyond demographic lines.

Need to Balance Old and New

Successful marketing in Japan and other parts of Asia requires recognizing the balance between the old and new markets. Despite its "Westernization," Japanese consumers continue to be more heavily influenced by tradition and culture than American consumers, as noted above. Companies need to be able to balance the impact of traditional and cultural values of the family with the influence of television, films, and other aspects of global culture. Companies need to spend more time in understanding these twin old-and-new streams in Japan than in other parts of the world where the market has undergone a slower evolution. As with the scenes in Asian countries of automobiles sharing the road with ox carts, the rapid transitions in Japan and other parts of Asia mean that the old and new are more likely to be found side by side than in parts of the world such as the United States, where this evolution from producer-driven to customer-driven economy occurred over a longer period of time. The compression of these changes found in Japan and throughout Asia means that the old has had far less time to move to the new through conversion or attrition.

Regulatory Changes Create Opportunities

Just as companies in the United States recognize that lobbying is part of doing business, Japanese firms need to recognize that the government will remain an important part of the business landscape. But as regulations are relaxed and become more open to change, the influence companies can have on shaping the environment increases. By looking for opportunities to change regulations and taking advantage of changes, companies can find new opportunities for building successful businesses in Japan. An important insight for other parts of Asia is the impact of changing consumers on regulations. This grassroots pressure can be far more effective than pressure from foreign governments in dismantling old regulations. At the same time, the experience with the heavily regulated Japanese economy can be an asset in moving into tightly controlled economies in other parts of Asia.

Some Asian markets, like post-war Japan, launched their economies through tightly regulated systems. As these economies succeed, they can be expected to reach the crisis Japan faced, resulting from a combination of internal and external pressures. Consumers become more active, regulations become more relaxed, and distribution systems become more open. Being aware of the possibility for these shifts in other Asian markets can help companies better anticipate them and take advantage of the opportunities they create.

The Economy Is Not the Market

While much of the world's attention in Japan and other parts of Asia is focused on the economy, companies also need to carefully examine market shifts. The economy certainly affects opportunities, but shifts in consumer behavior, for example, also create opportunities. That is why in a period of intense economic turmoil, sales of luxury goods in Japan continued to grow. It is important to appreciate both the market and the economy and identify opportunities in their interactions.

Reexamine Distribution

Whatever your distribution strategy in Japan and other parts of Asia, now is the time to reexamine it. Can you employ emerging distribution approaches or reinvent yourself through direct marketing, category killers, or electronic commerce? Given your target segment, what is the best way to reach it? Successful companies are balancing push-and-pull strategies more effectively. These changes in distribution also create opportunities for entry. Companies that may have stayed away from Japan because of distribution hurdles might want to reexamine their decisions in the light of recent changes. Which strategies that have been successful in the United States and other parts of the world might now be applied to Japan and the rest of Asia?

For companies that can navigate between the different perspectives of the old and new consumer, there are tremendous opportunities in these changes.

• Smaller families create demands for new products. For example, frozen food consumption in Japan grew 1.5 times between 1989 and 1994. Ownership of microwaves in the same period jumped twenty points, reaching a level of nearly 90 percent. There has also been a rapid rise in convenience stores.

• Increasing demands on the time of working women have led to a drastic change in shopping habits. Whereas the Japanese housewife used to spend an hour or so a day seeking out the best buys at local markets, she now has no qualms about picking up frozen food at the supermarket on her way home from work. This shortage of time has also created a demand for direct sales, which Amway and other companies have helped to fill. The rising individualism of Japanese consumers is creating new markets in a wide range of products and services.

- Comparison-shopping consumers create opportunities for new entrants to gain a foothold. Companies typically needed the backing of a large corporate brand or a long-standing relationship with the customer to move into the market. The new consumer is becoming more sophisticated and demanding. This gives imports a unique opportunity to challenge Japanese firms and creative new Japanese companies to make inroads against established rivals.
- The willingness to shop around has created opportunities for large retail stores outside of the metropolitan centers. It has also created increased opportunities for value pricing.
- Increasing value of brands creates opportunities to increase the importance of brand vision. For example, consumers can join the "Louis Vuitton Club," rather than just purchasing a bag.
- The benefits-oriented focus of consumers creates opportunities for problem-solving services. For example, Kinko's no-frills office services or the Gap's free return policy trade traditional courtesy for efficiently solving the customer's problems.
- An increased emphasis on family over work creates opportunities for family-centered products and services (such as Baby Gap and Toys "R" Us). It also gives an advantage to companies with family-centered policies in attracting young Japanese employees.
- Increased individuality creates increased opportunities for modularity and customization. For example, customers book airline flights and hotels separately rather than in a packaged tour and can purchase customized PCs or insurance.
- Changes in travel patterns in other Asian countries may contribute to similar shifts in markets. For example, Korean travel abroad was liberalized in the 1990s, compared with 1965 in Japan. As consumers increasingly travel abroad, this can be expected to accelerate the emergence of the new consumer. Increased travel also makes global compatibility more valuable, such as Citibank accounts that allow worldwide ATM withdrawals or AT&T calling cards that offer pre-paid long distance priviledges.

Points of Leverage

- Who are your customers? Are they the old Japanese consumers or new Japanese consumers? How does this mix change over time? Which are the unique segments and what are their changing needs?

- Which emerging segment of the Japanese market are you *not* serving today?

- If you are not selling directly to a consumer (such as to industrial organizations, etc.), how do changes in the consumer market affect your clients?

- How do the changes in Japanese society create opportunities for your specific product or service?

- What regulations pose the greatest threats and offer the greatest opportunities to your company?

- What regulatory constraints that held back your progress in the past are changing or could be changed?

- What are you doing to find out about regulatory changes and to seize the opportunities as they emerge?

- How effective is your current distribution system? Does it capitalize on changes in the Japanese consumer market as well as changes in distribution?

- How can you use the revolution in distribution to forge new channels and relationships with customers?

- What challenges have you faced in hiring good people in Japan? How do changing attitudes among workers create new opportunities for recruiting employees?

3

The Japanese Gateway to Asia

The Japanese economy rises like Mount Fuji in the midst of East Asia, far larger than the economy of any other nation in the region. The Japanese government and Japanese firms have been quick to recognize the opportunities for selling to and sourcing from Asia. Japan has become the center of Asian development.

While some Western companies have bypassed Japan on their way to Asia, they are increasingly recognizing Japan as a gateway to Asia. A 1998 survey of foreign firms in Japan found that 70 percent of them said their Japanese operations served as a marketing base for East Asia. Furthermore, the respondents said they expected to strengthen their Asia-wide functions for collecting information, conducting research and development, and overseeing unified operations. These results indicate, in the words of the Japanese External Trade Organization (JETRO), "that the firms entered Japan not only to develop the local market, but also to serve as East Asian regional headquarters in the longer run."[1] Similarly, a 1997 survey of foreign entrants to Japan found that an increasing number "have also cited the future potential of Asia and establishment of a production base as their reasons for setting up shops in Japan."[2]

Takeo Higuchi, a former senior executive of Mitsui Trading Vietnam, noted that "entry in Japan is a beginner's course for entering other Asian countries."[3] His advice on entering Vietnam— including finding a good local partner, understanding government restrictions, preparing for a slow response, and speaking the local language—sounds very familiar to any foreign firm that has worked to set up shop in Japan. If anything, the need for patience may be even greater. He comments that the Vietnamese time scale is much longer than that of the West and even than that of the Japanese. "They talk about ten years when we talk about ten weeks." Experience in Japan may be a good training ground for these challenges.

Japan is a trendsetter, investor, and builder across Asia. It offers insight into Asian culture and society and is a blueprint for development of other Asian markets. A presence in Japan provides critical insight into a lead market, relationships with key collaborators or competitors throughout the region, an R&D center, and a cash generator to fuel further Asian expansion.

Out of the Picture

This link between the fortunes of a company in Japan and its success in other parts of Asia can be seen in the case of Eastman Kodak, which entered Japan before World War II. Kodak initially dominated the market. But it didn't open an office in Japan until 1984, when upstart Fuji Film was already gaining strength. Kodak responded by creating its own distribution network, setting up a research center, and hiring a Japanese president. During the U.S. recession of the 1990s, it retreated from its investments, firing staff and rescinding offers to new Japanese engineering graduates. These moves damaged its reputation and made it easier for Fuji to gain ground.

This loss of ground in Japan helped create a competitor that challenged Kodak in other parts of Asia and around the world. Kodak had dominated the Thai market until the early 1980s. But stiff competition from Fuji Film, which entered the market in 1984, drove Kodak's share of the Thai photo market down to just 60 percent by 1992.[4] A weakness in Japan can shake a company's position throughout the region.

On the other hand, Procter & Gamble has benefitted from paying its dues in Japan. It exerts "Pan-Asian leverage" by developing products in Japan that are successful in Asian markets. Similar skin and lifestyles across Asian nations makes it easier to export concepts to other parts of Asia. Volkswagen, which is the top-selling import in Japan, is also doing quite well in China and other parts of Asia.

On a more anecdotal note, Michael Garrett, executive vice president of Nestlé and former president of Nestlé Japan, commented in an interview with one of the authors that his Japanese experience helped him immensely in running businesses in many other Asian countries. He said that in Japan, you have to play a lot of golf games without talking business before you can start building the business relationship. The same is true in building good business relationships in other Asian countries.

Japan is Part of Asia

East Asia is a diverse mix of religious, ethnic, and cultural backgrounds. Samuel Huntington, author of *The Clash of Civilization and the Remaking of World Order* (1996), contends that the Japanese civilization is distinct from both the Chinese (Sinic) and Islamic nations in the region.[5] There is also a debate about whether the concept of "Asia" itself is merely defined in opposition to the West. It is a truism that there is no such thing as an Asian market. The differences between countries in Asia are often more significant than their similarities.

In business, the similarities are more pronounced, from formalized relationships such as ASEAN to less formal business relationships and market trends across Asia. In *Megatrends Asia* (1996), John Naisbitt points out that there are trendlines that extend across Asia. He notes trends such as a turn from export economies to consumer economies, a distinction between modernization and Westernization, and a move from government-controlled to customer-driven markets.[6] Although each country is unique and heterogeneous, there are similarities in culture and market segments that unite the region. There are global segments, regional segments, and local segments. Japanese markets offer insight into all three, particularly the regional and global segments of the market.

From the standpoint of markets and economic development, Japan is clearly at the center of East Asian development. Japan is a leader in providing aid to the region, building manufacturing plants, selling products, and creating markets and trends. While it is important to recognize the differences among Asian nations, there are also important similarities among consumers and patterns in the development of markets, which provide insight into the secrets of success in Japan and Asian. Japan has many years of experience in moving from an undeveloped to a developed economy, and it suggests some of the stages a market will pass through in that development. The lessons of the Japanese market, if judiciously applied, can help avoid serious mistakes and offer strategies for success in other markets. If it is a mistake to treat Asian markets as homogenous, it is also a mistake to fail to see Japan as part of Asia.

Japan itself is not a homogeneous market. Thus, it is an oversimplification even to speak of uniform Japanese values. What is most interesting about Japan in the context of succeeding in Asia is the diversity of the market. It is a blend of East and West, a mix of the old and new, a market in transition. It is this complex picture that cannot be summed up in a simple recipe for "Asian" marketing success. It is this complexity that can be experienced in Japan and understood through a deeper knowledge of the current realities of the Japanese market.

Tilting Toward Asia

Japan's alignment with Asia is increasing. By the late-1980s, intraregional trade among Asian nations began to exceed exports to North America.[7] Japan is strengthening its position in Asia through foreign aid, commercial loans, technology transfer, direct investment, and preferential access to the Japanese market. By the mid-1990s, Japan accounted for more than half of official development assistance (ODA) in East Asia.

There are many reasons for Japanese interest in its growing neighbors. In addition to the attraction of emerging consumer markets in Asia, lower manufacturing costs are leading to the "hollowing out" of the Japanese economy as companies move their plants out of Japan into Asia. It may not be a deliberate tilt away from the West as much as a recognition of the opportunities to expand markets and decrease manufacturing costs that are making Asia such a focus of attention. Whether driven by trade pressures, a return to its Asian roots, or an awareness of the emerging opportunities, Japan has increased the Asian focus of its investments and its rhetoric.

Japan also has made more deliberate moves to assist in the development of Asia in the way it deliberately shaped its own economy. The Ministry of International Trade and Industry (MITI) announced a New Asian Industries Development Plan, designed to relocate Japanese businesses to lower-cost Asian nations. Former Japanese foreign minister Okita Soburo spoke of the pattern of Asian development as a "flying geese" formation (borrowing a term from pre-war Japanese economist Akamatsu Kaname). Like a flock of geese, the Japanese lead economy is closely followed by the Newly Industrialized Economies (NIEs) of South Korea, Hong Kong, Taiwan, and Singapore, and then by the ASEAN nations and China. As a Ministry of Finance report noted, "For the development of each of the three tiers, it is necessary that what Japan used to do should be done by the Asian NIEs, what the Asian NIEs used to do should be done by ASEAN countries, and Japan should enter into a far higher division."[8]

As one example of the shift from U.S. to Japanese leadership in the region, consider investment in Thailand. From 1970 to 1985, U.S. investment in Thailand was slightly higher than Japan's. Since then, Japanese investment sped past the United States, and its economic aid to Thailand had reached an estimated $500 million (¥60 billion) by the early 1990s, compared to less than $20 million (¥2.4 billion) from the United States. [9]

Asian leaders often welcome this investment. As Malaysian Prime Minister Mahathir Mohamad commented in a book coauthored with Japanese politician Shintaro Ishihara, "Malaysia's prosperity today owes much to Japanese investment, which created jobs and helped develop our capital market. These ties are mutually beneficial; Malaysia has in turn become a lucrative market for Japanese goods."[10] Japan, long aligned with the West, "has come home to Asia, and our neighbors have gradually encouraged Tokyo to play a more active role, politically as well as economically."[11]

Although the political and economic implications of this "tilt towards Asia"[12] are significant, this shift also has serious implications for marketing. As Japan strengthens its position at the center of Asian business, it becomes more important than ever for foreign companies to be in Japan and working with Japanese firms.

Japan as a Gateway

Japan serves in a number of ways as a focal point for the region, acting as:

- A trendsetter

- A source of insight into Asian culture and society

- A blueprint for market development

- A key competitor and collaborator

- A research and development center

- A cash generator

Japan as Trendsetter

Japan is a trendsetter throughout the region—from fashion to food to cars to karaoke. Teenagers in Kuala Lumpur and Bangkok collect photographs of Japanese actors in the way Japanese teens once collected Hollywood photos after World War II.[13] The Japanese public television drama *Oshin*, the story of a young woman who demonstrated values of selfless service and dedication, attracted 200 million viewers in China and was popular in Singapore, Indonesia, and Vietnam. Hashida Sugako, author of the television series, commented, "Viewers think, 'If we work hard, too, our country can be as modern and prosperous as Japan.'"[14] Although his comment certainly reflected a bit of nationalistic hyperbole, there is a small element of truth. In the way that Tokyo looks to New York, people throughout Asia look to Japan as a trendsetter.

A 1998 attitude survey of 1,200 women in six Asian cities found that 46 percent of respondents in Hong Kong and 42 percent of respondents in Taipei identified Tokyo as the city from which fashion emanates. The study by Dai-Ichi Kikaku Advertising Agency concluded that to produce hit products in Asia, a company must be in Tokyo and Hong Kong.[15]

Japanese companies and brands are highly valued throughout Asia. Even when China was closed to foreign trade, Japanese companies erected billboards to build awareness in and stimulate sales from travelers abroad. Japanese trading companies and retailers are a very important part of Asian business. While Japanese consumers look to Mercedes as a luxury standard, many Asian consumers see Toyota and Honda in the same light. Honda, for example, made an error in introducing a low-end automobile, the City, in Thailand. It eroded its luxury image with a smaller but more profitable high-end market in the country.

Both consumers and companies are looking to Japan as a model for business throughout Asia. "In factories across Asia, employees start the day by singing the company song and reciting its motto, and supervisors follow management methods honed in Tokyo and Osaka. From symbolic acts of loyalty to macroeconomic factors like cooperation between government and business, East Asians have borrowed chapter and verse from Japan's success story and have written their own versions."[16] Asian companies send delegations to

Japan to study their business models (even as these models are changing). Japan's industrial policies are being emulated throughout the region (even as these are also changing).

A cross-national study by Dentsu found that Japan was second only to the United States as the "country with which my country should create a close relationship," indicating the role that Japan plays as a pacesetter in the region. Japan far overshadowed England or Germany and even Hong Kong as a focal point of the region, as shown in Exhibit 3.1. With the exception of respondents in China, more than 70 percent of those surveyed in five other Asian countries said they "like the Japanese very much." In particular, they respected the Japanese values of hard work, business acumen, and technological achievement.

Given this attention to Japan, it might be fair to say that if you are not in Japan, Asians may not notice you. Just as the place to market to the United States is Madison Avenue in New York, the place to market to Asia may be Tokyo.

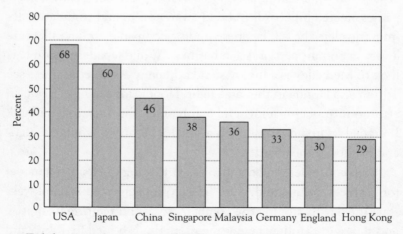

Exhibit 3.1. Countries and Regions With Which Respondents Feel Their Countries Should Create a Close Relationship (across six Asian nations)

Source: Dentsu, "Report on the First 'Comparative Analysis of Global Values,'" April 1997.

Insight into Asian Culture and Society

Asian leaders have made it clear that modernization is not Westernization. There is a distinction throughout Asia between a movement toward a more modern society and retaining cultural and societal values that are distinct from the West. This distinction has increased Japan's importance. It is the most advanced, most prosperous modern society that is not Western. If the United States is the model for Westernization, Japan is perhaps the best Asian model for modernization, reflecting a mix between Eastern and Western perspectives.

The leap from Japan to other Asian markets, is often not as great as the chasm that separates Asia from the West. Doraemon, a Japanese comic book character who lacks Superman's invincibility, has a broad following in China, South Korea, Vietnam, and other parts of Asia. But an English version failed in the United States. The idea of a vulnerable superhero was a small leap for Asian readers, but created a gulf for Western readers that even a superhero could not hurdle.[17]

Personal care products developed for sensitive Japanese skin, whitening powders, and other products can be brought more easily to other Asian markets. Rice-based cultures create similarities in some foods, appliances, and dishwashing liquids. Ajinomoto's monosodium glutamate, for example, sold in packets for consumer markets, is very popular with Southeast Asian consumers because of the primarily rice-based dishes in which fish sauce or soy sauce is used as the main seasoning.[18]

There are distinct differences between traditional Western and Asian cultural values. These differences lead to different marketing values, as summarized in Exhibit 3.2. As discussed, rapid changes in Japan and throughout Asia are shifting these traditional cultural and marketing values. Japan is now much more a mix between the East and West at the same time that Western markets are absorbing Eastern influences. For example, traditional Asian healthcare uses pharmaceuticals as a last resort, beginning instead with herbal

Exhibit 3.2. Traditional Western and Asian Cultural and Marketing Values:

Cultural Values

Classical Western
- Nuclear family, self, or immediate family
- Beliefs in competition, challenge, and self-expression

- Personal responsibility and independence
- Doing one's own thing
- Resentment toward authority
- Primacy given more to youth and change
- Control by "guilt" and conscience

Traditional Asian
- Extended family, blood/kinship/workgroups
- Beliefs in harmony, cooperation, and avoiding confrontation
- Shared responsibility and interdependence
- Public self and "face"
- Respect for authority
- Age and seniority important
- Value tradition
- Control by "shame" and "loss of face"

Marketing Values

- Brand segmentation; personal choice and self-expression through brands
- Presenters/testimonials important but more to draw attention to brands
- Seeding and diffusion from leading edge
- Belief in "understatement" of wealth
- Environmentalism

- Popular famous brands; confidence in brand and corporate names
- Imitation, emulation, and use of presenters as role models in ads
- Rapid adoption of successful brands
- Display of wealth and status
- Confidence in technology

Source: CRAM International, 1994.

medicines, acupuncture, and other holistic approaches. As Asia has adopted more Western approaches, the United States has moved to more Eastern approaches, with alternative medicines slowly becoming recognized by insurance companies and increasingly accepted by consumers.

Asian Youth: Not GenerAsian X

A 1997 study by advertising agency Ogilvy & Mather on the new generation of Asian adults indicates that younger Asians (twenty- to thirty-year-olds) are not merely adopting Western values or creating an Asian version of Generation X.[19] Instead, they represent a distinctly Asian perspective. The far-reaching study—based on 7,000 individual interviews and sixty-six focus groups in nine urban markets across Asia, as well as interviews with "trend gurus" in the regions—found that while these new Asian consumers are more independent than their parents, they are still more conservative and community-oriented than their Western peers. They are not adopting Western consumer values as a whole. Instead, they are combining traditional values with an increasing emphasis on individuality—in much the same way Japan has done (although Japan was not included in the study).

Ogilvy & Mather researchers called this young Asian generation "Genie" (GENeration who Independently Engage in society). They follow the rules, but still express individual independence. In this way, these young Asians contrast with Western Generation Xers, who have little respect for traditional values and social structures. "The study shows that the Genie are going down . . . a path that is true to their Asian roots as much as it is true to their ambitions for the future," said Mark Blair, O&M's Asian Pacific regional planning director.

The study contradicted much of the conventional wisdom about young Asian consumers, including:

Myth: Young Asians are consumed by materialism.

Reality: Asian values such as hard work and family are more important than materialism. They focus on using the best of the West rather than replacing Asian values with Western ones.

Myth: These "GenerAsian Xers" are disenfranchised.
Reality: They are committed to taking advantage of the new opportunities growing economies offer them.

Myth: Asia is too culturally diverse to characterize "Asian" youth.
Reality: The study found remarkable similarities among young Asians in different parts of the region, and much more similarity within the region than with Western peers.

Forty-four percent of the Genie (ages twenty to twenty-nine) said they would like to "stand out in a crowd," compared with 35 percent of respondents in their parents' generation (ages forty-five to fifty-four). But the 54 percent who thought children should never challenge their parents' authority was very close to the 59 percent of their parents, certainly much more similar to their parents than to the defiant Xers of the West.

A second study by Dentsu, which included Japan, confirms that Tokyo consumers share important similarities to those in five other Asian cities (Beijing, Bangkok, Singapore, Jakarta, and Bombay).[20] The study found that while the six Asian cities shared a common "orientation toward wealth," they also "are not willing to discard all their traditional values." Among the common values shared by Japanese and other Asian people are:

- A pragmatic view of health, family, and achieving wealth through economic growth

- A value on traditional virtues of politeness and hard work

- An increasing sense of equality between the sexes

- A high desire for a more democratic and equal society

- A rejection of wholesale adoption of Western standards (except in Thailand)

These younger consumers are a vital part of the emerging Asian market, not just because they are the future, but also because they account for such a large proportion of the market. Of the three billion people in Asia, half are under twenty-five years old.[21]

The Emerging Asian Middle Classes

While Asian youth share some characteristics, some segments of Asia are very global. The MTV culture and upscale segments tend to have more in common with their global peers than their compatriots. But the emerging middle class (or classes) share similarities across the newly industrialized economies of Asia. Unlike the Western middle classes, which emerged over long periods, the middle classes in Taiwan, South Korea, Hong Kong, and Singapore are primarily first generation and "have not crystallized in a strict sense."[22] A cross-national study of the emerging Asian middle class found evidence of a middle class as "an integral part of the capitalist development experience in post-war East Asia." This middle class is heterogeneous—in particular, most countries show the emergence of the old (salaried) middle class and the new (entrepreneurial) segment.[23]

Blueprint for Market Development

One thing Japan shares with the rest of Asia is its rapid market development. Japan's post-war rise to become one of the largest world markets shows a very different pattern of development than the gradual development of markets in the United States and Europe. Although other Asian nations have even accelerated Japan's rate, none have come as far along in their development. In this way, Japan's move from a struggling, tightly regulated local market to a wealthy, sophisticated, increasingly customer-driven market is a blueprint that other Asian nations are following.

As illustrated in Exhibit 3.3, there are two different paths to mature global markets—an individualistic model led by the United States and a collectivist model led by Japan. As shown by the upper arrow, the United States created a model for Western-style markets that is based on individualism. Europe followed the U.S. model closely, with emerging economies such as those in Eastern Europe and Latin America now moving along this U.S. path. In contrast, a more collective model of market development is occurring in Asian markets, with Japan as the pacesetter. In its path are Singapore, Hong Kong, Korea, China, and other Asian nations seeking to build mature markets on a different model than the West. Japan is seen as a blueprint for the development of these other Asian markets.

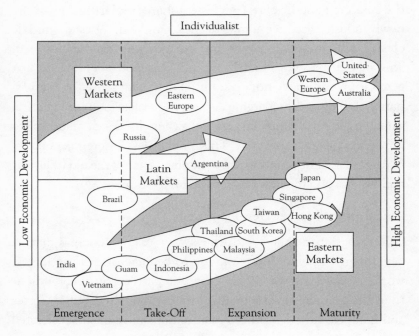

Exhibit 3.3. Global Market Dynamics
Source: CRAM International, 1994.

At the same time, these individualist and collectivist models are beginning to merge, with the extension of social networks for unemployment and other support systems in the United States and Europe. There is a balance between the market forces and social conscience that leads to dynamic changes in the structure of the economy and market.

These "collective" markets are based on distinctive Asian social structure, values, and attitudes, as summarized in Exhibit 3.4. The emergence of the market is based on extended families and a strong collective value system. As the economy takes off, the new rich begin to challenge family values and increase choices and aspirations. With the rapid growth of the economy, these values spread to an emerging middle class and modern values begin to emerge. In the mature or stabilizing phase of development, there is a shift toward a balance between the West and East, a rediscovery of traditional values, and a melding of traditional lifestyles with modernization.

What impact does this market evolution have on a specific product? Nippon Lever analyzed the specific benefits Asian women look for in a household cleaner. Traditional consumers might buy traditional products offering hygiene, purity, strong smell, and emphasis on hard work. The new Asian consumers are moving toward products with an emphasis on convenience and speed. As the market moves from a traditional to a more modern consumer, companies need to add products to their line and create new brands targeted toward these new Asian markets. Understanding the patterns of evolution in Japan can help in this process.[24]

Some aspects of the evolution of the Japanese market, summarized in Exhibit 3.5, will be seen in other parts of Asia. Japan offers insight into the pattern and impact of these shifts and the way market, societal, and family values interact.

While the evolution of every nation has its own trajectory, there are natural stages in the development of markets and marketing. As a rule of thumb, for example, consumers will purchase female

Exhibit 3.4. Collective Markets

	Emergence	Take-Off	Expansion	Maturity
Social Structure	• Extended family • Extrenched, privileged elite • Pyramidal hierarchy	• Emergence of new rich • Blue-collar growth • Urbanization • Decline of extended family	• Rise of nuclear family • Middle class • Development of young people • Rapid urbanization, pollution, traffic • Modernization	• Nuclear families • Egalitarianism • Lifestyle segmentation • Rise in single households
Values and Attitudes	• Traditional collectivism • Cooperation, group harmony • Duty, respect, self-sacrifice, and shared values • Traditional sex roles • Equality of rewards	• High aspirations • Overnight successes (new rich) • Choice, variety, access	• Western values • Emancipation of women • Materialism • Stress • Time pressure • New is good • Growth in environmental concerns	• Individualism • Balance of West and East • Return to roots • Quality time • Self-discovery • Leisure, nature • Health concerns • Aging population

Source: CRAM International, 1994.

Exhibit 3.5. The Japanese Blueprint for Asia

Traditional	Emerging
• Producer-driven	• Consumer-driven
• Close society	• Open society
• Homogeneous markets	• Heterogeneous markets
• Government control	• Deregulation
• Dominance of corporations	• Emergence of entrepreneurship
• Societal values shape consumer markets	• Consumer markets reshape values

sanitary napkins when the GNP per capita rises above $1,000 (¥120,000) and will purchase disposable diapers when the GNP per capita tops $3,000 (¥360,000). Unicharm, the leader in disposable diapers in Japan, established production and sales bases in seven areas in Asia. The Japanese disposable diaper market gives an indication of the potential. Created in the 1970s, the Japanese disposable diaper market has expanded to ¥80 billion in annual sales.[25]

Japan can be seen as forging a path of market development that other Asian nations are now following. Some of this is a result of deliberate imitation of the Japanese blueprint for development. In other cases, the natural evolution of markets—for example, the creation of consumers with disposable incomes leading to a more consumer-driven market—makes emerging markets follow in the Japanese pattern.

Korean retailers have seen a shakeout in their small mom-and-pop stores and rise in large-format stores, similar to the changes in Japan. Between 1995 and 1997, the number of grocery stores dropped by more than 7 percent.[27]

Perhaps because of these differences in market development, Japanese consumers place greater value on family than consumers in China and South Korea, as shown in Exhibit 3.6. In those nations, farther down on the curve, economy has gained priority over a

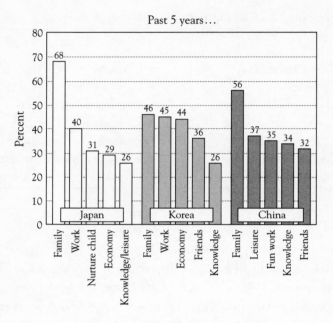

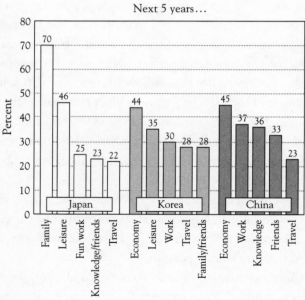

Exhibit 3.6. Values
Source: Human Studies, March 1997, pp. 23–28.

traditional family focus. The Japanese, in contrast, now have the luxury to pay increasing attention to family, leisure, friends, and travel.

Competitors and Collaborators

Japanese firms are at the center of Asian development. In Malaysia, more than 4 percent of its GNP is derived from Japanese manufacturer Matsushita alone.[28] Japan is one of the heaviest investors in most Asian economies.[29] Japan's more than $80 billion (¥10.4 trillion) in investments in Indonesia, Malaysia, South Korea, and Thailand at the end of 1997 was more than five times that of the United Kingdom, more than four times that of the United States, and nearly three times that of Germany.[30] Japan was by far the largest investor in Hong Kong, Taiwan, Malaysia, and Thailand (although it trailed behind the United States in South Korea and Singapore).[31] Any company entering other parts of Asia will come face to face with powerful Japanese firms, either as competitors or collaborators.

By the mid-1990s, Japan's exports to ASEAN nations accounted for more than a third of its total exports, surpassing exports to the United States. Asia also accounted for nearly one-third of Japan's imports. By 1994, 70 percent of VCRs and more than 40 percent of color televisions sold in Japan were sourced from Malaysia.[32]

Japanese companies have a long and enduring presence in Asia. Matsushita made its first move outside Japan with a venture into Thailand in 1961. Its "export center" in Malaysia was producing a quarter of its air conditioners and televisions by the mid-1990s and Malaysia accounted for a fifth of its foreign payroll. A joint-venture plant in Beijing established in 1989 was producing a million tubes per year by 1994.[33] Toyota created Toyota Motor Thailand Co., Ltd. in 1962 and started operations two years later. By 1996, its automobile plant became the first in the ASEAN region to produce one million vehicles. Honda created Asian Honda Motor in 1964 as a hub for developing motorcycle retailing in markets such as China, India, Taiwan, Thailand, Indonesia, and Vietnam (see box on

Honda's success in Vietnam).[34] Three years later, Honda became the first Japanese company to produce motorcycles and power products in Thailand. In 1984, it began automobile production in Thailand and later set up auto plants in the Philippines, Malaysia, Indonesia, Taiwan, and Pakistan. By the end of 1996, it had about one hundred auto outlets in its dealer network in Thailand alone and had a network of auto parts and systems plants in five Asian countries.[35]

Large Japanese manufacturing companies, facing increased costs of domestic production, moved their plants into Southeast Asia. They were followed by parts suppliers, and finally they created networks of Japanese firms. These Asian *keiretsu* networks have become a powerful force in many markets. *Asian Business* notes that in Thailand, "Local conglomerates, such as Siam Cement, have found it necessary to co-invest with the Japanese to ensure access to their own domestic market."[36]

Japanese firms control retail and trading networks throughout Asia that offer important access to Asian markets. Japan has about ten thousand trading companies engaged in foreign trade, the top six of which alone account for 4 percent of the world's trade.[37] As Trimble Navigation executive Mayumi Yamada noted, "The Japanese are currently building up their own networks in Asia, and in several years, an American company will find that a *keiretsu*-type structure will exist in Asia. Competing with the Japanese in Japan is the best way to stall their efforts elsewhere."

A presence in Japan offers opportunities to meet these firms on their home turf, either as partners or rivals. A Volvo executive commented that the company's absolute level of sales in Japan is not high (although the profit contribution is among the highest in the world). But a major reason for a presence in Japan is to keep an eye on tough Japanese competitors in their home market.

R&D Center

Japan also serves as an important research and development center for businesses in the region, although many companies, including

Signs of Change

Honda Means Motorbike in Vietnam

The road signs in Vietnam that read "No Honda" are not a sign of animosity toward the company but rather a sign of its widespread acceptance and success. The signs mean "no motorbikes," showing how the manufacturer has become synonymous with the product. How did Honda build such a dominant position?

Honda exported to Vietnam from 1965 until the government banned imports in 1970. Its reliable and economical four-stroke motorbikes were a great success. Honda's plans to build a factory in Vietnam were scuttled by the fall of Saigon in 1975. The plans could not be picked up again until 1996, after years of relentless effort. With government approval for a manufacturing joint venture, Honda opened the plant in December 1997. Despite the formal ban on sales, it is estimated that total Honda ownership in the country is 4.2 million. Some of the original Hondas from the 1960s are still on the road. Even when motorbikes could not be sold directly by Honda, they could be brought in as gifts from relatives, assembled as kits, or imported through government trading agents.

The keys to Honda's success are:

• A good product: The Honda Super Cub's reliability and efficiency accounts for much of its success.
• Persistence: Honda stumbled a number of times on its way to success. It humbly and patiently persevered.
• Consistent management: Part of its persistence was the key leadership of Honda Vietnam. Present CEO Mr. Takiguchi was involved from the beginning; he took one of the last flights out of Saigon in 1975 and came back to Vietnam to lead the firm in the 1990s.
• Asian way: Although Vietnam is very different from Japan, Honda's emphasis on building long-term relationships (business takes time), and a holistic rather than an analytical approach made it easier for the company to enter and succeed.[38]

Japanese firms, are setting up their facilities outside Japan. Japanese firms have a distinctive approach to innovation, which can best be understood through a presence in the nation.[39]

The demanding Japanese market can also be a source of innovations that benefit worldwide operations, in Asia and other parts of the world. When chipmaker Xicor entered Japan, its demanding industrial customers forced it to improve its delivery record and drop its smallest chip from two kilobit memories to just one kilobit. These innovations were then carried out to its operations in other parts of the world.[40]

As noted above, some of the specific products created in Japanese labs are eminently transferable to other parts of Asia. But the Japanese emphasis on high quality can be an impediment to success in markets that are willing to sacrifice quality for price.

Perhaps the most important role of having an R&D center in Japan is to understand a non-Western approach to research as well as new product development. It helps companies become aware of market innovations of Japanese competitors.

Japanese firms are also setting up R&D labs in Asia to better respond to specific markets. For example, Hitachi announced plans for using Singapore as a production base for DRAM chips and Sony announced a major alliance in R&D with Singapore's National Science and Technology Bureau. Toshiba also opened an R&D center in Singapore for digital TV and digital video disks. Toshiba, Mitsubishi Electric, Dai-Nihon Screen, and Hitachi are making similar research or production commitments to Taiwan.[41]

Cash Generator

Finally, because Asian markets will take time to develop, Japan offers a lucrative market that can help fuel future development in the region. Japanese consumers, even with recent economic instability, are still among the richest in the world. While investments in many parts of Asia—squeezed by a lack of disposable income, regulatory hurdles, and economic crises—are often operating at a loss,

Japanese markets are among the most profitable in the world. The investments in Asia are based on a hope for the future. Japan delivers current returns.

Although there other parts of the world in which to generate funds for Asian expansion, Japan offers these returns in addition to the strategic insights and connections that will help companies succeed in other Asian markets. Given this combination, a presence in Japan offers the resources and perspective needed to succeed in Asia. It provides a stepping stone to Asia and the cash to sustain an expanding Asian presence.

To Understand Asia, First Understand Japan

Understanding the changes in Japan—the revolution in its market and its impact on business model—provides insight into the current and future development of other Asian nations. Similarities in culture offer perspectives on approaching Asian markets. Contact with Japanese firms helps shape competition and cooperation in the region.

The changes in the Japanese market have tremendous implications for the practice of marketing in Japan. If these shifts, described in more detail later, are understood in Japanese markets, they can offer new insight into successful marketing to the new Asia. There are complexities and differences throughout Asian markets—and even within each market. But, given the central position Japan still has in Asia, companies that have no presence in Japan are at a disadvantage in other Asian markets. Understanding Japan doesn't guarantee success in Asia. But a failure to understand the lessons of Japan can set companies up for making the same mistakes in other emerging Asian markets.

Increasingly, companies are not focusing only on a Japan strategy or Asian strategy, but rather a global strategy. No company should ignore Japan or Asia as part of their overall strategy. Asia is the largest part of the world in terms of population, with enormous entrepreneurial centers and people, and extremely rich countries. Japan is the second-largest market in the world. Any global portfolio of activities should include a major presence in Japan and the rest of Asia.

As companies move more and more toward designing an integrated global supply chain, Japan and various Asian countries play a major role in this integrated global supply chain. As we saw, Japan can often act as the major R&D center, but it can also provide financing and managerial skills and serve as a very attractive market. Various Asian countries can, in turn, provide various raw materials, manufacturing, relatively cheap labor, as well as entrepreneurial skills and huge markets for products or services that are designed to meet Asia's changing needs.

Points of Leverage

- If you are in Japan, to what extent have you capitalized on your experience there to enter other Asian countries?

- Which strategies that succeeded in Japan have worked or failed in other Asian countries? What have you learned from this Japanese experience? Which strategies may succeed in Japan and other Asian countries in the future?

- If you are not in Japan, how could entry into Japan facilitate your entry into Asia? What lessons that you might learn in Japan would be applicable in other parts of Asia in the future?

- How does your understanding of the Japanese market help you understand trends in other parts of Asia and Asian culture and society?

- In what ways can Japan serve as a blueprint for development of other Asian countries?

- Which companies or individuals with whom you are working in Japan can be leveraged to form strategic alliances to enter Asia?

- What have you learned from competing in Japan that can help you compete against Japanese companies in other parts of Asia and the world?

- How can an R&D presence in Japan help in other Asian markets?

- How can profits from the Japanese market help fuel other initiatives in Asia?

- What role should Japan and other Asian countries play in an integrated global supply chain for firms such as yours?

4

Strategies for Entering Japan and Asia

"In uncertain economic times, value becomes more important. We expect this to continue."
Gary Steuck, president of Lands' End Japan[1]

In 1998, Williams-Sonoma ended its decade-old joint venture with Tokyu Department Stores and pulled out of Japan. It might be seen as yet another example of the daunting challenges for foreign companies entering Japan, particularly in the current economic environment. The only problem with this interpretation is that while Williams-Sonoma's business was flagging, Lands' End Japan's business was booming.

When Lands' End entered Japan in 1994, it established its own office to handle catalog production, warehousing, and fulfillment operations in contrast to Williams-Sonoma's joint venture. (In lifestyle mail-order catalogs, the experience of traditional retailers may not always be an asset.) Lands' End's local operations facilitated customization of the catalog to the market, more rapid response times and more control over the overall quality of the customer interaction. Also, Lands' End's single focus on direct mail seemed more successful than the divided focus of Williams-Sonoma on retail and direct mail. Lands' End tailored its product line based on sales. It also priced its products in yen and bought currency futures to insulate itself from currency fluctuations.

As has been the case throughout Japan's recent history, foreign entrants with seemingly comparable skills have widely divergent experiences. Coca-Cola thrived while Pepsi faltered. Domino's surged while Pizza Hut stumbled. Amway has been very successful in building its business through direct, door-to-door sales, but Avon has had a tougher time opening doors in Japan. Even some underdogs have risen to become dominant because of a better understanding of the Japanese market. Gillette, the leader in shaving products in most of the world, is a distant second to Schick in Japan, which has 70 percent of the market compared to Gillette's 10 percent. Kodak, which founded the Japanese film market, watched Fuji take over the market and become a powerful global rival.

The differences between winners and losers in this market reveal no simple recipe for success. In fact, they show the many intense challenges presented for foreign entrants. Ultimately, the new entrant who understands the traditional rules of marketing in Japan—and the ways these rules are changing—has a greater chance of success.

Starbucks: Brewing a Stronger Market Entry

Sometimes the same company can have two different experiences in Japan. Starbucks, for example, entered Japan in 1992 when the U.S. Marriott hotel chain became a franchisee. Marriott opened a Starbucks café in the Narita airport, but it had low awareness and a poor site. It withdrew in nine months.

Two years later, however, Starbucks returned with a vengeance. Not only was the global market for gourmet coffee beverages heating up, but Starbucks was much more strategic in planning its entry. It teamed up with Tokyo-based Sazaby Inc., which operated Afternoon Tea. This partner gave it experience in serving beverages to Japan, but what is even more important, the company had a focus on "proposing a lifestyle half a step ahead of the times." This was a partner tuned into the new Japan. Instead of the backwater of the airport, Starbucks established stores in premium metropolitan sites to gain awareness without advertising.

By the end of 1998, it had opened more than thirty stores in Japan and had accelerated its expansion to two new outlets per month. With its high-quality product and premium prices, it has displaced lower-cost chains. Even in this turbulent economic time, it represents an affordable luxury and a lifestyle statement for young Japanese consumers. Despite the costs of aggressive expansion, Starbucks expected its fifty-fifty joint venture with the Japanese partner to become profitable in 1999, and it had drawn up plans for 250 stores by 2004.

Thus, the same product from the same company fared very differently based on different entry strategies. For Starbucks, having a market-savvy partner in Japan, the right locations (facilitated by falling real-estate prices), and a critical mass of consumer awareness allowed the company to surge into Japan.

More Attractive Than Ever

For companies with the right strategy, Japan continues to be an attractive market. Despite a long recession and turmoil in the Japanese financial system, foreign companies are flooding into Japan. The Japan Bank reports that foreign direct investment in Japan climbed by 167 percent in 1996 to reach ¥5.5 trillion ($48 billion), as shown in Exhibit 4.1. A study of foreign firms in Japan by the Japanese External Trade Organization (JETRO) found that more than half saw sales rise in 1997 and, even with a worsening recession, more than one-third expected increasing sales in 1998.

A 1997 MITI survey of foreign-affiliated firms in Japan (at least one-third foreign ownership), found that 65.4 percent assessed their business as successful while just 1 percent characterized their business as unsuccessful. For the remaining 34 percent, the jury was still out. (The study didn't include businesses that had packed up and left.) Of those "successful" businesses, more than 70 percent were planning to

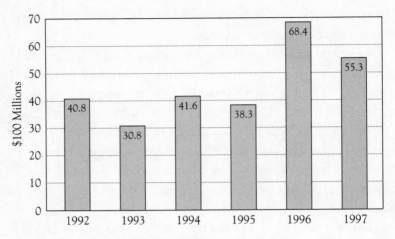

Exhibit 4.1. Foreign Direct Investment in Japan
Source: Compiled by JETRO based on application statistics at the Ministry of Finance, 1998.

expand their business activities over the next five years, despite the economic crisis. The primary area of expansion was sales and marketing activities. A full 85 percent of those companies that intended to expand their Japanese operations said sales and marketing was the primary area targeted for expansion.[2] This probably reflects an understanding that in the midst of the economic troubles, Japan's market revolution is still creating significant opportunities.

Foreign firms are coming into Japan in record numbers. Huge Western superstores are flying into Japan on the "tail winds" of the deregulation of large retail stores.[3] Toys "R" Us fought an uphill battle to enter Japan in 1991, but by late 1997 was posting annual sales of ¥100 billion, with 10 percent of the market. It had become the leading toy retailer in Japan, with plans to open 100 stores by 2000.[4] Resistance from a band of 500 small stores, which formed the Association of Toy Specialty Stores to combat this threat, had been unable to fend off this invasion, and its membership dwindled to just over fifty stores six years after Toys "R" Us arrived.[5]

With easing regulations making large stores even more attractive, other category killers are ramping up in Japan. By the end of 1997, both OfficeMax and Office Depot had established beachheads in Japan.[6] Office Depot opened its first store in Tokyo's Shinagawa in late 1997 and plans to open fifty stores by 2001. OfficeMax announced plans to have fifty stores with annual sales of more than ¥35 billion ($300 million) by the year 2000, beginning with a 2,000-square-foot store in Yokkaichi City, some 200 miles west of Tokyo. At the same time, Japan's small stationery stores are expected to drop from about 20,000 to just 5,000 stores by the end of the century.[7]

These new arrivals offer a much wider selection and lower prices than their smaller peers in Japan. The first OfficeMax, for example, carried 10,000 items. It sells ballpoint pens for 99¥ per dozen compared to a price of 80¥ to 100¥ for a single ballpoint pen at stationery stores. Copy paper, which retails for ¥5,250 at stationery stores, costs just ¥1,630 at OfficeMax. Because these large retailers often do business directly with manufacturers to cut costs, the growth of these stores is also sending shockwaves through the wholesale and distribution system.

Large foreign entrants are moving in on other sectors as well. Sports Authority opened in the summer of 1997 and plans to have 100 stores by 2003. Foot Locker opened its first store in Funabashi City, with Athlete's Foot close on its heels.[8] Consumer computer direct marketer Micro Electronics opened its first Japanese office in November 1997, encouraged by the successes of Dell and Gateway.[9] Some of these entrants are summarized in Exhibit 4.2. Takuya Okada, chairman of Jusco, a large retailer, commented that for these global superstores, "Distribution is not a domestic industry. They will ride the waves of globalization and go anywhere."[10]

Many of these entrants are bypassing traditional joint ventures and trading companies to launch wholly owned subsidiaries in Japan.[11] Pitney Bowes, for example, established a subsidiary in Japan in 1995. CEO Shoya Imura estimated the Japanese market

Exhibit 4.2. Rushing Into Japan—A Sample of Recent Foreign Entrants and Expansions

Entrant	Headquarters	Business
Toys "R" Us	United States	Toys, 70 stores
The Gap	United States	Casual clothing, 30 stores
L.L. Bean	United States	Outdoor clothing, 16 stores
Office Depot	United States	Office supplies, 3 stores
OfficeMax	United States	Office supplies, 3 stores
North Coast Medical	United States	Direct mail, products for elderly
Greenery International	Netherlands	Fruits and vegetables
Cold Water Creek	United States	Direct mail, clothing
City Chain	Hong Kong	Watches
Tallies	United States	Coffee shop
James Mead	United Kingdom	Direct mail, clothing
British Petroleum	United Kingdom	Gas stations
Bergdorf Goodman	United States	Direct mail, general
Marks and Spencer	United Kingdom	Department store
Carrefour	United Kingdom	Department store
adidas	Germany	Sporting goods
Walgreen	United States	Drug store
Cosco Wholesale	United States	Membership discount wholesale
Rooms to Go	United States	Furniture
American Malls International	United States	Shopping centers
Crate and Barrel	United States	Furniture
Foot Locker	United States	Athletic shoes and apparel
Athlete's Foot	United States	Athletic shoes and apparel

Source: Nihon Keizai Shinbun, November 12, 1997 and Nihon Keisai Shimbu, January 1, 1999, P. 25. Number of stores, where indicated, are as of 1999.

could produce sales of around 300,000–400,000 units and he is launching a low-priced postage metering system to attract smaller firms.[12] United States pharmaceutical firm Allergen first entered Japan in 1976 through a joint venture with Santen Pharmaceuticals to market lens cleansers and preservatives. It established a wholly owned subsidiary in 1985 to market an internal lens for patients suffering from cataracts. Allergen dissolved its partnership with Santen. The company not only felt it could operate alone, but also planned to recruit directly from Japanese colleges, showing the increasing acceptance of foreign firms.

A 1998 survey of women aged (18–59) in the Tokyo metropolitan area found that close to half used foreign-brand cosmetics.[13] In addition to the expected success of Christian Dior and Chanel, young Japanese women have propelled newcomer MAC into third place in consumer awareness. Among teenagers, it is the top brand. Its sales strategy and lower price are geared toward younger audiences, trading formal uniforms of its in-store personnel for individually distinct dresses and make-up and keeping packaging simple. This distinctive positioning to target younger buyers shows the power of effective marketing in rapidly building brand awareness.

Why this rush into Japan? According to a 1998 survey by JETRO, the business environment for foreign firms is improving in many dimensions, including greater opportunities to secure good employees, less prejudice against foreign firms, relaxing regulations, and greater chances for mergers and acquisitions, as shown in Exhibit 4.3. Eased restrictions of the large-scale retail trade laws, decreased prices of land, and a voracious set of consumers are all making Japan a more attractive market for foreigners. While interest in Japan in the early-1990s focused more on Asian entry, there is increasing awareness of the market itself. A survey of 206 foreign firms by communications firm LBS, Co., LTD. found the percentage of firms entering Japan principally because of the attraction of the market increased from 77 percent to 87 percent between 1994 and 1997.[14]

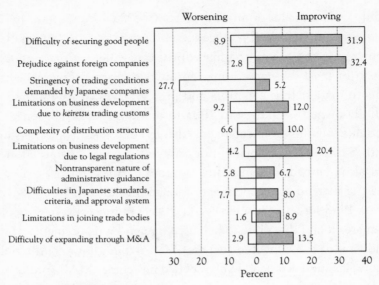

Note: Multiple responses

Exhibit 4.3. Changes in Business Environment
Source: Attitude Survey of Foreign Corporations Toward Direct Investments in Japan, JETRO, November, 1998.

The Emergence of Mergers and Acquisitions

JETRO called 1998 "a watershed in the emergence of full-scale M&A activity in Japan."[15] A wave of mergers and acquisitions has been driven by the combination of "big bang" financial reform, financial difficulties of some Japanese firms, and foreign companies' increasing interest in Japan. Japanese firms' high stock prices and tax rules that made acquisitions and mergers difficult in the past are no longer as significant obstacles. The close ties of the *keiretsu* are weakening.

M&A activity among Japanese firms and between Japanese and foreign firms has steadily increased since 1993. Daiwa Securities reported that there were 700 M&A cases involving Japanese firms, up eighty-three from the year before. Nikko Securities estimated that the number would reach 800 by 1998. The major areas of activity are finance, communications, and distribution.

Merrill Lynch has rapidly expanded its Japanese business through acquisitions, including purchasing thirty-three branches of the defunct Yamaichi Securities, once Japan's fourth-largest brokerage. GE Capital expanded its business with the acquisition of Toho Mutual Life Insurance Company's 500 sales offices.

The increasing instances of mergers and acquisitions offer more opportunities than ever for foreign entrants to move into Japan. But selecting the best entry strategy from these complex and changing options has become more difficult.

Growth Markets

Despite the economic downturn in Japan, there are still parts of the economy that are expected to grow, as shown in Exhibit 4.4. Some are driven by technology, such as the projected increases in electronic commerce. Other markets such as lifestyle and culture, expected to more than double by 2010, are being propelled forward by demographic changes in the Japanese market. There are still other bursts of growth, such as the expected 267-percent increase in distribution and logistics, expanding because of structural and regulatory changes in the market.

Challenges of the Japanese Market

Although Japan is becoming more hospitable to foreign entrants, it continues to be a challenging market. A 1997 survey of more than 200 foreign firms with offices in an average of thirty countries found that 64 percent believe they face greater difficulties in Japan than in other parts of the world. Only 3 percent felt it was easier to do business in Japan than elsewhere.[16]

A 1995 survey of foreign-affiliated firms found the following obstacles were among the most commonly cited, although many of these concerns have been mitigated by recent changes in the Japanese market:

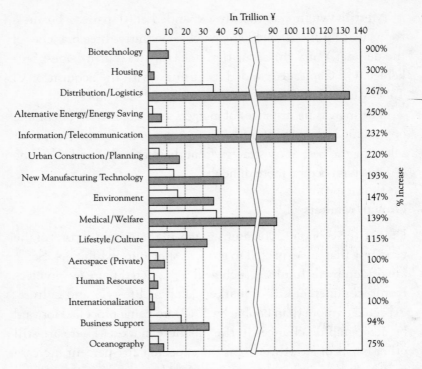

Exhibit 4.4. High-Growth Markets
Source: Compiled by JETRO from "Action Plans for Change and Creation of Economic Structures" (Cabinet agreement on June 15, 1997) and the follow-up on the Cabinet agreement on December 14, 1997. Note that market-size forecasts may fluctuate depending on technology advances.

- High business costs (82.3 percent). Today, many of these costs have significantly decreased.

- Japanese-style infrastructure (66.7 percent). New distribution systems and consumer attitudes are dismantling much of the traditional, cumbersome infrastructure.

- Strict customer demands (61 percent). Consumers have remained strict but are more willing to make compromises for value.

- Difficulty hiring and keeping capable employees
  (47.6 percent). The changing attitudes of recent
  college graduates are making it easier for foreign firms
  to hire Japanese employees.

- Administrative procedures (34.9 percent). Relaxing
  regulations and eased consumer pressures are making
  the red tape less burdensome.[17]

As shown in the survey, the most serious obstacles to Japanese entry
are the high costs of labor, real estate, logistics, taxes, utilities, and
other expenses. (This may have been particularly emphasized
because the survey was conducted during a period of significant
appreciation of the yen against the dollar.)

The recent economic downturn has actually reduced many of
these costs for foreign investors as exchange rates have become
much more favorable. This helps mitigate what has traditionally
been the most significant obstacle to establishing Japanese operations. Foreign real-estate investments soared with the drop in prices,
as American vulture funds increased their investment in Japanese
properties by fivefold in 1997, up to $20 billion (¥2.42 trillion).
Companies such as Goldman, Sachs and Bankers Trust are purchasing Tokyo assets for as little as 10 percent of their peak prices.[18]
This was so widespread that the Japanese media began decrying the
American "invasion," reminiscent of how the U.S. media responded
to Japanese real-estate and business acquisitions in the 1980s. Many
foreign entrants are finding that the real-estate crash has made it
possible to enter Japan at fire-sale prices.

Government restrictions and administrative limitations,
as noted in Chapter Two, are being dismantled in many areas, making Japan more open to business. Similarly, the limitations created
by Japanese-style business practices such as *keiretsu* relationships and
complicated distribution channels are being bypassed by new supplier relationships and more direct distribution.

These changes may explain why there has been such a tremendous influx of new investment into Japan and why this flood of entrants has not abated, despite Japan's economic decline.

On the other hand, when nearly two-thirds of foreign companies in Japan say the market is tougher there than the rest of the world, new entrants should take note. The obstacles identified in the 1995 report continue to be important factors in Japanese entry that can make or break an entering company.

Strategies For Japanese Market Entry

If past experience is any indication, half of the companies rushing into Japan today will fail and half will succeed. Some will fall to domestic competitors. Others will be beaten by similar foreign entrants using superior strategies. What will separate the successes from the failures? Although some advisers propose simplistic formulas for success factors in entering Japan, the reality is far more complex. Some companies succeed with local management, others with foreign management. Some use partners while others go it alone. Some carefully tailor or remake their products while others exploit their foreignness.

While we do not offer a prescription for successful Japanese entry, we will examine some of the most important issues and examples of companies that have succeeded or failed in moving into Japan by using the following strategies:

- Tailoring to the market by adapting to cultural and structural differences

- Finding opportunities in declining markets

- Not underestimating local competition

- Offering a unique product and positioning

- Using foreignness as an advantage

- Using alliances strategically

- Using Japan as a stepping stone to Asia

Tailor to the Market

Perhaps the biggest obstacle to entering Japan is the inability of outsiders to see the continuing differences in the Japanese market. Companies that are wildly successful in other parts of the world have stumbled badly in Japan. Others have been successful by tailoring their offerings to the market. For example, tiny U.S. direct-mail retailer Paul Frederick Menswear built an $8 million (¥960) business in Japan, exceeding sales of much larger catalogs. How? While major retailers only offered sleeve lengths at the American standard of 32 inches, Paul Frederick, noting that Japanese men wore shorter sleeves, produced shirts with 31- and 30-inch sleeves. These shirts were instant hits. The company also responded to different color preferences of Japanese customers. It translated its English-language catalog into Japanese and saw its sales jump.[19] When REI translated its catalog into Japanese, it saw an 80-percent increase in sales.

In contrast, a survey found 70 percent of Japanese customers who ordered from a foreign catalog experienced some problem with their order. Some ordered catalogs that were delivered eight weeks later, only to find out when they placed an order that the items they wanted were no longer available. When mail order was a novelty and the yen was high against the dollar, many mistakes were forgiven, but now the catalogs rise or fall based on their ability to satisfy the market.

As this is basic marketing, it almost goes without saying, except that so many new entrants fail precisely because they neglect to tailor their products or services to the Japanese market. Why is this? Perhaps it is because companies that moved with relative ease into

European markets expected to do the same in Japan. They see signs of globalization and expect Japanese markets to be more like the West.

American automakers stumbled when they failed to make relatively simple changes to their products, such as right-hand steering, improved body finish, or Japanese-language owner's manuals. They ignored these differences at their peril.

As in any global market, there are parts of the Japanese market that are represented by global tastes and styles. Some Japanese drivers, for example, prefer left-hand drive cars. For products and services directed toward this global segment, local tailoring may not be as important. But for other products and services, this awareness of and response to local demands is crucial.

Different types of products also require different approaches for success. Coca-Cola's worldwide success is based on products that are targeted toward youth and leisure-oriented markets. In contrast, Nestlé products are part of the culinary culture, and because attitudes toward food and cuisine differ by culture, its lead products vary in different markets. While Coca-Cola takes a global strategy to market segments, Nestlé succeeds with a more regional strategy tailored to local tastes.

Tailor to Culture

Japanese consumers have distinctive tastes. Domino's tailored its product to these tastes, with distinctive toppings such as octopus. It also sells $20 million (¥2.4 trillion) worth of *mayojaga* pizza, combining bacon, onion, potato, and mayonnaise. In understanding and responding to Japanese tastes, Domino's quickly built its position in a market in which others pitching standard Western products failed. Two other examples are Dunkin' Donuts and Mr. Donuts. Both companies have struggled in Japan for the simple reason that Japanese consumers don't eat donuts. This is a serious obstacle for companies that are built around this one product. Mr. Donuts has successfully addressed this challenge by expanding its offerings to include curry, something it probably doesn't offer in many other places. McDonald's also introduced rice-based fast foods—meaning the Big Mac outlet is no longer identical throughout the world. It is this awareness of and response to local tastes that is the key to their success.

There are also preferences that may or may not be culturally based but are significant. For example, the widely used tranquilizer Valium is in low demand in Japan. However, digestives are in far greater use than in the United States. Japanese businessmen who eat too much ingest enzymes to relieve the symptoms. A preferred product form is a pelletized product which is dissolved in water and is then consumed.

Coca-Cola adjusted its product to Japan using a smaller-sized can to reflect the Japanese preference for a shorter drink. With Sprite, Coca-Cola also had to adjust the taste to make it competitive with Kirin's Lemon and other domestic brands. Nestlé entered Japan in the 1960s and gained more than 70 percent of the market for instant coffee by the 1990s. But the company has built its business by responding to changing tastes, packaging, and other factors. Nestlé used strong brand images for Perrier, Valvert, Maggi, Buitoni, KitKat, Milo, and other brands, rather than relying on its corporate brand.[20] Toys "R" Us Japan developed unique merchandising techniques such as offering Barbie dolls that appealed to Japanese consumers and incorporating new store designs to win the hearts of customers. Companies have had to make subtle changes such as lowering scent levels in soap, decreasing creaminess and sweetness of chocolate, and modifying toothbrushes for smaller hands.

It is very easy for foreign companies to miss the subtle cultural differences. There is the now-famous example of the Western firm that developed cake mix designed for the Japanese rice cooker. The mix worked well, but failed in Japanese focus groups because the developers didn't understand the significance of rice in the culture nor the reluctance of the Japanese to sully their rice cookers with flavored batters.[21]

Snapple, one in a long string of failed entrants, withdrew from Japan after its cloudy beverages failed to catch on in the Japanese market.[22] Similarly, a toothpaste maker ran advertising and distributed thousands of free tubes of its product to households throughout Japan. The only problem was that it hadn't tested whether Japanese consumers liked the taste of the toothpaste. They didn't, so each sample that had been distributed further eroded the company's reputation.[23]

Tailor to High Standards of Quality

Many companies also have to adapt their products and service to Japanese standards of quality. Despite an interest in lower prices, customers are unwilling, for example, to accept a car with minor scratches in the finish or to purchase consumer goods in dented

---

Signs of Change

Not Your Average Coke Machine

Japanese products are diverse, quite different from Western varieties, and they are rapidly changing. A peek inside the ubiquitous Japanese vending machine offers a glimpse of the extremely different tastes of the Japanese market. Japan is one of the only markets in which canned coffee is sold. Other offerings include *amazake* (a sweet drink made from fermented rice), consome/potage/corn soup, *tonyu* (soy bean milk), *satsuma imo* (sweet potato drink), *miso shiru* (miso soup), *tonjiru* (Japanese-style pork soup), and *sake chazuke* (rice and salmon doused in hot tea). This is in addition to soft drinks, juices and sports drinks. Japanese consumers drank ¥1.3 trillion (about $11 billion) in soft drinks from vending machines in 1997. Carbonated beverages were overtaken by the tea category in 1996, and a reported 500 new items are introduced and disappear annually.[24]

packages. A Japanese women's magazine ordered clothing from several Western catalogs and produced scathing reviews of the quality of some of the merchandise with loose threads or stitching. In contrast, retailers with good product quality, such as L.L. Bean or Hanna Andersson, benefit from their reputations.

Tailor to Market Structure

New products or services need to address the peculiar cultural and structural demands of the Japanese market. Failure to do so is one of the most common sources of entry failure, and among the easiest to identify and rectify if companies take off their domestic blinders.

Kodak failed to see the importance of channel equity in developing its position in Japan, and this is where Fuji had an opportunity to surpass its large foreign rival. Although channel equity is less important in the emerging customer-driven Japanese market, it is still more important in Japan than in the United States.

Domino's also had to tailor its Japanese business to the complexity and narrowness of streets in Tokyo. It developed a sophisticated computer mapping system to guide its delivery people to their destinations and employed smaller-sized vehicles to move its product through Tokyo traffic.

Find Opportunities in Decline

While many foreign entrants fail to see differences in Japanese markets, many domestic competitors may fail to see or neglect to capitalize on available opportunities. Industries in which Japanese competitors are out of touch with the market or are considered unattractive may offer great opportunities for Western companies to enter with little resistance. Declining industries in Japan may be due to unalterable market conditions, or they may be a sign that Japanese firms are failing to meet the needs of the market. By examining these industries and looking for ways to revive them by changing the value proposition, entrants can profit. The motion picture industry, as described in the upcoming box, is a good example of the opportunities that may lie hidden.

In another example, Merrill Lynch & Company drove aggressively into Japan's turbulent financial services industry. In 1998, in what it called "Project Blossom," Merrill took advantage of bank failures to hire thousands of experienced employees and build a nationwide branch network in a period of a few months. Other U.S. firms have also found opportunities in the changing Japanese market, such as Fidelity Investments' push to sell mutual funds by telephone and direct mail. In just two years, Goldman, Sachs & Company's mutual funds business grew to be the ninth-largest in the nation. GE Capital became the first foreign firm to break into the Japanese life insurance industry.[25]

The movement of these U.S. companies into Japan has also accelerated the growth of foreign advertising agencies. Ogilvy & Mather Japan's billings, for example, grew by 179 percent in 1997. As L. B. Lazarus of Ogilvy & Mather commented, "The Japanese subsidiary's billings rankings in Japan rose from number 41 to number 26 in the past year. Major global corporations are reducing the number of agencies in order to foster a common global brand. . . . The brand is becoming more important than ever."[26]

The recession environment itself is seen as an opportunity. As Arthur Serkoviz of DDB Needham commented, "We have the experience of devising advertising strategy during recessions in the United States and other markets. We can advise Japanese corporations who are suffering under adverse economic conditions."[27]

Major Japanese railway companies are entering the funeral business in Japan, consolidating what has traditionally been an industry of small, regional companies. Companies such as Keikyu, Seibu, Tobu, Nagoya, and Hankyu Railways have built on their accompanying businesses by offering taxis and memorial gifts. This plan also utilizes the companies' excess of land and employees.

In considering opportunities for entering Japan, examine industries that are in decline. Is the decline because of lack of marketing

Signs of Change

A Hollywood Ending

By all measures, the Japanese motion picture industry was in decline. Its peak gross attendance of 1.1 billion in 1958 had dropped to just 170 million by 1997. Its 7,500 movie theaters had dwindled to a mere 1,800. With audiences dropping more rapidly than theaters were closing, the industry problems seemed destined to worsen. Most of the failed theaters were part of the a *keiretsu*, showing only films made by their own studios and offering only single screens. Viewers now preferred to stay home and watch videos.

Japanese studios responded to the decline by cranking out more films. However, AMC and Time Warner employed a new model to succeed in this declining Japanese market. By 1997, Time Warner's joint venture called Warner-Mycal had opened eleven cinema complexes, and AMC had opened thirteen, with many more in the works.

The two Western companies challenged outdated Japanese regulations that prohibited multiple screens within a single building. The law was changed in 1992. Time Warner created a set of large suburban theaters, taking advantage of the increased mobility of Japanese viewers. AMC, on the other hand, took its multiplexes directly into the heart of the cities. Although studios were miffed, viewers flocked to the new theaters. In one example, the new Warner-Mycal theater in Ebina surpassed Nippon Gekijyo theater in Central Ginza for attendance. A remarkable 940,000 people visited its facility in the first year. With Ebina's population of just 110,000, this means every citizen visited the theater an average of nine times in a year. (The Japanese national average for theater attendance is slightly more than one visit per year.)

Now that the market for multiplexes has been opened, many Japanese competitors are rushing into the fray, including Namco, Jusco, and Sony. But the foreign entrants that saw an opportunity in decline got a head start on the competition.

savvy? Are there ways to revive the market through different approaches? Can regulations and other obstacles be removed?

Don't Underestimate Domestic Competition

An American appliance manufacturer closed its office in Tokyo after it faced unexpected local competition in its market for CFC-free refrigerators.[28] After achieving success in Europe and the United States, it had seen Japan as a major outpost in carrying its business empire into Asia. But it had not anticipated the strength and speed of local competition. Given this opposition, the company failed to gain more than 1 percent of the market, and it quickly withdrew its office to Singapore.

Many new entrants' innovative products experience initial success. But the market merely tolerates these products—once the market is recognized, Japanese competitors come in with their own products, offering superior features and lower prices. The original entrant sees its promising start derailed. This phenomenon is referred to as "the three-years miracle." The companies that have been able to survive this have truly learned Japanese business practices and continue to improve their products.

A clearly differentiated product or service was one of the key factors for successful entry identified in a 1994 study of 436 foreign companies by Hideki Yoshihara of Kobe University.[29] Coca-Cola and McDonald's introduced a new product concept to Japan, making it easier for them to gain a foothold. Procter & Gamble faced far greater opposition in entering the detergent market because Japan already had a strong competitor, Kao, which fought aggressively for the market. Toyota has recently successfully battled back against BMW and Mercedes with new luxury brands.

Offer a Unique Product and Positioning

It used to be that a powerful corporate brand in Japan, with a reputation that took ten to fifty years to build, was the key to success. Now, Japanese consumers are much more likely to try an unknown brand. This makes a unique product or positioning more powerful in entering Japan. The Gap went from being an outsider to being a household name through its product offerings and positioning. Instead of taking advantage of market power, companies can more readily take advantage of lifestyle changes to find new niches for their products.

By stressing individualism, Reebok made a strong entrance in Japan in 1986, setting off what became known as "the Reebok phenomenon."[30] In contrast to its position as an athletic shoe for female aerobics students and office workers in the United States, Reebok positioned its product in Japan as New York chic. This image, reinforced by upscale pricing and advertising that stressed individualism, appealed to trendy, young office workers in their twenties. (As new competitors entered the market, however, Reebok's share plummeted and it began to emphasize health and physical fitness. Eventually it introduced lower-cost shoes.)

Tiffany's initially entered Japan through department store Mitsukoshi, but the jewelry company had only moderate success. In 1993, it set up its own boutiques. Where its department-store partner had primarily pushed moderately priced jewelry, Tiffany's emphasized its upscale image and its expertise in diamonds and platinum. Through its unique product and service offering, Tiffany continued to grow through the economic downturn. By 1998, it had opened forty-four outlets in Japan. Michael Kowalski, president and CEO of New York-based Tiffany & Co., commented, "The Japanese consumer, despite economic difficulties, seems ready to recognize good design and act accordingly."[31]

Utilize Foreignness

In some cases, as with Reebok, the entrant's foreignness can be an asset. This is particularly true for fashion items, but it can also be true for technology entrants. Deutche Telecom Tokyo entered Japan in 1990, after the arrival of British and American telecommunications companies in the 1980s. To stand out, it emphasized its German connections by offering direct communications to Germany. It also brought its highly developed ISDN technology to Japan and began renting cellular phones at Japanese airports based on the European GSM standard. This allowed travelers to communicate with people in Europe and other countries using systems based on the standard. Through these strategies, it turned its foreign reputation, know-how, and connections into assets.[32]

Levi's stood out from a host of firmly entrenched foreign and domestic competitors by equating its product with America. Its "heroes" campaign, linking its product with rugged American individualists such as James Dean and John Wayne, took it from an unknown brand to the dominant jean brand in Japan. Another lesson learned through Levi's experience in Japan is that the entrant's global reputation may be of little or no value in Japan. Although Levi's was well-known in other parts of the world, it was unknown in Japan. Assumptions such as this can be a tremendous disadvantage

---

Signs of Change

"High School Gal Talk"

The Japanese fascination with the West, as well as their ability to absorb and change it is evidenced in a new, hip dialect popular among Japanese teenagers. This *ko-gyaru-go,* roughly "high school gal talk," takes English expressions and transmutes them into Japanese phrases. For example, the greeting "Check it out, Joe" becomes *chekaraccho.* Teenagers' cool, loose socks become *roozu sokusu* and a "dangerous" (difficult) test is *denjarasu.* Teenage boys croon *wonchu* (I want you) to teenage girls. The language allows teenagers to converse without being understood by their parents, as well as convey a hip, international image.[33]

for successful global firms that show up in Tokyo expecting to be welcomed by customers. However, foreignness and a lack of reputation can also be opportunities to create a distinctive definition in Japan.

Use Alliances and Japanese Leadership Only When They Truly Provide a Better Understanding of the Market

Some argue that for foreigners to understand the market, they must have Japanese executives and Japanese partners. There is certainly great truth in this insight, but there are also many times when Japanese staff and alliance partners are not necessary and can even be a liability in market innovation. To the extent that new entrants need to connect with the traditional market—distribution channels, consumers, et cetera—Japanese partners and executives are a crucial asset. To the extent that entrants are using market innovations and focusing on new consumers, the Japanese perspectives become less important and even a disadvantage. This is not to say companies with this focus shouldn't utilize their Japanese partners and executives, but they should first carefully consider the advantages and disadvantages of partnering.

The advantage of hiring Japanese executives is also acquiring relationships with Japanese partners, suppliers, bankers, and others vital to the success of the new venture. The downside is that Japanese leaders often have a harder time convincing corporate headquarters to take the radical steps necessary to succeed in Japan. Without this trust, the Japanese operation is hampered.

This may be the reason why many foreign entrants succeed under foreign leaders. Hal Roberts, who was flown in from Georgia, created the phenomenally successful Coca-Cola business in Japan. Roberts's savvy in committing to the market as well as his relationship with central headquarters—which allowed him to take more unconventional approaches—were vital to Coca-Cola's success. Chris Walker, president of record retailer HMV, despite being a *gaijin* (foreigner), has built a tremendously successful Japanese operation through his intimate understanding of emerging Japanese tastes. His experience as a marketer and his extensive and painstakingly developed knowledge of Japanese consumers have given him deep insight into the market. He notes that being an outsider can sometimes be an advantage in challenging conventional business practice, because it is more accepted coming from a foreigner than from a Japanese executive.

The type of business also affects the decision of whether native or foreign managers fare better. Foreign managers can be an asset for niche businesses with a foreign cache. Yet in manufacturing, the advantages of Japanese management and skill will probably be more of an advantage.

Opportunities for partnering with Japanese firms are increasing as the tightly linked *keiretsu* and other relationships begin to weaken. For example, although Tokyo Mitsubishi Bank was the principal stockholder in Nikko Securities, Nikko went to Travelers for a new alliance. In an increasingly competitive market, Nikko preferred a foreign partner that had the technical expertise it needed to compete.

Partnering Versus Going It Alone

The same tradeoffs apply in deciding whether to partner with a Japanese firm. Although traditional wisdom about Japan is that foreign entrants need a Japanese partner to succeed, companies have been successful entering alone. Some of the most successful companies—including Coca-Cola, McDonald's, Nestlé, Johnson & Johnson, BMW, and Procter & Gamble—have found their own way through the Japanese market.

But these entrants have often relied upon relationships with Japanese suppliers and distributors even if they were not joint ventures. For example, Coca-Cola's strength was its establishment of a relationship with Kirin bottlers. Once Coke locked in the largest bottling company in Japan, and then developed a strong product line and distribution strategy through vending machines, Pepsi faced an obstacle it has never been able to overcome. Coca-Cola still controls more than 70 percent of the cola market, with Pepsi trailing at barely 10 percent.

Joint ventures with Japanese trading companies, in particular, have become less popular as foreign entrants find the trading companies bring trading expertise, but not the *marketing* savvy needed to achieve success in Japan. It is much easier for foreign entrants to make their way directly into Japan, given changes in regulations, distribution systems, and other factors. There may be other reasons to create a partnership, particularly to leverage research and knowledge bases in industrial markets, but they are less compelling than before.

On the other hand, Eddie Bauer's very successful retailing entry into the Japanese market, described in the introduction, was built on a strong joint venture with the direct-mail division of Sumitomo Trading Group, Sumisho Otto. The Sumitomo corporate brand was an asset in attracting talented staff, creating an effective distribution system, and understanding the demands of the local market.

AT&T, which had found it difficult to enter the Japanese telecommunications market alone in the past, announced a joint venture with British Telecom in 1999 to enter through a capital investment in Nippon Telecom. With Nippon Telecom share prices falling to half their value three years earlier, the investment became much more attractive. Other major global competitors, including Germany-France Telecom Group and MCI WorldCom, have also moved into this market, which is second only to the United States in size.[34]

Some entrants use the partnership as a stepping stone toward creating an independent business in Japan. For example, Sandoz and Bayer entered Japan through joint ventures with Japanese firms, but set up independent Japanese operations and exited the original ventures. Procter & Gamble initially entered through a joint venture and then built a powerful independent business. Volvo began selling cars in Japan through a joint venture in 1974, but established a wholly owned Japanese subsidiary in 1986. In some cases, the foreign entrant even sold out to the Japanese partner (for example, Southland's 7-Eleven sold to Itoh-Yokado).

Although most joint ventures end amicably, the foreign entrant's position in Japan can be damaged for many years to come if the venture sours. Borden had entered Japan through a joint venture with Meiji to produce ice cream and margarine. Although the venture was financially successful, it broke up and each of the partners accused the other of bad faith. Scathing articles about Meiji were published in the United States. And when Borden approached another potential partner, Morinaga, articles in the Japanese press accused Morinaga of selling out to a badly behaved foreign firm.[35]

Most of the ventures that lasted for decades were between partners who were not a threat to one another, such as Fuji Xerox and Taito-Pfizer. Of thirty joint ventures that survived from the 1950s into the 1980s, only three were foreign firms with large Japanese players in the same industry. Most of these enduring ventures were between small companies, trading companies, or banks, partners that would be unlikely to threaten the balance.[36] More recent alliances are often based on looser links than a formal joint venture. Companies collaborate in certain areas—for example, IBM and Toshiba in research and development or Kellogg and Ajinomoto in sales and marketing—without creating a formal structure.

As with any alliance, the Japanese partner should provide complementary skills and assets. Toys "R" Us partnered with McDonald's Japan for its experience in site selection, logistics, and recruiting. Sandoz teamed up with Sanyo to improve its sales force management in Japan.

In assessing the importance of Japanese partners, it is crucial to consider the nation's unique market conditions. Western companies often underestimate the role of trading companies and other aspects of the Japanese infrastructure that seem unnecessary but are actually quite important for successfully conducting business. One Western firm, noting the high costs of conducting business through a trading company, decided to bring the trading processes in-house, including foreign exchange, transportation, and marketing. It found, however, that it was far more costly, given the complex Japanese distribution system, to handle these issues in-house rather than through the domestic trading company.

Investing for the Long Term

Success in Japan requires a far greater commitment than in the West. One of the reasons German automakers have been so successful in Japan is that they stayed in the country when American companies pulled out during challenging times. It is this consistent presence, the long-term relationships, and the process of building that become the greatest strength of a new entrant.

Many Western companies find that a focus on short-term profits works against the market. A U.S. semiconductor production equipment manufacturer entered a joint venture with a Japanese company. The partners spent two years developing prototypes and attracting letters of intent from major Japanese manufacturers. At this point, however, the U.S. firm's stock price soared and it sold out to another firm, leaving behind its Japanese partner. Such U.S. ventures may be successful from a short-term financial standpoint. But for long-term success in the market, the relationship with Japanese partners and commitment to building the market need to take precedence over harvesting gains quickly.

The Challenges of Franchising

One way companies quickly build their presence in markets is through franchising, but some firms that franchise in other parts of the world own their outlets in Japan. McDonald's franchises its restaurants in most parts of the world, but its operations in Japan are wholly owned. Similarly, Domino's franchises its U.S. businesses but owns its operations in Japan. Why? When does franchising make sense in Japan? Den Fujita of McDonald's Japan notes that the advantage of owning restaurants is that his operation is not under the same pressures as the U.S. operations where disgruntled franchisees can exert pressure of the corporate parent.

In many cases, it is difficult to find franchisees because the drawbacks of franchising outweigh the benefits. When the company needs the flexibility to move in new directions to meet market demands, it might want to own its business. Also, because of the close relationship required between the headquarters and franchisees, an understanding of the Japanese market and Japanese business owners is essential. These relationships are often much easier for a Japanese firm to develop than a foreign entrant.

Japanese-owned convenience stores, particularly 7-Eleven Japan, have used a franchising strategy more effectively. At the time 7-Eleven was building its network of convenience stores, many small local stores were going out of business. Therefore it was an attractive proposition to offer them a franchise for their locations. Often these stores held coveted liquor licenses that could not be transferred, another reason to franchise the business. For these reasons, franchising made sense, particularly because the company built the information systems and other infrastructure to tie its franchised operations together.

Developing an Entry Strategy

The best strategy in entering Japan is tailored to the specific needs of the company, its product or service, and its strategic objectives. The biggest problem in entering Japan is the misconceptions about the market. If companies are basing their decisions on these myths rather than the current reality of Japanese and Asian markets, they will very likely make strategic errors. These myths are so firmly entrenched in the minds of foreign companies that even the most experienced firms have fallen victim to them.

Companies that believe they have no hope of distribution without a Japanese partner might end up with a partner who, in fact, contributes little strategic value. Yet changes in retailing, the emergence of cyberdistribution, and other channels create more opportunities than ever to move products to consumers more efficiently. Companies that believe Japanese consumers are inherently different might neglect market research that could offer tremendous insights to guide market entry. Companies that believe customers will not buy from foreign brands might underestimate the importance of building their own independent brands.

Determine Strategic Goals

There are many reasons to be in Japan, including direct sales to the Japanese market, research and development, or as a basis for moving into other Asian markets. The strategic goal will shape the strategy for entry. Another strategic issue is the role of Japanese entry in the company's overall global strategy. Some products and services, such as Starbucks coffee or Kinko's business services, allow for a more global strategy while others require regional tailoring. One of the common mistakes made by successful global corporations entering Japan is to assume that Asian markets are all alike. Levi's initially developed an "Asian" jean produced in a Hong Kong factory. It wasn't until it gained a deeper understanding of the Japanese market that it was able to adapt its jeans to the Japanese market.

Partnering

Another key decision in developing an entry strategy is whether to partner with a native firm or go into Japan alone. As noted previously, some of the compelling reasons for partnering, such as access to complex distribution, are no longer as compelling. But other reasons for partnering, such as understanding the emerging Japanese consumer, are still significant. Foreign firms should be very careful to assess the current market insight of potential partners or acquisition targets rather than their past successes, which could have been based on realities that are no longer valid. Today, the costs of building independent networks are lower and the challenges of hiring employees are decreasing, making it far easier to go alone than it has been in the past.

Integration Into Asian Strategy

The company's Asian strategy should be built into its Japanese strategy. Successful entry in Japan may not guarantee success in other parts of Asia, but it can certainly facilitate that entry. As discussed in Chapter Three, the Japanese market provides a blueprint, a stepping stone, and insight about important competitors and collaborators in the region. It can also be the company's base of operations for further Asian expansion.

If the company needs a Japanese partner to succeed in other parts of Asia, it might consider partnering in Japan, even if the Japanese market itself doesn't require it. This relationship can serve as a network for a broader partnership in Asia.

New Wisdom of Japanese Market Entry

While market entry in Japan must be tailored to specific products and markets, there are some general principles for new entrants to keep in mind, now and in the future:

• Empower local management. Coca-Cola recently gave its Japanese office full authority for new product introduction decisions. It sped up the time for the launch by six months. You also need a reliable and credible negotiator with headquarters. Den Fujita of McDonald's, Rainer Jahn of Mercedes-Benz Japan and Kakutaro Kitashiro of IBM Japan, are examples of talented local management who have made a difference. These leaders understood the Japanese market and were able to make their cases to headquarters. They are essential for bridging the gap between the corporate world and the new approaches needed for Japanese market.

• Hire passionate expatriates. Successful expatriates are, generally speaking, committed to Japan. This interest in Japan is far more important than speaking the language. Successful expatriates are sensitive to the trends of the society.

• Money isn't everything. In fact, it is less of a motivator in Japan. Customers won't accept lower product quality to save money. You cannot hire a good person simply by offering high pay. Salary, while important, is not the highest priority in Japan. For example, Nobuyuki Idei of Sony is paid less than ¥100 million yen (less than $1 million).

• Being American isn't enough. Japanese consumers are now less U.S.-oriented than those in the other parts of Asia. Simply being from the United States doesn't make everything easy. J-pop (Japan-made Western music) is more popular than American music. Comic books are all Japan-made. Many of the most favored brands, such as Gucci and Luis Vuitton, are from Europe, not the United States.

• Choose employees and advisers carefully. Assume that there is no such thing as specialists except in engineering and finance. Look for outstanding people beyond the border of industry and function who understand the customer. Your ad agency and other consultants should understand you, be committed to you, and know the market well. They should also excel at creative execution, something that traditionally has not been a strength of many Japanese agencies.

• Be prepared to make a solid upfront commitment. A sincere show of commitment is a must. Japanese distributors and employees will watch closely to see whether the entrant is truly committed to the market. The depth of a company's commitment may be a self-fulfilling prophecy. The greater the commitment, the greater the chance of success.

• Have a focused target. Companies need to be very clear about their target market. Simple analogies to similar markets in the West do not always work because Japanese lifestyle segments are very different.

• Be tenacious. Don't give up at the first effort. KFC, Starbucks, and Kao's Attack detergent all stumbled at their first attempt, but came back with successful businesses.

Points of Leverage

- Given these changes, what are the implications for your strategy in Japan?

- What are the assumptions on which you are basing your Japan strategy? In light of the discussions of myth and reality, how much of your strategy is based on myth or the new realities?

- What are the marketing strategies that might be possible for you to use now?

- Is this a time for increasing your investment and involvement in Japan? In what areas? Why or why not? As you continue to read through the book, you may want to consider whether the changes described here warrant a change in your initial strategy for investment and involvement in Japan.

For foreign firms considering entering Japan:

- What are your goals for entry?

- Given the discussion here, what strategy for entry will be the best?

- What partners will help you most in this process?

- What criteria should you establish for evaluating and selecting entry strategies and partners?

For foreign companies in Japan:

- How successful has your entry strategy been?

- If you are going to expand your current operations in Japan, would you consider new entry strategies?

- Are your current partnerships and alliances still serving you well? In the light of the discussions here, should you consider changing your strategy in Japan?

- Does the leader of your Japanese operation correctly understand the implications of the changes in the market? If not, how are you going to take advantage of the opportunities created by these changes?

For Japanese firms in Japan:

- Given your objectives and strategies, what opportunities are there for you to partner with foreign entrants?

- Where are you susceptible to attack from new foreign entrants, given the entry strategies available?

- What strategies should you consider to preempt new entrants to reduce your vulnerability?

The same sets of questions could be applied to entry into Asia as well as Japan.

From "Tap Water" Marketing to Tapping Markets

"The responsibility of a meritorious corporation was to make a superior product and educate the consumers as to its qualities and lead them to it."
Akio Morita, founder of Sony

In Japan's former producer-driven economy, marketing was on the periphery. Until 1983, the University of Tokyo had no marketing department. Most companies in Japan did not distinguish between marketing and sales. Top leadership of Japanese firms rose up through engineering. Companies collected research on audience ratings, brand awareness, and, later, on store audits. But these were all concerned with the "share" and not with the "why" of consumer demand. Even focus groups, which are now in vogue in Japan, were not utilized until the 1970s. Although Japanese global corporations were pacesetting marketers in other parts of the world, marketing at home was marginalized.

It is no wonder that Japanese companies "have been notoriously poor marketers."[1] This is because there was little need for this kind of discipline in a producer-driven economy. What need was there for point-of-sale (POS) data or market research? Create the product and send it to the market. What need was there for branding and positioning? A decent product from a well-established company was a shoe-in. If it wasn't, there were always plenty more products to replace it, as long as one controlled the distributors' shelf space.

Many foreign entrants, even experienced marketers, had learned to focus primarily on the structural challenges of the Japanese market. They had learned that the key to success in Japan was gaining access to distribution channels. They had learned that market research that worked in other parts of the world was useless in the homogeneous markets of Japan. They had learned that branding strategies they perfected elsewhere were pointless in Japan, so they focused instead on building powerful corporate brands. For example, Procter & Gamble, the master of branding strategies in other markets, gave much more attention to its corporate brand than to its individual brands in Japan.

Today, however, marketing is moving from the periphery to the center. Marketing expertise, once an afterthought, is now a central strategic necessity in rapidly changing Japanese and Asian markets. The practice of branding and segmentation, pricing, new product development, advertising, and marketing research have undergone fundamental transformations. These changes, as discussed in the following chapters, have tremendous implications for the critical success factors in entering Japanese and Asian markets. Overall, these many changes have made marketing more central to success in Japan.

A decade or two ago, domestic and foreign companies could succeed in Japan without a sophisticated marketing capability. A strong corporate image, technological expertise, local connections, and a broad distribution network were enough. It wasn't necessary to understand the customer or the market. Today, with increasingly demanding customers and savvy marketers in Japan, few companies can succeed without strong marketing abilities. These skills and insights are crucial to winning in Japan and Asia. Those companies that do not have a highly developed understanding of marketing are at tremendous risk. Those global competitors that have well-developed marketing capabilities have an unprecedented opportunity to apply these skills to their advantage in Japan and Asia.

Tap Water

In the initial post-war era, Japan was desperately behind in quality of life. Consumers focused on the "three Cs"—cars, coolers (refrigerators), and color televisions. Konosuke Matsushita, founder of the Panasonic brand, once described his strategy in Japan as "tap-water merchandising." In a rapidly developing economy, in which demand outstripped supply, a quality product flooded the market like water from a tap, and thirsty consumers drank it up. The more the company could pour out, the greater its chances of success. Perhaps as much as culture or habits, this top-down structure had a powerful impact in influencing Japanese marketing.

Matsushita used the "tap water" strategy to build a large network of retail outlets. This network helped Matsushita's VHS videotape format become the industry standard, despite the technical superiority of Sony's Betamax. Japanese marketers were obsessed with shelf space. The more products one could produce to fill the shelf, the greater the probability of keeping out the competition.

Understandably, marketing was not a central function in Japanese firms. Companies had market planning departments, but they were primarily focused on selling. They had little strategic influence and received minimal attention from senior leaders of the firm. A company's R&D and distribution strategies were far more important than marketing.

For example, before the launch of its successful dry beer, Asahi was focused primarily on its distribution network. The customer was virtually ignored. Now, the company is very attentive to customer needs. Competitor Kirin also has had to respond to its rival's success. Similarly, supermarket Kao was more marketing-oriented, so rival Lion had to develop its marketing skills to remain competitive. The presence of increasingly effective marketers in Japan raises the bar for all competitors.

The Inscrutable Japanese Consumer

One of the reasons companies ignored the customer was a belief that conventional marketing principles did not apply in Japan. When foreign executives tried to apply Western marketing to the Japanese market, they were told that the Japanese consumer cannot be understood through Western methods. The Japanese market is different. The Japanese culture is fairly homogenous, so individual tastes and concerns are not that important.

When marketers in Japan sought to assess customer reaction to a new product, they typically looked to themselves or their families for feedback. The theory was that any Japanese consumer was representative of the entire market. In many ways, the market behaved as if this were true.

When foreign companies entered the Japanese market in the 1960s, marketing professionals were perplexed with the reluctance of their Japanese counterparts in commissioning research. A typical exchange between a Japanese executive and a Western colleague might have gone like this:

WESTERNER: "Let's test this product for consumer acceptance."

JAPANESE: "That's unnecessary. Let's hand them out to the staff and have them ask their wives. We could limit the cost to just the products."

WESTERNER: "But that would not be a representative sample. The information would be meaningless."

JAPANESE: "Not at all. Our staff and their families are typical Japanese. Besides, I'm Japanese, so I have a pretty good idea whether the product would be acceptable."

WESTERNER: "I'm an American, but I wouldn't dare take the risk of launching a new product in the United States without testing it with the consumer. I couldn't assume to know how all consumers feel."

JAPANESE: Well, unlike the United States, Japan is a homogeneous society, so we don't get a spread of opinions. We will be wasting our money on research. If it worries you that much, let's get our salesmen to go around to the retailers and ask their opinions."

This attitude was so pervasive that Japanese managers sometimes even tried to apply it to U.S. markets. John McCreery, a marketing consultant, describes his frustration when his Japanese colleagues asked his advice as a "typical" American:

> It has happened again. A Japanese colleague has an idea and has come to ask the resident American, i.e., me, "What will Americans think of this?" Once again, I am stumped. I can tell him what one middle-aged American male, born in Georgia, raised in Virginia, educated in Michigan and Upstate New York, an ex-Lutheran WASP of mixed Scotch-Irish-Franco-German descent thinks. If he wants to know what my parents, wife, or daughter think, he will have to ask them. And the idea that I could speak for Hispanics from Texas, Blacks from Harlem, cowboys, construction workers, or any other ethnic or occupational category in the jumble that America is today seems highly dubious to say the best.[2]

Obviously, the Westerner faced an uphill battle in pursuing a market study, unless he worked in a fully owned subsidiary. Otherwise, most market research in joint ventures had to be pushed through over the objections of the local staff.

This view of a fairly homogeneous Japanese market may at first appear to be a marketer's dream. But it actually made marketing more difficult. Consider the following assessment of the Japanese market in the early 1990s:

> Japan is a country where the people of a single ethnic origin live on isolated islands . . . . Culturally homogeneous and economically relatively wealthy, it might seem that she [Japan] represents an 'easy'

case for marketers in a textbook sense. This, however, is not the case. Japanese experience shows that homogeneity in an advanced economy could be a liability rather than an asset to marketers. . . . Importance of emotional dimensions, others' influence, and decisions at the point of purchase are among the factors making marketing in Japan a difficult job.[3]

Marketing Without Comparison

Japanese advertisers maintained that comparative advertising went against the grain of Japanese society. This assumption was long held because it could not be tested. The structure of the Japanese advertising industry, in which advertising firms handled competing accounts, made agencies reluctant to engage in comparative ads. When Pepsi-Cola ran a comparative television ad against Coca-Cola in 1989, there were no signs of shock and disgust from Japanese consumers. Although the advertising had to be modified slightly for the Japanese market, it was clearly comparative. According to research, consumers were not only unoffended by the approach, but they found it highly entertaining. When Western firms broke the "taboo" and ran comparative ads, they revealed that the restriction had more to do with Japanese business than Japanese culture.

Once the door to comparative advertising was opened, General Motors took the next step with a press campaign comparing its products to those of a Japanese firm, Nissan. Again, there were no signs of outrage from consumers. Finally, Japanese brands joined in the fray, with computer manufacturer NEC launching a comparative campaign for personal computers against IBM.

It is easy to see how these attitudes stunted the growth of marketing in Japan. If the market really was fundamentally different, it would not be possible to apply standard marketing approaches to Japan. This attitude, however, turned out to be a myth. The combined forces of trailblazing companies that were willing to apply new approaches to the market shifts that demanded them exposed the myth of the inscrutable Japanese, thereby forcing the emergence of marketing in Japan.

Similar arguments have been suggested about other Asian markets' uniqueness. Local experts argue that they are fundamentally different and that traditional Western approaches cannot be applied. The Japanese experience offers important insight into the necessity of marketing and the danger of wholeheartedly accepting such statements.

Reversing the Tap Water Flow

The advent of a new marketing era in Japan can be seen in Panasonic's "tap water" marketer Konosuke Matsushita's response to the 1990 recession. The company's traditional reaction to a downturn was to send out an army of salespeople to promote its products, priming the pump for its future "tap water" strategy. In 1990, its response didn't appear much different—on the surface. Matsushita sent out more than 10,000 dealers to personally visit a declared target of twenty million homes.

It may have looked like the same strategy, but there was an important difference. These representatives were not selling consumers on their products, but listening. They arrived hat-in-hand to ask consumers what they wanted. Through a questionnaire, Matsushita found out that consumers felt burdened by the numerous functions on their electronic equipment, and that they longed for simpler equipment at a lower price. Until that point, manufacturers had vied with one another to provide the most functions on each model. With Matsushita's questionnaire, it became clear that Japanese consumers were no longer willing to pay for these features.

The attention of Matsushita, and the rest of Japan, had turned toward consumers. The flow of information was no longer a one-way stream from manufacturer to customer. And customers, no longer content with arranged marriages to large corporations, expect to be wooed by companies. Japanese customers were making their choices known, and companies were sitting up and listening.

Listening to the Market

Companies are using their superior understanding of the market to develop successful businesses that respond to the needs of customers. While Blockbuster Video has struggled in Japan, a similar company, Stya, has created a new concept for "culture clubs" that has struck a chord among Japanese youth. These sprawling outlets combine video rentals with books, CDs, and cafés. The stores deliver an experience targeted toward this youth segment. With increasing marketing successes of domestic and foreign companies in Japan, the movement of marketing to the center of Japanese firms should accelerate.

Exceptions to the Rule

While marketing before the 1990s was marginalized among most companies in Japan, there were important exceptions. Companies such as Itoh-Yokado were among the most aggressive firms in the world in using point-of-sale (POS) data. Firms such as Kao were early in adopting a more strategic perspective on marketing. Kao saw marketing as a total concept driving the company and infused that objective throughout the organization. Today, every employee is encouraged to visit a supermarket at least once each weekend to view how customers choose products. In this way, all employees, whether in accounting or product development, gain direct perspectives on marketing.

Some Japanese business leaders, such as Akio Morita, also demonstrated extraordinary genius in relating new technology to customers. His insight to create the Sony Walkman was a combination of a direct understanding of the target market from observation and an understanding of the possibilities of the emerging technology. These insights were primarily applied to world markets; beyond these marketing "geniuses," the systematic use of marketing research and tools was largely underdeveloped in Japan.

Many Japanese companies have highly developed marketing capabilities abroad. Internationally, they concentrated in a narrow band of industries, such as automobiles and electronics, where domestic competition was intense.[4] Success in these areas created a surplus of visible trade, instilling the myth that Japanese marketing is superior. Only one or two Japanese pharmaceutical companies are in the world league. Practically none of its glass, paper, or software companies make the grade. Telecommunications and advertising giants draw their strength almost entirely from the domestic market. There are outstanding marketers in Japan, but they are not representative of the whole.

The Rise of Marketing

Many companies in Japan are recognizing the rising importance of marketing and are investing more heavily in it. Companies are tracking consumer preferences with POS data and tailoring their products to consumers rather than "leading" customers to existing products. They are using segmentation, positioning, and branding. They are involving customers in new product development.

Signs of this shift also are apparent in the leadership and structure of Japanese firms. In the 1990s, Toshiba passed over its engineering department to appoint someone from sales and marketing as its new president. Sony's new CEO is also from a marketing background. Honda, Toyota, and Nissan have all reorganized their Japanese advertising, dealer management, and product planning into one integrated department. Companies now recognize that their success increasingly depends upon their marketing strategy.

Whereas large companies once poured out new products for thirsty consumers like tap water, now they are learning to tap markets in order to understand and respond to customer demands. Among the signs of increased attention to marketing are:

A Growing Attention to Branding and Segmentation

As will be discussed in Chapter Six, a 1998 survey found that nearly 60 percent of Japanese and foreign companies in Japan said they were actively working to build their brands. While more than half segmented their markets by demographics, more than 80 percent recognized the need for more sophisticated approaches to segmentation in dimensions such as values and lifestyles.

A Shift from Employees to Customers

Where Japanese companies have traditionally placed employees above both customers and investors, this emphasis is turning. As customers and investors are placed ahead of employees, understanding the market becomes increasingly important.

Increases in Marketing Staff

As companies recognize the importance of marketing, they are increasing their marketing staff as well as placing more emphasis on the marketing function in the organization.

Increase in Marketing Education

Marketing has found its place in the curriculum not only at Japanese business schools but also in other parts of Asia. For example, by early 1999, Tsinghua University in China had five marketing faculty members. Some thirty or forty students wrote their theses on marketing topics, compared to just six or seven students five years earlier.[5]

Growth in Advertising

Advertising expenditures rose from just under ¥3 trillion ($13 billion) in 1985 to nearly ¥6 trillion ($49 billion) in 1997.[6] At the same time, Dentsu and other major advertising firms have undergone fundamental restructurings to be more responsive to customers, introduce new advertising approaches, and respond to the rise of electronic commerce.

Rise in POS Systems

POS systems were introduced in Japan in 1978 and took off when 7-Eleven Japan Co., Ltd., the nation's largest convenience chain, started using a POS system in 1983. The rapid growth of POS systems in Japan, increasing at an annual rate of 100 percent per year, is fundamentally changing relationships between manufacturers and retailers. These changes "may abolish the existing system completely."[7] Traditionally, companies have watched the Neilsen Retail Index to understand their marketshare versus that of rivals. Individual purchasing patterns were not of much interest. Instead, companies examined their weekly sales. Now, with the rise of POS data, they can monitor purchasing patterns more closely.

Importance of Marketing Information

A 1997 survey of more than 200 foreign firms in Japan found that market information is crucial to success in Japan. A lack of information was cited as a problem by more than 21 percent of respondents and a full 13 percent added that this issue, in particular, was a serious stumbling block to market entry.[8]

Importance of Market Relationships

Market relationships also are important, as reflected by the stress on understanding the strict customer demands (cited as an obstacle for 61 percent of the firms who participated in the 1997 survey), hiring employees (an issue for nearly half of the companies), and understanding Japanese business practices (an issue for more than 66 percent of the firms).

IBM Moves to the Market

IBM Japan built its early market through a product-driven strategy focused on mainframes. When the mainframe market bottomed out and the yen became stronger, the company's performance went with it. By 1993, it was in the red. IBM turned its business around by shifting to a market-driven strategy.

IBM expanded into new services, including systems development, systems integration, preventive maintenance, outsourcing, and software (Lotus and Trivoli). It also increased marketing for its full product line—from mainframes to PCs—to serve all the information needs of Japanese clients.

While some of the strategies are similar to those employed by IBM to revive its business in other parts of the world, these were specifically tailored to the needs of the Japanese market. As Kakutaro Kitashiro, CEO of IBM Japan, commented, "IBM Japan is responsive to Japanese customer needs because the management is Japanese and the majority of employees are Japanese. Since we have our own technologists and our own research facilities, we can request help from the United States but also do developmental work that is not possible in the United States."[9]

This market-driven strategy has been very successful. Beginning in 1994, IBM Japan entered a period of double-digit growth. Software and service grew to more than half its business, accounting for most of this growth. After posting a loss of ¥18.4 billion ($170 million) in 1993, the company turned a ¥10.4-billion ($100 million) profit in 1994. By 1996, it had recaptured its position as top earner among foreign capital companies with a profit of over ¥55 billion ($500 million). Despite the recession in the personal computer industry in 1997, IBM Japan's profits continued to grow to ¥68 billion ($560 million).

IBM Japan has been helped by the strengthening yen and because it moved its manufacturing into Southeast Asia. However, its comeback also was a result of a more market-driven strategy.

Management Implications: Marketing Advantage

For companies with strong marketing capabilities, this rise in the importance of marketing creates new opportunities for them to use their skills in Japan. For companies that have survived up until now without essential marketing skills, there is a compelling need to develop them.

For companies that have modified their market-driven approaches to more producer-driven markets in other parts of Asia, there are also important lessons to be learned from the changes in Japan. They need to be careful not to get so deeply entrenched into a producer-driven view of the market that they fail to see shifts that make marketing more important. As assets and knowledge are focused primarily on distribution and other factors that are vital to producer-driven markets, it becomes more difficult to see the need for marketing insight.

In Japan, as in other parts of the world, there were voices in the wilderness advocating a more market-centered approach long before it was widely accepted. These front runners often gained a substantial advantage because it was not until the wisdom of their approaches was proven in their superior performance that others followed their example. By then, these pioneers had established strong positions. Moving early provides considerable advantage.

Among the key issues in developing a marketing strategy in the new Japan and other emerging Asian markets are:

Distinguishing Between Culture and Structure

Ultimately, the shift in the market calls into question how much of the conventional wisdom of the Japanese market is based on deep cultural values and how much is based on market structure. Many Japanese executives, like the Japanese manager who shunned market research in the exchange noted previously, attribute to culture what very well might be a result of infrastructure and tradition. The manager in that case made the assumption that there was no need for market testing because all Japanese consumers are alike. In fact, there was no need for testing because the views of consumers made little difference in a production-driven marketplace. The strategy of not testing may have been right, but for the wrong reasons. As regulations and infrastructure change, these mistaken assumptions may result in lost opportunities or costly mistakes. Managers should carefully discern how much of the current marketing reality is shaped by the structure of the market and how much is truly due to slower-changing cultural differences.

Looking for Opportunities to Apply Innovative Approaches

Changes in the market mean that methods (such as Western practices) that did not work in the past may work in the future. Even if no other firm is providing money-back guarantees, focusing on value pricing, or engaging in comparative advertising, there may be opportunities to do so. Managers should not assume that just because these approaches have not been tried in Japan or other Asian markets that they cannot be used there effectively. Sometimes it is one firm that disproves the rule. Outsiders, with knowledge of other markets, are in a particularly good position to inject these new approaches into Japanese and other Asian markets.

Not Assuming Domestic Partners Know Better

Despite the enormous value of domestic partners in understanding the market, don't follow them blindly. Foreign entrants often have greater marketing skills but hold back because of an unwillingness to contradict local experts and partners, who are expected to better know what will work. These local experts, however, may have their own misconceptions about the market and marketing practice. Companies would do well to question the value of this advice, particularly when it undermines the principles and practices that have led to success in other markets. Companies should listen to this advice critically, with an understanding that these partners may know traditional markets but not emerging market segments and creative new approaches that have not been tried. Given the heterogeneity of Asian markets, it is vital for companies entering Asian countries to use marketing capabilities to understand and respond correctly. This is the best way companies can tailor their products and approaches to the specific demands of the market and identify untapped opportunities.

Recognizing the Shifts That Make Marketing More Important

Many Asian markets may start out highly regulated and controlled, with little apparent need for traditional marketing. Relations with government officials may be more important than marketing for success in China, for example. But as the market emerges, as the middle class grows and is not simply interested in raising the collective standard of living but also in personal choice, marketing will become more important. Companies in these other Asian markets should pay attention to shifts that change the significance of marketing. By being alert for changes in the market and the role of marketing, companies can avoid sticking with old approaches when the market demands new ones and they can better anticipate when to apply marketing strategies from other parts of the world to the market.

Marketing as Corporate Philosophy

Overall, these changes mean that the divide between Western, consumer-driven marketing and Japanese marketing is beginning to close. Many distinctive features of Japanese culture, business, and government continue to shape competition and marketing in Japan. Like customers in any other market, Japanese customers have unique demographics, culture, and history. Japanese businesses have distinctive approaches to competition and unique structures for competing. Japanese government continues to play a powerful role in the nation's economic development. But it is now clear that Japanese customers are no longer docile sheep, herded in the direction dictated by corporate leaders.

Although marketing in Japan will not replicate that of the West, the differences in techniques will no longer be in substance but in emphasis. (This is particularly true because Western marketers have been adopting some of the approaches of Japanese marketers.) Japanese businesses have distinctive approaches to competition and unique structures for competing.

As true consumer markets emerge in Japan and throughout Asia, marketing is the way they will be won. Companies will win or lose based on their marketing skills as well as other capabilities. Increasingly, this is where the competitive battles will be fought.

To begin to move marketing to the center, managers need to begin their strategic planning with the market and moving outward. Instead of starting with a product and then seeking a market, they should start with the market and move to the product, answering the following questions:

1. What is the real customer need? Any corporate decision should start with understanding the real customer needs. Developing a business proposition depends upon coming up with unique positioning for the product and services that address the ways to create value for customers.

2. What product or service offerings will meet the target segments' needs and offer a sustainable competitive advantage? Given this customer need, how can it best be satisfied?

3. What strategies and programs, resources, capabilities, and processes are required to develop and effectively implement the product and service solutions? If the company does not have these resources and capabilities, how can it best develop or acquire them?

By inverting the product-centered approach, the company creates a marketing philosophy. This shift in perspective, particularly markets undergoing rapid change as in Japan and other parts of Asia, can open many new avenues of opportunities. It also can give the company a tremendous advantage in identifying and meeting these market needs.

Points of Leverage

- How important is marketing to your overall strategy in Japan? Do you need to increase resources for marketing? How can you give marketing a more central role in your strategy and organization?

- To what extent are your marketing resources and partners based on expertise in the old Japanese market, and to what extent do they understand and address the new market?

- To what extent is your top management in Japan and the organizational culture of your Japanese subsidiary customer-oriented? Are they prepared to take advantage of the changes?

- Given the changes in the Japanese market, how do you need to reshape your marketing strategy?

- Do you leverage opportunities in the interface between marketing and other business functions such as operations?

6

From Power to Finesse—Segmentation, Positioning, and Branding

As briefly discussed in previous chapters, until the late 1980s, Kirin lager was synonymous with beer in Japan. The entire market was viewed as a homogeneous single unit. Japanese were considered one market and they all liked Kirin. Taste was not important. Brand image was not important. All that mattered was that the beer came from a respected corporation. This made Kirin the dominant brand, and it was assumed there was no reason to offer anything else.

As a tiny beermaker fighting for its life, Asahi had little to lose. So it took the risk of introducing a new, dry beer in 1987. Asahi Super Dry was a rapid success, dominating this new segment and raising Asahi from a marginal player to one of the market leaders. In 1985, Kirin had held 60 percent of the total beer market compared to 10 percent for Asahi. By early 1998, Asahi had risen to 39 percent while Kirin's leadership eroded to just 41 percent. The single segment was beginning to be deconstructed.

Asahi's sharp and dry taste went better with Western food. This newcomer stood for something—new ideas, individuality, foreign tastes. Asahi demonstrated the power of branding, positioning, and segmentation in putting products on the map. This superior marketing strategy allowed it to run circles around Kirin.[1] A powerful corporation and dominant market share were no longer sufficient for success. Asahi had proven that branding, positioning, and

145

segmentation could be used like a slingstone from a tiny David to bring Goliath to its knees.

Segmentation and Positioning Put Honda in the Driver's Seat

Toyota's popular Mark II was squeezed out by smart segmentation by Honda and other companies. Driving a white Mark II hardtop to a country club in suburban Tokyo was once considered a modest sign of success among Japanese white-collar workers. Toyota sold as many as 20,000 Mark II automobiles in 1990, most of which were white. But then its target market began to demonstrate more diverse tastes.

A new Mark II model introduced in 1997 did not fare as well. Its market was eroded by the rise of sport utilities, small wagons, and stylistic imports. Honda introduced a series of sport utility vehicles, starting with the pioneering Odyssey. Honda also carefully targeted other market segments. It created the Odyssey for style-conscious families, its Step wagon for drivers who needed more space, and the SM-V and Capa for young individualists looking for space and price. By carefully positioning its new models, Honda was able to chip away at Toyota's monolithic white Mark II legacy one customer segment at a time. Honda's careful segmentation and positioning made it one of only two auto companies (with Suzuki) that recorded increased sales in Japan in 1997.

The Old Corporate Brands

The old "corporate brands," such as Kirin's lager beer and Toyota's Mark II, were dominant in a market where individual taste didn't matter as much. Like Kirin's ubiquitous lager, these large and bland corporate brands were comfortable and stable. They may not have been completely satisfying, but they were familiar. As the Japanese consumer continues to exhibit a wider range of distinctive tastes, successful firms will be the ones that can cater to these tastes through careful segmentation, positioning, and branding.

Japanese companies traditionally used their corporate identifications as a brand umbrella across a wide range of products. Kao slapped the same corporate brand on products ranging from detergents to computer disks. This traditional Japanese practice of corporate branding was in sharp contrast to the practice of many U.S. firms that built their brands around products (Ivory rather than Procter & Gamble, Buick rather than GM). The association of these brands is with the benefits of the product rather than the credibility of the corporate parent.

With a lack of individual brands, the corporate logos became a more important part of Japanese branding. For example, a 1990 study of Japanese and Korean television commercials found that they tend to display corporate logos more frequently than commercials in the United States and West Germany.[2]

As diligent students of the Japanese market, Western firms adapted their branding to place greater emphasis on their corporate brands. Procter & Gamble, which had built its company around powerful product brands, had to adapt to a market with small regard for individual brands. It began increasing the prominence of its corporate identity at the end of its advertising, in sharp contrast to its emphasis on brands in the United States. For example, a television advertisement for Pringles potato chips ended with a full-screen P&G logo in its closing, a practice that is quite different from its U.S. advertising. Similarly, an advertisement by Nippon Lever for Lipton Ice beverage ends with a full shot of the corporate image.

Rise of Individual Brands

The power branding strategy ("big and ambiguous") was well tailored to the demands of the market. The old consumer had little interest in brands. Products with different brand names were almost completely substitutable from the customer's perspective. Companies, in turn, viewed the Japanese market as a large, homogeneous market, a view which largely ignored customer differences and made segmentation difficult, if not impossible.

This lack of differentiation became a problem as customers became more price-sensitive. Without differentiation and branding, similar products could only be differentiated based on price. This led to destructive price wars that undermined profits. Tired of endless price competition, manufacturers finally became serious about building brands with a specific vision of a focused customer target segment. As price competition intensified, the need to build strong brands became more imperative. At the same time, product lines were pared back, so companies could no longer rely on innovation as a substitute for building brands.

The new successes, as Asahi and Honda demonstrated, are "small and smart" strategies, using finesse to tailor the product to the specific needs of market segments with brands that say something about the product and the purchaser. (It is interesting to note that the tag line of Honda's 1998 advertising campaign was "Small and Smart.")

Another success in building brand identity at the product level is Toyota's Prius model. A hybrid car (gasoline and electric), this model has quickly become one of the strongest ecological brands in Japan. It is branded as "Prius by Toyota," combining the individual identity with the corporate brand.

There is a fundamental shift in viewpoint, from "The beer is good because it comes from a good company" to "The beer is good because it tastes good to me," or because it provides other benefits. A large, undifferentiated market is giving way to clear positioning. Large corporate brand umbrellas are giving way to sharply focused and cultivated brand images. A focus on selling individual products is being subsumed by a focus on selling brands.

Traditionally, Japanese companies have focused on building large, ambiguous corporate brands, so the "what" of brand positioning has been very difficult to pin down. In a market perceived to be homogeneous, the "whom" of brand positioning has also been very difficult to determine. In effect, the "what" and "whom" of Japanese brand positioning—other than an overall sense of quality and stability—were essentially "all things to all people." Today, this is changing. Companies are moving closer to the approach advocated by marketing authors Al Ries and Jack Trout "to plant one and only one key word in the minds of customers."[3]

The declining importance of the "big and ambiguous" corporate brand can be seen in the decreasing size of corporate logos in advertising. Even as P&G discovered the importance of corporate brand building, Japanese marketers were beginning to develop strong individual brands. Japanese companies began nurturing brands and decreasing the emphasis on the corporate logo. Subaru emphasized its strength in sport wagons. In more recent Toyota advertising for its Scepter model, the brand name is three times as large as the corporate logo.

Sharpening Corporate Brand Definition

In addition to creating more individual brands, companies are also building more personality into their corporate brands. In contrast to Western corporate brands such as BMW, Nestlé, or Nike that have clearly defined images, most Japanese corporate brands tend to have a much less obvious brand personality. Kirin sold beer and orange juice under the same brand umbrella.

In many cases, global Japanese firms have clearer brand images abroad than they do at home. Shiseido, Toyota, and Panasonic have much better brand images abroad where their marketing is more sharply focused than in Japan, where these brands are stretched thinly over a vast array of products. In Europe, Shiseido cosmetics are comparable to those of Christian Dior. The company did not traditionally have that image at home, although it is working to change it.

In Japan, Shiseido used to be a nebulous brand that embraced products from a 100-yen bar of soap to cosmetics costing more than 10,000 yen. The company has begun to sharpen its brand identity through the image of "successful aging." It weeded out outliers from its line and launched new individual brands such as Ayura and Ipsa with different identities from the Shiseido parent.

Sony, as a major global player, had been a pioneer in using this strategy. Its brand identity evolved from an image of "small, accurate, and high quality" products to an image of "digital dream kids" that describes the aspirations of its customers.

SECOM is another company that has successfully refined and deepened the meaning of its corporate brand. It began by offering building security services. It expanded its services to include remote medical services, home shopping, and integrated home security services. The expansion of its services were built around a shift from offering a specific security service to providing total "care" to a family.

Sometimes Japanese brands developed and clarified abroad are then reverse-imported back to Japan. When Matsushita found its "National" brand was already registered in the United States, it switched to Panasonic, a brand that later came back to Japan for consumer electronic products. Thanks to its international experience, the brand had a sharper image when it came back home. Similarly, Kenwood and Konica brought brands developed abroad back to the home markets.

Rising Interest in Brand Building

Japanese companies are responding to these new opportunities with an intense interest in brand building. A 1998 survey of thirty-four major Japanese and foreign firms in Japan along with twelve advertising agencies found that the majority of companies were building brands. Some 60 percent of all Japanese companies said they had already started their brand-building efforts. Japanese companies are still behind their foreign rivals in Japan, 85 percent of which have started brand building efforts. (And, what may be a troubling sign for Japanese advertising agencies, clients were more interested and involved than their agencies in brand building, as shown in Exhibit 6.1.) While the agencies felt brand building was

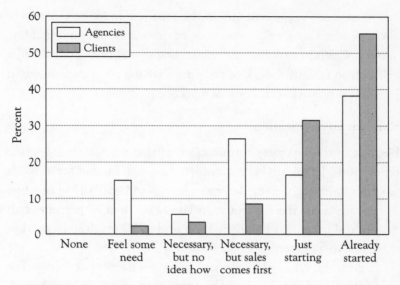

Exhibit 6.1. How Much Interest Does Your Company Show in Brand Building?

Source: Hotaka Katahira, "Advertising and Brand Building in Japan," working paper, University of Tokyo, 1998.

necessary, they were far less likely to believe that brand building had already begun.

Another telling sign was the assessment of the success of these brand-building initiatives. Only 11 percent of the respondents engaged in brand building felt they were doing so successfully. Approaches to segmentation were also relatively unsophisticated. Half the respondents segment their markets by simple demographics, even though most were aware of more sophisticated segmentation strategies. In contrast, all of the foreign companies segmented the market in more sophisticated ways such as by lifestyles and values.

The perceived need for brand building and the lack of ability to do it effectively, as shown Exhibit 6.1, indicate a great opportunity for the future. The survey shows a widespread belief that companies with the ability to use branding and segmentation effectively can create tremendous advantages in the Japanese market. The survey also indicates that foreign firms have an advantage in brand-building activities. Where building individual brands was once considered a distraction from the work of creating a strong corporate image in Japan, it is now a central task of marketing.

Random Diversification

Because of the Japanese consumer's traditional focus on corporate reputations, Japan has been considered a tough market for individual brands. Of the ten top detergent brands in 1987, all but one had disappeared from the list four years later. Less than 10 percent of all new brand launched between 1988 and 1990 resulted in market share above 5 percent after the first year.[4]

A given brand would thus tend to have a fleeting existence. For example, Exhibit 6.2 shows the trajectory of a new beer brand, which exhibits the typical loss of share. It takes off very quickly,

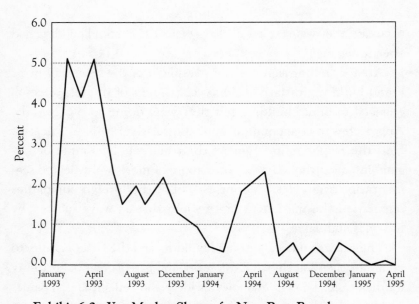

Exhibit 6.2. Yen Market Share of a New Beer Brand

reaching a high of just over 5-percent share in three months, then it fizzles.

In the absence of strong individual brands, the corporation often became the stable brand in Japan. While brands look so volatile in Exhibit 6.2, the market shares of "corporate brands" are surprisingly stable. A typical, traditional, Japanese consumer doesn't care what brand, but asks if the product is from a large, respected company.

Under brand umbrella, a steady stream of products can come and go without forcing the company to build a brand from scratch each time. (Western industries with short product cycles, such as IBM and Philips, employ a similar strategy.) This diversity creates serious challenges for product-line management. Beneath the corporate umbrella, brands are relatively unimportant. In fact, because products come and go so quickly, it is important that the consumer not become too attached to the brand.

The undifferentiated view of the Japanese market led to what Masahiko Yamanaka, deputy general manager of Ajinomoto Co. Ltd., refers to as "the random diversification trap." If the marketer believes consumer consumption is random, he has no choice but to constantly and aggressively diversify. The Japanese word for diversification—*tayohka*—has two meanings. The first is "variety" and the second is the "creation of randomness."

Opportunities in Branding, Segmentation, and Positioning

This rising importance of branding, segmentation, and positioning has created new opportunities. In addition to Asahi and Honda, other nimble companies are taking advantage of the changes in the market to identify and capture specific segments of the market:

• Mujirushi-Ryouhin, a specialty chain selling apparel, household goods, and food, has created the ultimate brandless brand. Its name literally means "No Brand, High-Quality Item." It sells 100-percent store labels at prices that are not necessarily low. The concept has primarily appealed to young women looking for no-frills and the

value of understatement. Sales grew by more than double digits
annually since the early 1990s.

• Newcomer in toothpaste Sangi increased market share from next
to nothing to 6.5 percent in early 1996 by emphasizing the benefits
of the toothpaste's whitening power. The Sangi toothpaste was
based on a chemical process for whitening teeth. It costs about ten
times that of competitors, but for young buyers who wanted whiter
teeth, it was worth it. Meanwhile, the established toothpaste makers such as Lion, Sunstar, and Kao lost market share. These incumbents fought back with new similar products in the same price
range. (Sangi later suffered against this renewed opposition, but it
is worth noting that its segmentation did allow it to overturn the
market leadership of the leaders, even for a short time.)

• Sumisho Otto, a mail-order company, built its position by focusing on fashion-conscious working women. It offered quality, variety, and a stylish image (complete with supermodels in its catalogs)
at acceptable prices. It keeps its prices down through a broad global
operation covering fourteen countries. A joint venture between
Sumitomo Corporation and Otto, a German mail-order leader,
Sumishi Otto was established in 1986 and posted $270 million
(¥25 billion) in annual sales by 1995, with an annual 35-percent
increase in sales.[5]

• As women become a more definable segment of the market, companies are developing products specifically targeted toward this
group. Asahi, for example, targeted a new beverage for young, pro-
gressive women called Asahi First Lady. Its advertising was the first
to feature multicultural models (black, white, and Asian women),
appealing to the interest in diversity and individuality among hip,
young women in Japan.

• Subaru, with its Legacy sports wagons, has cultivated and dominated the four-wheel-drive sports wagon segment. This clear segmentation and positioning allowed Subaru to grow despite the
handicaps of having only a few dealers, a perception of mediocre service, and poor fuel economy. Instead of going head-to-head with

Toyota and Nissan, Subaru shifted to a more focused, sporty position for a growing group of Japanese consumers attracted to this image.

• MosBurger overcame its significant disadvantages in competition with McDonald's by cultivating a tasty, made-to-order menu. Its positioning convinced customers to put up with slow service, poor locations, and prices that were often more than twice those of its larger fast-food rivals. Its positioning was so strong that even when McDonald's ran a 100-yen (under a dollar) Big Mac campaign in late 1994, cutting its price by more than half, Mos saw no sales drop; overall, its sales increased over the year before. CEO Takao Shimizu built the business by carefully studying customer needs, right down to what they throw away. He notes that the store trash bins are a "treasure box" of customer information, providing insight into customer satisfaction and dissatisfaction.

These companies took one real strength, focused on a target market, and worked to build a brand without a large corporate presence in Japan. This seemed to violate all the accepted principles of Japanese marketing. But the success of these firms and others shows that the rules of branding, segmentation, and positioning are changing.

Stirring the Pot: Anjinomoto's Use of Careful Segmentation

Soup maker Ajinomoto employed careful customer segmentation based on use of its products to redesign its product line. For example, it differentiated among customers who buy soup for breakfast versus those who purchase it for dinner or a drink. This approach allowed Ajinomoto to cut its existing products by half while simultaneously introducing new products. By 1988, it offered fifteen different kinds of soup through its Knorr division, but its top five varieties accounted for more than 80 percent of total sales.

The company surveyed housewives, female office workers, and female high school students to understand their perceptions of Knorr's products and those of its competitors. The researchers found that high school students separated soups into two categories (tasty and not tasty) while housewives could discriminate among seven categories of products. Ajinomoto also found that customers sought different benefits for different occasions—breakfast, lunch, dinner, or snack. Based on this research, Ajinomoto was able to reduce its product offerings from fifteen to just seven.

It then reshaped its shelf plans by examining different patterns of displays through simulations. This analysis also showed that seven or eight products in its shelf space produced the best results not only in profits but also in sales. So both the analysis of customer perceptions and their buying behavior led to the conclusion to cut its product offerings in half.

Segments of One

In some categories, businesses in Japan have successfully moved from a mass-market single segment to a segment of one. For example, Nestlé has created the Nestlé's Club. Members, typically working women in offices, receive monthly personal letters inviting a response to products and communicating about new coffee, chocolate, pasta, and other products.

Japanese companies have traditionally been masters of relationship marketing. Young high school students receive their first lessons in make-up from Shiseido. Those same students receive a card from the company when they turn forty. Car salesmen are not rewarded for their first sale but for repeat sales. In the past, however, these connections have been based on personal relationships rather than customer information and customized offerings.

Japanese marketers have just begun to use more high-tech relationship marketing approaches, making full use of information technologies. For example, all the airline companies have now started offering frequent flyer programs on a full scale, department stores issue loyalty cards, and petroleum companies have begun individualized discount programs based on past usage.

It must be admitted, however, that the technology levels are five to ten years behind those in the United States. This fact adds to the attractiveness of entry in Japan for companies from abroad with expertise in this area.

Balancing the Corporation With the Brand

Brands in Japan must still be balanced against the corporate image. Failure to see the continuing importance of the corporation can be just as damaging as the failure to see the increasing opportunities for creating independent brands.

By emphasizing the brand too much, the company can alienate and confuse customers who are attached to the corporation. Kirin found this out when, in response to the loss of market share to Asahi in the 1980s, it tried to expand its position in lager beer to a line of four beers with different tastes. Kirin realized it needed to more directly segment and position its products. In 1989, it renamed its Kirin Beer as "Kirin Lager" and then launched a diversified line of four other beers—fine pilsner, fine draft, cool, and malt dry—to give it a brand in each segment. The new flavors were based on the results of taste tests of more than 100,000 respondents.

Kirin also abandoned its standardized "one-size-fits-all" sales approach, using proposal-type sales activities tailored to the customers and needs of the specific retailer. The sales force went from collar-and-tie salary workers to salespeople in shirt sleeves and jeans riding motor bikes. The goal was to gain direct insights into local markets.

The initial full-line strategy was not a great success. The newly launched brands reduced the size of the corporate name on the labels and advertising. The launch not only failed to attract consumers, but actually eroded consumers' confidence in Kirin. The labels of the new brands were interpreted as the company's loss of confidence in its formula and its corporate name. After an abysmal year, the four brands were pulled from the market and Kirin launched a campaign to restore confidence in the company.

Kirin replaced the four beers with a single premium offering—Kirin Ichiban. The new beer label and advertising emphasized the Kirin company name. The name Ichiban means "first squeeze," contrasting it with common beers that also use the "second squeeze" of ingredients. The new brand was not differentiated based on taste but rather on the company reputation. The campaign emphasized that Kirin was back. Kirin Ichiban outperformed the four brands it replaced. Kirin had underestimated the importance of its company name and reputation, and had failed to see that Western-style approaches to segmentation and branding could not always be applied directly to Japanese markets.

A similar pattern is seen in the disastrous case of Mazda's multi-brand strategy in the late 1980s. The Mazda brand was completely replaced by four new brand names: Infini, Eunos, Autorama, and Autozam. The strategy was an instant failure and the company went bankrupt shortly afterward. Ford came in and returned to the Mazda brand, with much better results.

On the other hand, Kao was more successful with a line of products launched under the Sophina brand. Rather than roll out all the products at once, as Kirin did, Kao gradually added new products under the brand to create the full line.

The power of corporate branding sometimes causes companies to make mistakes by stretching their brands too far. Suntory, with a strong reputation in whiskey, failed to gain a following in beer because consumers couldn't make the leap from one category to another. On the other hand, Coke was more successful in moving to coffee with a separate "Georgia Coffee" brand, yet it was still sold in Coke machines, giving it a brand umbrella of the parent corporation while creating a strong independent brand for the beverage.

Hybrid Branding Strategies

Given the need to balance corporate and product-level branding, Japanese companies are applying a variety of approaches. These range from the more traditional corporate branding to two-story branding to narrow individual brand positioning.

Corporation as Brand

The traditional corporation as brand strategy remains a viable approach in Japan. New and existing players such as Mercedes, BMW, and the Body Shop are effectively using the corporation as their brand.

Independent Branding

Companies are also using more Procter & Gamble-style branding, in which each brand has a clear positioning independent of the company. This is the approach Kao took in launching its independent Sophina brand. It allows the company to target a new market without carrying all the baggage of its corporate parent. Shiseido also spun off new brands such as Ipsa and Ayura. Sadao Abe, senior executive director of Shiseido, noted that they introduced these brands not only for their own sake but also for protecting the purity of the Shiseido brand umbrella.

Two-Tier Branding

Companies create an individual brand under a corporate umbrella. For example, Toyota's corporate brand tells customers that they would receive quality, friendly service, and the backing of a large and reliable company. Beneath this first tier, the individual brands of Corolla and Celica are focused on specific markets, attracting customers with their fuel economy, flawless finish, and acceleration ability.

Co-Branding

Co-branding is actively used in the mobile telephone industry. NTT Docomo, the market leader, launched a service called "i-mode" that lets users make restaurant reservations, transfer money, or conduct other transactions or information searches through a wide screen on the phone. Providers of the services that can be accessed through the new phone are joining forces with Docomo. For example, JAL and Docomo started a joint advertising campaign promoting the use of i-mode to make reservations on JAL flights. NEC has joined forces with Docomo to promote its "Mobile Gear" handheld PCs in conjunction with Docomo's mobile telephone.

All of these approaches exist side by side in the Japanese market and all are effective in some markets and specific situations. The successful use of the narrow-positioning approach, however, is a fairly recent development. The increasing emphasis by Japanese firms on brand leverage is less focused on fitting new products to the brand. Instead, the company tests whether a proposed new product contributes to the positioning of the brand or detracts from it. If the new product doesn't enhance the positioning of the brand, it should be launched through a different brand name.

No matter what the strategy, a weak brand image is a liability. While high-end brands are now sharing the market with private brands and other value-priced offerings, it is still dangerous to be caught in the middle of these two extremes—positioned as neither a low-cost product nor a luxury product. The Olay cosmetics brand, which has succeeded in every part of the world except Japan, may be a victim of intermediate pricing and poor brand image. It was positioned as a premium product but was offered it through self-service channels (rather than using the expensive beauty consultants of traditional Japanese channels). This distribution decision conveyed a mixed message about the quality of the product. Even after P&G bought Olay and launched it under its successful Max Factor entity, sales were sluggish. A test in the Kinki region achieved only 33 percent of targeted sales.[6] Clear positioning and segmentation are crucial to product success.

Implications: Building Brand Equity

With shifts in the Japanese market, companies can create brand loyalty by emphasizing benefits to customers. This erodes some of the traditional dominance of large corporations with strong brands and allows companies to launch new brands without the backing of a huge company. An increasing ability to segment the market and position products allows companies to more carefully target their offerings. This reduces the need for an inefficient, scattershot approach to new product launches.

Among the implications of these shifts for marketers working in Japan or entering the market are that:

- It is imperative to build strong brands. In contrast to the disposable brand strategies of the past, companies can gain more than ever from creating and managing strong brands. This is particularly true for new entrants and product launches. A powerfully developed brand with a careful focus on a particular customer segment can create a powerful advantage for the companies that use them.
- The problem may not be the market but your brand. While U.S. automakers complained about trade restrictions, the most serious problem could be their brand image. A study by the Tokyo office of J.D. Powers and Associates found that only 0.4 percent of 1,000 people surveyed named Ford as their first choice for their next car. The percentages were even lower for GM and Chrysler. By contrast, BMW garnered 15.1 percent and Mercedes-Benz acquired 14.3 percent, higher than domestic manufacturer Mazda (with 14.1 percent).[7] While German automakers made more than a decade of investments in Japan of over $1 billion in building their brands, Ford, the most active of the Big Three, spent just about $100 million in building its own brand.
- Companies need to understand the market segments and create products to meet their needs. Marketers need to collect better information about market segmentation and identify products to meet the needs of different segments. Companies need to work against the homogeneous view of the market and carefully examine the nuances of these emerging segments. This is where the greatest opportunities are to find unserved segments.

- Companies should not forget the corporate brand. As the Japanese market evolves, corporate brands continue to play a more important role in marketing in Japan than in other parts of the world. While building new brands, don't forget that for some consumers (particularly older ones) the backing of a large corporation still carries more weight than the brand itself. (Even beyond the need to emphasize the corporation to sell products, foreign companies may continue to emphasize the corporation to attract employees, who want to work for established and recognized firms.) These beliefs are changing, but companies still have to be aware that corporate image continues to be important in Japan.

- Success demands focus, focus, focus. All of the above examples of successful branding, positioning, and segmentation illustrate that focusing on one target segment and acting effectively on it is the key to success. Transition from being "everything to everyone" to a focused position is strongly warranted within the current Japanese market.

- It is beneficial to use a portfolio of brand strategies. Companies should develop a portfolio of strategies, using local branding in some cases and global branding in others. The choice depends on the market segment being addressed. Sometimes they will combine elements of the two.

A Final Note on Brand Translations

Branding in Asian markets is as idiosyncratic as the markets themselves, as can be seen by looking at the language differences between nations. Sometimes these language differences work against brands, giving them unintended negative connotations. This was the case with Exxon, a word that translates as "stalled engine" in Japanese, which is the reason why the company retained its old "Esso" brand in Japan.

But these differences in translation also sometimes work fortuitously. By careful selection of Chinese characters to represent the brand in translation, you can make the language work in your favor. For example, BMW is represented by two Chinese characters sounding like "bao ma," meaning "treasure horse." Japanese liquor manufacturer Suntory is called "San De Li" meaning "three benefits and profits" in Chinese. Other examples follow:

Signs of Change

Brand Translations

Brand	*Chinese name*	*Meaning*
Ford	Fu Te	Special fortune
Benz	Ben Chi	Running freely and fast
Coca-Cola	Ke Kou Ke Le	Drinkable and enjoyable
Pepsi Cola	Bai Shi Ke Le	Everything made enjoyable

Points of Leverage

- Do you have brands that are focused on each of the important emerging customer segments? If not, how can you develop them?

- How do customers in each of these segments view your brands?

- Can you use changes in the market to rethink your positioning?

- How important is your corporate brand to your customers? What combination of corporate branding and individual product branding will be most effective?

- Do you have the optimal portfolio of segments?

- Do you have the optimal positioning? Does it address critically important problems facing your target customers?

- Do you have strategies in place to maximize brand equity?

Signs of Change

A True Individual

George Tokoro—game show host, singer, songwriter, and profes-sional pitchman—is the most popular celebrity for pitching American products in Japan. His appeal, particularly among young consumers, may be precisely because he is the opposite of the traditional Japanese salaryman. He is boyish, with a slapstick sense of humor and an uninhibited ability to express his own personality. His bug-eyed, off-beat endorsements helped General Motors jump-start stalled sales of its Chevy Cavalier and helped reverse a slump in Coca-Cola sales.

Companies once used foreign box-office celebrities as icons of respectability in their ads, but now are using homegrown talent to shape a product image of quirky individuality. Where companies might once have relied on the power of corporation to sell the prod-uct, they are now using personal persuasion focused on connecting with certain customer segments.[8]

7

Starting With the Customer— Developing Products and Services

"We manufacturers looked at the competition rather than to our customers. So, if we found that somebody had introduced a feature that we did not have, we would hurriedly include it."

Professor Hajime Karatsu, former senior executive at Matsushita

In 1990, Coca-Cola was selling nine out of every ten colas in Japan and had captured 30 percent of the total soft drink market (including noncarbonated beverages). But by 1994, it saw its position erode under a barrage of new teas, fruit-flavored sodas, and fermented-milk drinks from Japanese rivals. Coke successfully responded with a series of new product entries of its own, launching more than thirty new drinks in less than three years.[1] It realized that a powerful brand is not enough to hold the Japanese market. A company also has to keep the new products flowing.

Japanese consumers, used to rapid new-product rollouts, demand high levels of innovation. Rapid product development traditionally has been one of the great strengths of Japanese firms and one of the challenges for foreign entrants in the Japanese market. Any company that wants to succeed in Japan needs to recognize this characteristic of the market and learn from Japanese approaches to R&D and then use rapid product development as a competitive advantage.

While rapid innovation still is more important in Japan than in Western markets, the increasing customer focus in Japanese markets has reduced its significance. As companies better understand the needs of specific segments, they can be more focused in designing products to meet those needs. As they use more sophisticated marketing research, they can move away from scattershot experimentation.

The radical changes in the Japanese market, discussed in Chapter Two, are creating more heterogeneous segments. To meet the needs of these more individualized and demanding customers, companies need to build their products around the customers. Rapid prototyping and virtuosity in technical research is no longer enough to win the market.

Research and new product development centers in Japan also are a good place to begin keeping track of the strategies and advances of Japanese rivals. Many Japanese companies are masters of new product development, as can be seen by the diverse areas in which Japanese companies lead in global markets (shown in Exhibit 7.1).

In addition to honing skills in rapid product launches, a research presence in Japan also helps attune new product development to the needs of Asian markets. This makes Japan an ideal center for research and development of new products and services for Japan and the rest of Asia. An R&D presence in Japan offers insight into critical new product innovations that could be useful around the world. But to successfully establish an R&D foothold in Japan and Asia, companies must understand the distinctly Japanese approach to new product development and how it is beginning to change.

Foreign companies can understand the market as well as Japanese companies. Some of the top new products in 1998 were from foreign firms.[2] They succeeded because they were able to develop or adapt their products to local tastes or concerns. These include Coca-Cola's Ulon tea in a plastic bottle, a new blend of Nescafé coffee, Haagen Daz Royal Milk Tea, and P&G's Joy disinfectant kitchen detergent.

Exhibit 7.1 Japanese Products That Currently Hold Top World Market Share

Home appliances, and electronic instruments	Electronics materials or components	Machinery or systems
Color TV	Silicon	Automobile
Video tape recorder	Anti-epokishi for	Bicycle
CD Player	semiconductors	Ship
MD player	Ceramic package	Camera
DVD player	for ICs	Watch
Video camera	Crystal displays	Copy machine
Digital camera	Lithium ion battery	Building machine
Car navigation	CD-ROM activation	Industrial robot
system	system	Semiconductor
TV game	Floppy disk activation	production
(in-house)	system	machine
Calculator		Semiconductor
		refinement machine
		DP machine for mini-
		laboratory usage
		Automatic knitware
		weaving machine

Source: Nikkei

Japanese companies that understand the opportunities for products and services based on the changing market are in high demand. For example, Sazaby used its astute understanding of the market to build a conglomerate of boutiques, bakeries, cafés, and restaurants with annual sales of more than $345 million (¥41 billion). Its secret is to analyze trends in other markets and then adapt them to Japan. Founder Rikuzo Suzuki spends part of his year abroad, engaged in "big-city watches"—cruising the streets of Paris, London, and New York looking for new ideas to take home to Tokyo.[3] In addition, Sazaby has helped to adapt global brands such as Starbucks to the distinctly Japanese market. In an increasingly diverse and fast-changing market, this skill in being able to tailor offerings to the emerging market is very valuable.

Hit Products

This responsiveness to the market can be seen in Dentsu's annual survey of hit products. Its 1998 list reflects such changes in the market as an increased concern for value, a focus on individuality ("the desire to enjoy individuality"), the changing concerns of single women, the decline in birthrate, as well as a continued fascination with technology.

A Concern for Value

"Budget performance," such as inexpensive *kaiten* sushi shops that allow customers to select sushi as it passes before them on a conveyor belt, affordable compact utility wagons, and low-fare airline tickets have gained in popularity. "Affordable luxury," such as premium facial tissues that cost four to five times as much as ordinary tissues, ready-to-eat meals in department stores, and compact home appliances are also on the rise. All these items offered moderately priced luxury.

A focus on Individuality

Japanese consumers showed "the desire to enjoy unconventionality" in increased sales of such gender-bending products as unisex cosmetics, beauty magazines for young men, and large-displacement motorcycles for their middle-aged peers. Tired of the constraints of the past, these individuals also helped create fashion fads for camisoles and comfort shoes (with wider soles adapted to the feet).

The Changing Concerns of Single Women

Single women helped drive sales of aquarium jellyfish, stuffed pillow dolls, and virtual pets. They also became a prime part of the market for apartments, as lower real-estate prices and changing values allowed them to rent or purchase their own homes.

The Decline in Birthrate

A declining birthrate, far from decreasing interest in children's products, only made the remaining children more worthy of lavish attention. Products such as children's car seats, ear thermometers, and premium baby foods took off. With an increase in dual-career households, services such as handsets to allow parents to keep in touch with children, hourly day care, and even pubs with built-in nurseries became popular.

A Fascination With Technology

High technology continues to have an intense attraction for Japanese consumers, who recently favored such products as wrist-watch PCs flat-screen TVs, and satellite cellular phones.

Faster is Better

New product development in Japan used to be technology and shelf-driven. In this environment, Japanese firms developed an unparalleled capacity for rapid product innovations, churning out new products and variations at a breathtaking rate. Japanese companies continue to have tremendous capabilities in rapid product innovation.

This level of innovation is higher than product launches in the United States, although it varies by product category. As shown in Exhibit 7.2, in some categories such as beverages, the absolute number

Exhibit 7.2. Number of New Products in 1990 By Category

	Japan	United States	Japan per capita Pop.: 123	United States per capita Pop.: 248
Beverages	720	642	5.9	2.6
Food	1,249	3,489	10.2	14.1
Household Products	269	451	2.2	1.8

Source: Hiroshi Tonaka, "Branding in Japan," in Brand Equity Advertising, 1993.

of new product launches is greater in Japan than in the United States. In other categories, such as household products, the number of new product launches relative to the size of the market is larger in Japan than in the United States. In a few categories, such as foods, Japan lags behind the United States in producing new products.[4]

Traditional Benefits of Rapid Product Development

This rapid product development allows Japanese firms to use market experiments as a substitute for marketing research and gives them first-mover advantages that are even stronger than in other markets.

Using Rapid Product Development as a Substitute for Marketing Research

The choice criteria of Japanese consumers is complex and changing rapidly. The U.S. approach to such cross-sectional variability would be niche marketing. United States marketers would find segments of the market in which the company has advantages over rivals and concentrate on those markets. But because Japanese consumers have traditionally been hard to segment and consumer choices have changed quickly—and, in many cases, randomly—Japanese firms instead developed a "rapid fire" approach to marketing to deal with the tremendous variability of their markets.

In contrast to the U.S. "sure hit" approach of cautiously studying the needs of target markets and developing products to meet those needs, Japanese marketers tend to study consumer trends by looking at small samples of consumers and continuously introducing new products. As the manager of a major electronics manufacturer commented, "Don't waste money on market research."

Because of this philosophy, Japanese firms have traditionally used new product introduction much more than U.S. companies as a means of defending market share (see Exhibit 7.3).[5] In contrast, U.S. marketers rely on a balanced approach of new products, nonprice competition, and price reductions.

Exhibit 7.3 Means of Defending Market Share (unit percent)

	Japan	United States
New Product Introduction	69	47
Nonprice Competition	37	41
Price Reduction	29	41

Source: Hiroshi Tonaka, "Branding in Japan," in *Brand Equity Advertising,* 1993.

With the increasing use of market research, companies can be more clearly focused in their new product development in Japan.

First-Mover Advantages

One of the reasons for this rapid product development capability— or perhaps one of the results of it—is that being first to market in Japan is more important than in the United States. In Japan, the rule seems to be to enter first or not at all. A study of retail buyers sponsored by the Marketing Science Institute found that pioneer brands have an even greater advantage in Japan than in the United States. The research on more than 103 supermarket buyers in Japan and 139 customers in the United States found a sharp difference in the emphasis on pioneer brands as opposed to followers. Over half of all new brands offered to the buyers in Japan were pioneer brands compared to just 14 percent among U.S. buyers. Japanese suppliers offer more pioneer brands and fewer late followers.[6]

Product innovation also is seen as a key competitive weapon in Japan. When Honda declared war on Yamaha in motorcycle manufacturing, it was Honda's phenomenal ability to churn out product innovations—113 in less than two years compared with Yamaha's comparatively anemic thirty-seven product changes. Yamaha eventually waved the white flag of surrender. It was product innovation that won the battle.

Traditional Strategies for New Product Development

To support this strategy of rapid innovation, Japanese companies adopted a distinctive approach to new products. In contrast to the linear, "relay race" process of Western firms, Japanese companies created overlapping stages in a "rugby" strategy that compressed cycles of new product development.[7] When Fuji Xerox inherited the linear product development system of its parent, it was able to restructure the process to cut development time for a new copier from sixty to twenty-nine months.

How have Japanese firms been able to avoid the high costs associated with many new product failures? They have used nested technology and "make-up" technology (a platform technology used across many new products) to reduce the costs of failure.[8] This use of a single core technology can be characterized as a "Mount Fuji" (single-peak) approach. American firms, in contrast, tend to focus on a "saw-ridge" (multiple peaks) approach. The advantage of the saw-ridge approach is it provides variability in the basic technology, but at a high cost. Japanese markets, on the other hand, demand variability in the products rather than technology. So the Mount Fuji approach could better satisfy this demand for variation while keeping costs down and quality up. Many American and European firms have recognized the importance of this approach by establishing product development functions in Japan.

Many Patents, Few Nobel Prizes

Japanese R&D focused on developing many new patents, rather than fundamental breakthroughs. Japanese companies have traditionally measured the success of their R&D departments based on patent output. "A large number of applications is regarded as a symbol of both a company's and a department's efforts toward research and development."[9] This emphasis on volume may contribute to the Japanese practice of filing many small patent applications, which also forces other companies to cross-license inventions.

Japanese patent applications have been the world's highest since the 1950s and they continue to grow each year. The steep rise in Japanese patent applications began to level off and decline in the 1990s, remaining close to 370,000 early in the decade. The number of applications granted hovered around 90,000. Even in the United States, Japanese share of patents has grown from 8.8 percent in 1975 to 22.5 percent in 1992.[10]

Relative R&D spending is also higher in Japan than in the United States. In 1993, its total R&D expenditures amounted to 2.9 percent of the GNP compared to 2.5 percent for U.S. firms, as shown in Exhibit 7.4. In 1994, more than a third of the fifteen largest corporate spenders on corporate R&D worldwide were from Japan.[11]

Yet, the list of Nobel Prize recipients in the field of natural science includes the names of 159 Americans, sixty-five British, sixty Germans, but only five Japanese.[12] The implication is that much of this energy is focused on innovations that are not setting the world on fire. In fact, a survey by Nomura Research Institute concluded that only about 5.5 percent of Japanese patents were for highly original or creative technologies, compared with 17 percent in the United States. Most were small refinements of existing technologies.[13] (It should be noted that this tendency to file for patents on

Exhibit 7.4. R&D Expenditures

	Total (¥ billion)	Government Funds (as percent of total)	Ratio to GNP (percent)	Per Researcher (¥ billion)
Japan	13,709	21.6	2.91	21.4
United States	17,875	42.3	2.53	—
France	4,025	45.6	2.43	29.1

Source: Japan 1996: An International Comparison, 1995 Science and Technology Agency.

minor innovations is not just a result of the Japanese focus on continuous innovation; it also reflects differences in patent laws and legal actions in the United States and Japan.

Speed and the Japanese Option Glut

The customer used to be virtually ignored in this endless process of innovation. At the height of manufacturer-driven R&D in Japan, companies in the late-1980s added so many features and products that the consumer was virtually buried in new offerings. In 1989, Kao offered 600 items in its product line before it started cutting back. Matsushita offered 220 types of televisions. Sony offered 250 varieties of its Walkman.[14] Around 700 new soft drinks were launched in Japan each year in the late 1980s; but 90 percent disappeared within twelve months.[15] This also resulted in increasingly complicated products, as companies continued to add bells and whistles to the core product.

Finally customers had had enough. In the early-1990s, the most successful VCR was a stripped-down, low-cost model by Aiwa. It met the demand for simplicity and low-cost from increasingly value-conscious consumers. It had fewer buttons. Japanese companies found that, contrary to the conventional wisdom of the time, less was more. They began to rapidly strip down their product lines.

It should be noted that some creative business leaders in Japan were extraordinarily adept at understanding the needs of the market. Akio Morita's development of the Sony Walkman demonstrated deep insight into the needs of customers. But with the exception of a few innovators such as Morita, the majority of systematic R&D in Japan was driven by the engineers and technicians rather than marketers. Customers were not part of the process.

Faster Isn't Always Better

Faster innovation doesn't always mean better products. Researchers found that Japanese companies were not consistently high performers in product integrity (measured by total product quality—a composite of such indicators as total quality, manufacturing quality, design quality, and long-term market share).

Overall, Japanese product integrity was about the same as in Europe and the United States. Japan had both top-ranked and bottom-ranked players, as did U.S. and European groups. But because of its advantages in speed and efficiency, Japan had some all-around high performers (leading along all three dimensions). Researchers found that European companies that focused on the high-end of the market could achieve product integrity and market success through slower and less "efficient" product development.

Rapid product innovation is becoming less important to success in Japan. It is increasingly important to develop products that satisfy new or unmet customer needs and achieve higher levels of value. This shift erodes some of the advantage that less market-savvy, technology-driven Japanese firms have had over foreign rivals. It also creates opportunities for Japanese firms to build their product and service lines by emphasizing customer benefits.

There are examples of very successful radical innovations. As cited briefly before, Toyota introduced its Prius model in late 1997, creating a revolutionary hybrid gasoline-electric car that was truly ecology oriented rather than an incremental improvement. Despite a higher price tag, the product was very successful. Toyota had planned to sell 1,000 per month but sold more than 2,000 per month because of the high demand. Toyota is also engaged in fierce innovation battle with Daimler-Chrysler, GM, Ford, Honda, and other carmakers to develop the first commercially viable fuel-cell car.

Emerging Approaches to New Product Development

The rise of Western-style marketing research and the evolution of consumer-driven markets may be beginning to slow the frenetic development and launch pace of new products in Japan. Food maker Ajinomoto launched an average of thirty-one new kinds of frozen foods each year in the late 1980s, but in 1992 it launched only nineteen. In 1988, Matsushita had 5,000 audio products on the market. In 1993, it sold only 1,000. It also trimmed its seventy-two kinds of rice cookers in 1989 to just thirty-eight in 1993. Kao, which launched seventy new products in 1988, dropped to just twenty products in 1992 after boosting its market research to target its new product launches more carefully.[16]

Japanese companies continue to be masters of rapid product innovation, but they increasingly realize that this strength in new product rollouts is not enough. They have to be able to innovate in ways that matter.

Start With a Champion—Involve the Customer

One of the big changes in new product development in Japan is a more customer-driven approach. For example, Suntory started with the customer when it developed a new alcoholic beverage called Cocktail Bar, which was a big hit in Japan. Rather than starting with the product and looking for the market, Suntory started with the market and developed a product for it. Its success was a result of its focus on a specific target market: single women living alone in the Tokyo suburbs, who came from the countryside in Japan and now worked in large companies downtown. By starting with the target consumer and creating the product, the company came up with the best products for her.

This process is not entirely customer-led, but rather involves a product champion or team that represents the lead user. As part of shaping their understanding of the product and the market, this team then goes directly to customers for insights. Honda's new minivan Odyssey began with the vision of the product champion to create a "personal jet with four wheels." The Honda team clearly wanted to separate it from current minivans in Japan, which were black-smoke-spewing diesels with poor ride quality and inhospitable interiors. To shape the concept, the new vehicle development team went to the beach and the mountainside to speak with potential customers. In this way, the core concept of the champion was refined and polished through *gemba*, or "market reality." It took them a year to boil down the concept and determine the target market. It was a combination of engineering vision and customer input that shaped the minivan.

The ultimate vision was not initially realized because the president did not want to build a new assembly line for the Odyssey. This forced designers to downsize their plan to fit the line. It still turned out to be a dynamite hit in Japan, reviving Honda's faltering sales. Later, when Honda needed to build a larger Odyssey for the upscale U.S. and Japanese markets, the original vision was dusted off and made a reality. The team spent quite a bit of time in the United States to learn about minivan drivers there. The resulting Odyssey was launched in mid-1998 and was an instant success.

Fuji used a similar process to create its hit digital camera, Pix 700, which became the best-selling digital camera in Japan in 1998. The team developed products they would be proud to own and use themselves, with the constraint that the final product had to fit into the breast pocket of a dress shirt. This "impossible" challenge, and a subsequent demand to reduce noise, helped lead to a very creative and successful design.

Tying the new product development process to the market, as Suntory did with its Cocktail Bar beverage, is the key to success. It was not just a coincidence that the designer-in-chief happened to be very similar to the target customer. This creates opportunities for companies in Japan and new entrants to develop products uniquely tailored to the market.

The Japanese market is becoming increasingly concerned with more than speed and variety. The strategy of churning out a lot of product variations that customers don't care about has increasingly been undermined by the move to a customer-driven market. Customers are demanding products that offer not only newness but also true benefits. This is changing the approach to new product development in Japan, but it is important to understand both the traditional approach and how it is changing.

Reorganizing Around the Customer

To create more customer-centered products, companies are also reorganizing their new product development processes. Japanese companies are moving toward using cross-functional teams—with representatives from R&D, sales, the factory, suppliers, sometimes even dealers and wholesalers—to develop new products. This allows them to combine data, hands-on information, and passion. When the managers who launched Kao's successful Attack detergent were asked to identify the person responsible, their reply was that the entire team was responsible.

Honda's product development used to be organized around a visionary product manager. The chief product designer had a vision for the future and the car was designed to the needs and specifications of this lead designer. A new process, such as the one used to create Honda's Odyssey, has moved to focus on needs of the market rather than on the technology of the designer. The development process relies upon a team of technical people, product engineers, and sales and marketing people. It is more likely to be based on marketing research. This is a shift from a top-down view of the market to the view of design and R&D as an interactive process with the market.

Successful New Product Development

Research on new product development shows the following factors are key to success in Japan:

Development Vision

The development vision is driven by the personal desire of the project leader, who is among the most knowledgeable target customers. The project leader should be a demanding customer, be proactive, passionate, and tenacious, and be technically and professionally competent.

Cross-functional Integration

Development teams need a high level of cross-functional information sharing, coordination, and joint involvement in conducting new product development activities.

Learning From Market

Successful new product launches also reflected a high level of competence in competitive and market intelligence generation. The project development team understands the customer purchase decision and price sensitivity and is aware of competitors in the marketplace. In addition to quantitative research, equal emphasis is placed on qualitative approaches, including focus groups, observing and listening to customers, and visiting retailers and users' homes.

Experienced Product Team

A high quality technical development process with a proficient project development team.

A Laboratory for Studying Japan and Asia

Conducting R&D in Japan not only keeps the research closer to the market but also provides early warnings of new products developed in Japan. Although Japan may lag in Nobel prizes, as discussed above, it is a myth that the Japanese only copy existing products, as P&G and other companies have learned by hard experience.[17] This myth may have held some truth in the post-war era and for a few companies (Matsushita's Japanese nickname means "products which have been copied"). However, this belief also tends to minimize the attention foreign companies pay to monitoring Japanese products and technologies.[18]

P&G's initial dominant position in disposable diapers in Japan was eradicated by aggressive product improvement by Kao, which launched a super-absorbent disposable diaper that gave it market leadership in Japan in 1983. P&G was surprised by the rapid and successful attack, but quickly rolled out its super-absorbent Ultra Pampers in the United States, forestalling a potential attack by Kao in its home market. It is unlikely P&G would have responded so quickly if it had not seen the impact of the innovation in Japan.

Kao found an enzyme in the soil near its Tochigi Laboratory, an element that became the basis for the first compact detergent, called Attack and launched in 1987. Kao's share rose from 33 percent to 45 percent. Again, P&G and other U.S. manufacturers again saw the threat in Japan and were able to move quickly to blunt a potential entry into America.

Other Western firms have benefitted from product ideas discovered in Japan. Molex uses Japanese miniaturization techniques in its portable electronics. Otis Elevator used a mid-range product developed in Japan. S. C. Johnson maintains a research facility in Oiso, Japan, one function of which is to keep an eye on technical and product developments throughout East Asia. Significantly, the head of Johnson's Japanese operation reports directly to the CEO, the same reporting level as the company president. Coca-Cola learned important process improvements in bottling in the 1960s through its Japanese subsidiary.[19]

Japanese companies are leaders in innovations in mobile phones, videogames, electronics, and diverse other markets. A presence in Japan offers a front-row seat on key developments and innovations.

Implications for Managers

A slowing pace and an increasing focus on customer-driven products is changing new product development in Japan. It is also changing the requirements for success. New products must be more directly focused on the demands of the market, so the process needs to be defined in a way that connects. For companies that can focus their R&D toward producing benefits in the market, this change creates opportunities. Innovations that are focused on generating greater value for customers are also more likely to succeed in today's markets.

As companies develop new product development strategies in Japan, they need to consider the following issues:

• Carefully monitor new product pacing. Companies need to be closely attuned to the demands for innovation of the Japanese market. Is the company's pace of innovation and the speed of its new product launch fast enough to keep up with Japanese rivals? How could competitors use rapid product launches (as was the case with Coca-Cola) to erode your market share?

• Use customer focus for advantage. Companies need to carefully examine how they can use a more customer-focused approach to new product development to create more targeted products. How can you use this customer focus as an advantage over rivals with more rapid product development capabilities?

• Examine implications for Asia and the rest of world. Companies should consider the strategic role of their R&D operations in Japan for success in Asia. How can they offer insight and capabilities that are crucial to success in other Asian markets? How can they help in competition with Japanese firms in other parts of the world?

Points of Leverage

• How can you get customers more involved in the new product development process?

• What implications do the shifts in the Japanese market have for your R&D initiatives? What new products will respond to these changes? Which new ones will you need to develop to meet emerging needs?

- Is your current R&D structured for speed at the expense of deeper connections to the market? To what extent is it technology-focused? Market-focused?

- How can you use research centers in Japan to develop products for other parts of Asia, particularly in competition with other Japanese firms?

- To what extent do you integrate the new product development function in Japan with those in other parts of Asia and around the world? How are you trying to accomplish pan-Asian leverage of R&D?

- Is your new product development staff in Japan instrumental in identifying, understanding, and interpreting your target customers in the Japanese market? What have been the challenges in recruiting, training, and motivating capable development staff in Japan? How has your approach changed to reflect changes in the Japanese lifestyle?

- How focused have you been in targeting your customers in new product development? Are you going to improve this focus?

- Are you rethinking your product and service offerings to allow for customization?

8

The Discovery of Value— Pricing and Promotion

"Our focus now is value for money."
Shinya Iwakura, director of Honda Motor Company[1]

Anyone who thought Japanese consumers were insensitive to prices was disabused of that notion in October 1992 when a bargain men's clothing store, Aoyama Shoji, landed like a bombshell in the middle of the prestigious Ginza shopping district. Far from turning up their noses at this low-brow entrant, more than 200 customers lined up in front of the store by 7 A.M. on opening day to purchase suits priced at just ¥10,000 ($80), jackets at ¥2,300 ($20), and shirts at ¥500 ($4). Latecomers had to wait patiently in lines that stretched past the noble façades of the old Japanese department stores, as the Aoyama store managers exercised crowd control by periodically closing the doors. The store's opening-month's sales topped $3 million (¥363 million), ten times that of its average sales. The menswear sections of the adjacent department store were virtually deserted.

Pricing had arrived in Japanese markets. However, Aoyama's experience teaches a second lesson: Low prices alone will not cut it. After its initial success, Aoyama's "cheap" image caused the store to self-destruct. Japanese customers were less willing to compromise quality in exchange for discounts. They wanted good quality *and* low prices. Japanese consumers expect to give up little on quality in exchange for decreases in price. This continued demand for high quality makes discounting in Japan far more challenging than in other parts of the world. The traditional wisdom that "where Americans argue about a centimeter, Japanese argue about a millimeter" continues to hold true.

Although Aoyama and early discounters failed, the impact was already made. Mainstream departments stores cut their prices in response. Next door to Aoyama, the Matsuya department store slashed its prices on suits from around $800 to $550–700 because of competitive pressures. (Its prices were still far above Aoyama's average price of $280.) These innovative entrepreneurs taught customers to be more demanding about price and more concerned about value than ever before. Pricing in Japanese markets would never be the same.

New Approaches to Pricing and Promotion

In addition to the rise of discounting, there are a variety of other changes in pricing and promotion strategies in Japan. Rather than focusing on long-term market penetration, the focus has shifted to customer value. It is used increasingly as a competitive marketing tool. Among the many recent innovations in pricing and promotion:

Rise of Price Busting and Private Brands

As Japanese discounters began price busting, mainstream retailers created their own private brands. Although Japanese consumers are less willing to accept poor quality for low prices, they are increasingly concerned about price in purchasing decisions. McDonald's used a very successful 65-yen hamburger campaign to drive the growth of its Japanese business. After research found that customer satisfaction increased from 30 percent at 210 yen to 120 percent at 65 yen, the company slashed prices on its hamburgers and cheeseburgers (80 yen), with similar discounts on its full meals. The rise of the "100-yen store" is another sign of the increasing importance of price in Japan. These stores, which are packed with products priced at just 100 yen (similar to dollar stores in the United States) are expanding rapidly. In a deflated economy, discounting was a powerful force in driving the continued growth of the fast-food chain in Japan.[2]

Bundled Products and Services

Price is not single dimensional, but multidimensional. Companies are realizing that they can bundle the prices of products and services, for example, including financing. The majority of new consumers are now taking the total price approach to evaluate the value of the product. Marketers are taking excellent advantage of it, offering a total pricing package. BMW Japan, for example, offered customers benefits such as low-interest loans and extended warranties in addition to fair prices. BMW offered these benefits at below their value as an added incentive to purchase a car.

Customer Time and Money Tradeoffs

Another factor in pricing is time. Although customers want value, they are willing to trade low price for convenience. The growth of convenience stores is one sign of this trend. Another is the acceptance of pizza delivery, which more than doubles the price of a pie.

Increasing Price Transparency

The price and value of products and services is being made more explicit. Even such traditionally unmentionable costs such as the fees for funeral arrangements are being broken down. With the consolidation of the Japanese funeral business by the railways and other large firms, detailed price sheets have emerged that list prices for coffins, limousines, reception, cremation, and even the honorarium for the monk who officiates.

Polarized Pricing

Some segments are very price sensitive and others are price insensitive. Many consumers are more than willing to pay six times the price of local mineral water for a foreign brand. Premium-price products have fared very well, despite the recession in Japan. For example, Mercedes sold more than 9,000 of its new "A Class" model, hardly inexpensive at ¥2.65 million ($22,000), by November 1998, far exceeding its goal for the entire year.[3] Expensive brands such as Christian Dior and Hermes continued to post increasing sales. The luxury buyers are at both ends of the generational spectrum—young women and retired couples.[4] According to a survey of household savings by the Prime Minister's Office, the average savings of those over sixty was approximately ¥22 million ($169,000) at the end of 1997, about twice the savings rate of those in their forties (¥11.9 million or $91,000).

Some pricing strategies that are successful in the West have failed in Japan because customers were not used to them. For example, when airlines offered lower price for passengers who booked ahead, customers were upset and annoyed that the same seats on the same flight were being sold for different prices. The airlines had to drop the discounts.

Money-back guarantees also haven't always been successful because this is an implicit admission that there could be a defect in the product, something Japanese companies with "zero-defect" policies are not willing to acknowledge.

Causes of the Pricing Revolution

The rise in interest in pricing was driven by growing global travel and awareness, a tighter economy, the declining importance of the relationship between the buyer and seller, and the emergence of more demanding customers.

An analysis by three Japanese economists of the cost of protectionist policies estimated that these policies cost consumers about $110 billion (¥16 trillion), or 3.8 percent of Japan's GDP, at the end of the 1980s.[5] These studies confirmed what thousands of Japanese travelers had seen with their own eyes—almost everything costs more in Japan. Until the 1980s, Japanese consumers accepted these higher prices. For example, a 1986 study of Japanese executives and German expatriates in Japan ranked price sensitivity as the key factor in German markets but only ninth in Japanese markets.[6] An August 1988 study of new car preferences conducted by *Nikkei Industrial Daily* found that fewer than 9 percent of Japanese men and women gave reasonable price as a reason for their new car purchases.

Initially, these higher prices were not considered a problem. The Japanese bureaucracy has traditionally viewed consumers as naive creatures who need to be protected from the vicissitudes of price competition. Aggressive pricing would only cause these consumers to buy products that were not needed or lower the quality of the available products. Higher prices were believed to support the economic growth of the nation. But then, this "childlike" Japanese consumer, whom business and government leaders had tried to protect, finally grew up.

International travel became an opportunity for global price comparisons. These world travelers, one of the segments of the market with the most money to spend, were no longer willing to accept the explanation that the higher prices were good for the country. Their rallying cry was *naigai kakakusa*, meaning "the difference between domestic and overseas prices." The more acutely aware they were of this discrepancy, the more pressure they created for lower prices in Japan.

Parallel imports, in areas where they were allowed, showed consumers directly how much they were paying for inefficient distribution. The same products were offered at a significant discount.

At the same time, retailers were becoming more aware of customers. Point-of-sale systems made the consumer's view on prices and products much easier to track.

Price-sensitive Consumers

Japanese consumers are becoming more price sensitive, as shown in Exhibit 8.1. Between 1992 and 1998, the percentage of customers citing "cheaper price" as a reason for selecting a store increased across diverse product categories. Fashion items such as handbags and men's suits were a bit more resistant to price pressures but, even here, price played a greater role in the purchase decision. Female fashion (not shown in exhibit) was also less price sensitive, with only 31 percent of respondents citing price as the reason for choosing a store.[7]

A survey of Japanese consumers in the early 1990s found that 76 percent felt prices in the supermarkets were too high and nearly 50 percent said store preference and distance would not matter if they could obtain the same product at a cheaper price. Fifty-nine percent indicated that they would be willing to trade traditional consumer service for a lower price. But few were willing to sacrifice such culturally conditioned values as store atmos-

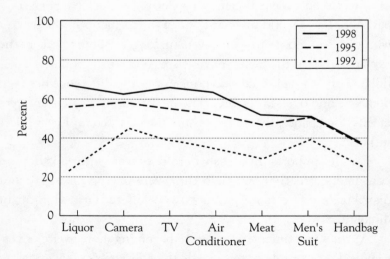

Exhibit 8.1. Increased Price Sensitivity: Proportion of Consumers Citing "Cheaper Price" as a Reason for Selecting a Store
Source: Economic Planning Agency, November 1998.

phere and packaging just to cut prices.[8] Japanese consumers also reported that they would expect products from newly developing countries to be priced about 30 percent lower to be attractive.[9]

At the same time that consumer attitudes were changing, entrepreneurial companies were responding to these new demands. Discounters like the previously mentioned Aoyama Shoji have appeared throughout Japan, shaking up the current retailers. Large manufacturers and retailers have, sometimes reluctantly, been forced to embrace these new rules. They have slashed their own prices and introduced low-priced private brands to compete with their premium offerings.

Japanese unit prices continued to move downward in 1997 and 1998, particularly among deregulated items, as shown in Exhibit 8.2. Although Japanese retail prices are declining, Tokyo prices still remain higher than in other major world centers, as shown in Exhibit 8.3. Except in a few categories such as healthcare, education, durable goods, and public utilities, it is more expensive to live in Japan.

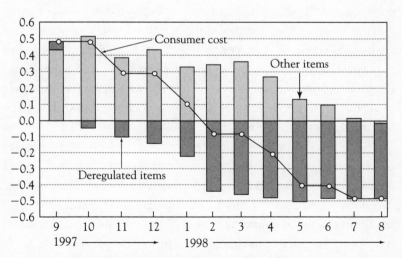

Exhibit 8.2. Deregulation and the Decline in Consumer Cost
Source: Nikkei.

Exhibit 8.3. Retail Prices (1996)

	Tokyo	New York	Berlin	London	Paris
Commodities	100	75	81	78	84
Food	100	69	60	58	65
Durable goods	100	81	119	105	120
Clothing and footwear	100	60	93	64	78
Other goods	100	76	90	87	99
House rent	100	57	83	75	65
Public utilities*	100	58	127	70	103
Transportation and communications	100	83	106	94	95
Health care	100	137	30	53	68
Education	100	109	93	164	86

* Fuel, light, and water charges
Source: Japan Planning Agency, November 1996.

Price Busting and Private Brands

This rising tide of consumer unrest over high prices had a logical consequence in the market: price busting. *Kakaku hakai,* or price busting, became a key focus of competition for new discounters and traditional retailers. A survey by the Prime Minister's Office found that two-thirds of Japanese citizens approved of price busting and less than a fifth of those surveyed felt it had a negative impact.[10] Most respondents, looking at their own pockets, found that price busting had a positive impact.

Established retailers responded by creating low-priced private labels. In the early-1990s, Daiei, a major supermarket chain, fired one of the first volleys in the price war with the introduction of a private-label orange juice. Daiei had determined that customers would buy orange juice as frequently as milk, if the prices were comparable. It dropped the price of its orange juice from over $3 to around $2. It had to scour the world to find oranges at a price that would allow it to earn a profit. Japanese consumers responded enthusiastically. Daiei originally estimated it would sell about $2 million (¥190 million) worth of orange juice, but by 1995, it had already sold nearly $300 million (¥28 billion) worth.

Daiei also introduced its own brand of detergent, Savings, at the unheard of price of $3.50. When competitor Ito-Yokado brought its price down to the same levels, Daiei lowered its price to just about $3.[11] In the scuffle, the price of market leader Kao's product, Attack, slipped from its list price of about $9 to a shelf price of below $5.

Like Aoyama, Daiei's initial success was undermined by concerns about quality, forcing the company to rethink its discounting strategy. But along with its discounted orange juice, the customer had also gotten a taste of lower-priced private brands.

Price busting has moved beyond commodity items like detergents and orange juice to luxury items. A bottle of Old Parr liquor can be purchased for about $40 at a discounter, about half of the price from a department store. Chevas Regal, priced at about $33 was sold for about $26. Dom Perignon, which used to start at more than $150, was offered for about $67.[12]

Seikyo, which began its life as a nationwide association of buying cooperatives, has rebuilt its strength by focusing intensely on price cutting and private brands. With efficient methods of inventory management, it has evaluated all of its 17,000 product lines to identify 200 of its best-selling items for potential private branding. To produce these brands, it entered into negotiations with sixty manufacturers. Membership in the buying co-ops topped 17 million and its sales increased to nearly $30 billion in 1994.

Price busting in the travel industry is also contributing to the further education of Japanese consumers on world pricing. The fastest-growing segment of overseas travel is the one catering to economy travelers. These tourists take shorter holidays, handle many of their own arrangements, and pay less for the services of agents. As lower prices allow more Japanese to travel, they become more aware of global pricing, and the cycle of declining prices builds upon itself.

Automobile customers are also seeking lower prices. Manufacturers began cutting superfluous features (for example, automatic vibrating side mirrors that shake off rain) from economy models. When Honda cut the cost of its 1993 Today (an economy model) by $440, its quarterly sales rose 21 percent above target.[13]

Some manufacturers had initially sought to use their power to undermine the growth of discounting and private brands. Shiseido, for example, stopped shipment to discounter Kawachiya and Kujiki, claiming "breach of contract." It asserted that the retailers had violated their contracts by offering steep (20 percent) discounts on their products. This case was later brought before the Federal Trade Commission (FTC) in Japan and Shiseido resumed shipping. The large manufacturers later seemed to adopt an attitude of "If you can't beat them, join them." The manufacturers began working with retailers in producing private label brands and offering products directly, without going through the traditional networks of middlemen.

Discounters Have Their Day

In addition to private labels, discounters have grown as a result of the increased interest in pricing. As the names indicate—*disukaunto stoa* (discount stores), *auto retto* (outlet), *horusera kurabu* (wholesale clubs)—are largely imports from the West. Traditional Japanese discounters focused on disposing defective goods at a cheaper price. As long as the goods were not seriously damaged, they could be sold at a discount. These outlets were primarily frequented by students and eccentrics seeking finds. Most Japanese considered these stores inferior.

The discounter of the early-1990s was different. This new *ofu puraisu stoa* (off-price store) carried top designer brands that were selling for far higher prices at the department stores. Through parallel importing and streamlined distribution systems, the same items were offered at a substantial discount.

While these discounters face increasing competition from falling prices at mainstream retailers, they continue to be a strong force in shaping marketing—particularly pricing—in Japan. One projection saw discounters increasing from 37 to 60 percent of the market by the year 2000. Generic drug sales are expected to increase from 13 percent of the total market to 25 percent by 2000.[14] Whole shopping centers filled with discounters—called *pawa senta* (power centers)—have been developed.

Factory outlet stores also are on the rise, popping up around major cities. Their growth has been driven by a tough economy and more value-conscious consumers. Stores such as J. Crew and Eddie Bauer are offering discontinued merchandise at bargain prices. These outlet malls, popular in the United States, are growing rapidly in Japan. For example, a thirty-store mall in Osaka saw its sales rise by 23 percent in 1998 at a time when Japanese department store sales were falling.[15]

No Skimping on Quality

Japanese consumers have given up the belief that high price equals high quality, as reflected in the expression *yasukaro, warukaro* (you get what you pay for). But the new focus on value doesn't mean the Japanese have lowered their demands for quality, particularly their intolerance of defects in the physical appearance of products.

Whether it is dented boxes or tiny imperfections in automotive paint, the Japanese consumer is still more finicky and less willing to sacrifice quality for cost than U.S. consumers. Foreign automakers still need to run their new cars through import facilities to make sure they meet the stringent demands of the Japanese market. Initial attempts to market private brand products—such as Seikyo's ¥100 cosmetics (under a dollar) during the 1970s—ended in failure because quality was not maintained. Even Aoyama's low-priced image in apparel began to work against it, and it later had to emphasize high quality and upscale image to try to regain lost ground. But now, as high-quality products are offered at lower prices, Japanese consumers have demonstrated that they are much more willing to shop around for lower prices on comparable products.

Itoh-Yokado, which had forged a partnership to procure low-cost products from Wal-Mart in 1994, began phasing out the products when it found Japanese consumers were too fussy about quality to accept inexpensive U.S. goods. Unlike consumers in the United States, most Japanese are in the middle and upper classes, so there is almost no low-income market for cheap, low-quality goods.[16]

The mineral water market grew by leaps and bounds, but only at the high-priced end. Japanese consumers were not willing to accept low-priced, low-quality mineral water. The ideal is lower prices and undiminished quality due to improved efficiency. Failing that option, brand-equity based on quality control becomes the winning idea.

The traditional gift-giving periods in Japan add another dimension to pricing. The cost of products is a sign not only of quality but also of generosity. Johnny Walker Red Label scotch ruined its market position when it dropped its price from ¥5000 to ¥4000. The company failed to realize that the scotch was given as a gift during the semi-annual corporate gift period and a less expensive product was a less meaningful gift.[17] But now, Japanese consumers are more accepting of price cuts on premium brands. After all, a bottle of Chivas Regal is still Chivas Regal, no matter what the purchaser paid for it.

This willingness to accept lower prices—even in gift giving—can be seen in changes in the array of gifts offered by major retailers. The department store Matuzakaya cut thirty-one items priced over $50 in 1994 and added thirty-four items at lower prices. Tokyu added twenty-one items priced under $30.[18]

Consumers also are willing to give up some of the personal attention they have received from companies in the past. The acceptance of self-service products, discussed in more detail in Chapter Twelve, has allowed discounters to significantly reduce their prices.

More Fluid Pricing Strategies

Japanese pricing has traditionally been far more static than in the West. Japanese companies rarely change their suggested retail prices over the life of the product. Japanese car makers set a price for a model that usually holds until the introduction of the next model. Japanese companies do not use list price adjustments as a competitive strategy in the same way as companies in Western marketers.

Although list prices remain unchanged, manufacturers would adjust rebates to the sellers. With a focus on sustaining market share rather than profits, companies would adjust these rebates to maintain share, even at the sacrifice of short-term profits. These were not consumer promotions, but the savings were usually passed on to consumers through lower prices by retailers.

Mark-up Pricing

A survey of pricing decisions by twenty-two managers at leading Japanese firms by Ichiro Furukawa of Osaka University found that most firms used a "mark-up pricing" strategy.[19] This approach, used by 90 percent of the companies in the study, reflects the full cost of the product including R&D, production, advertising, and sales promotion, plus a given margin. The margin would typically run between 20 and 40 percent for consumer goods.

Image-premium Pricing

Another less popular approach for price setting that Furukawa found was "image-premium pricing," in which price is used to shape the image of the product. Here the pricing is based on psychological factors. Furukawa also identified two primary strategies for managing the evolution of market price over the life of the product. The first is maintaining a relatively stable pricing pattern. The second is developing a pattern of rapidly declining prices, where pricing drops almost to the average unit cost of production. The study found that this "competitive price" strategy—a high initial price driven down rapidly—seemed to be the most typical approach in Japanese markets.

A Move to Open Pricing

One of the casualties of the new price wars has been the tradition of official pricing by manufacturers. Manufacturers used to call the shots in pricing, but more of the power has shifted to retailers. In December 1993, Hitachi and other leading appliance makers opened pricing for 346 products. This, in turn, has forced them to scrap their standard rebates to major distributors to allow their *keiretsu* stores to compete with discounters. Matsushita, Toshiba, and others have followed suit.

The manufacturer's suggested retail price (MSRP) was traditionally set by cost plus profit, based on the most inefficient retailer. Factory prices and wholesale prices were set as a percentage of the MSRP along the channel. But customers now have their own opinion of what products are worth, which has forced manufacturers to move to open pricing.

When it introduced its private brands, Daiei also created a radically different approach to pricing. Instead of manufacturer-based pricing, it organized a customer board meeting, where its patrons developed the price for new products. Daiei's challenge was then to develop a quality product that could be produced for this price. This was one of the first cases where the consumer, not the producer, determined the price. The flow of pricing had been reversed.

Manufacturers are also changing their pricing policies. Kagome, a packaged-food manufacturer, has restructured its messy rebate system. It reduced the number of items from 120 to sixty and shifted from an "increasing returns" rebate to a flat rebate. It also offers retailers their discounts on the spot, rather than the traditional "pay back later" approach.

Increasing Use of Promotions

Promotions—both trade and consumer—are much less important in Japan than in the United States. Without list prices for products, it is difficult to define what a promotion is. Most pricing and discounts were left to the discretion of the wholesaler, based on rebates passed down from the manufacturer.

A mixture of explicit restrictions against promotions and traditional approaches to marketing have stunted the growth of promotions in Japan. Sales promotions have been virtually ignored in Japan because of regulations against them and lack of experience among Japanese companies. Coupons and refunds were banned outright. Even as the total ban has been lifted, there are still regulations against coupons in magazines and newspapers. Free premiums are restricted by law as well. Having little experience in trade promotions, Japanese firms have been reluctant to use them. With the complexities of rebates and distribution systems, it is harder to establish broad trade promotions.

Japanese companies have traditionally chosen media advertising over sales promotions. In 1992, mass media advertising accounted for more than 63 percent of average advertising expenditures of Japanese firms, while sales promotion accounted for a little more than 36 percent, as shown in Exhibit 8.4. This is quite different from patterns in the United States, in which trade promotion alone accounted for 45 percent of advertising budgets compared with less than 30 percent for both media advertising.

While direct mail accounted for half of U.S. advertising expenditures in 1992, it amounted to just 11 percent of Japanese budgets. In contrast, Japanese companies spent 19 percent of their budgets on billboards and other outdoor advertising compared to just 2 percent in the United States. The Japanese approach to marketing is much more of a broadcasting of general knowledge compared to the U.S. approach of communicating to individuals.

The types of sales promotions favored in Japan are also different. U.S. companies tend to use price promotions such as discount coupons, but a study by the Japan Marketing Research Center (JMRC) found that Japanese companies rely on quiz or contest prizes that do not require purchases, promotions and events introducing new products, and lottery-type premiums. (The focus was on national promotions, so this study ignored the local promotions,

Exhibit 8.4. Distribution of Advertising and Sales Promotion Expenditures (by percentage)

Media	1986	1987	1988	1989	1990	1991	1992
Total advertising and promotion expenditures	**100.0**	**100.0**	**100.0**	**100.0**	**100.0**	**100.0**	**100.0**
Advertising expenditures in the four mass media	**66.0**	**65.7**	**66.3**	**64.6**	**64.2**	**63.8**	**63.6**
Newspapers	25.1	25.0	25.5	25.1	24.4	23.5	22.3
Magazines	6.5	6.5	6.7	6.6	6.7	6.8	6.7
Radio	4.5	4.4	4.3	4.1	4.2	4.2	4.3
TV	29.9	29.8	29.8	28.8	28.9	29.3	30.3
Sales promotion expenditures	**33.9**	**34.1**	**33.5**	**35.2**	**35.6**	**36.0**	**36.2**
DM	3.9	3.9	3.8	3.6	3.5	3.5	4.1
Inserts	6.2	6.1	5.8	5.9	5.9	5.9	5.9
Outdoor	6.5	7.0	7.0	6.9	6.9	6.9	6.9
Transportation	4.4	4.3	4.3	4.4	4.5	4.6	4.9
POP	3.2	3.0	2.7	2.8	2.7	2.8	2.7
Telephone directory	2.1	2.1	2.1	2.0	2.2	2.5	2.9
Exhibitions, visuals, etc.	7.6	7.7	7.8	9.6	9.9	9.7	8.8
New media advertising expenditures	**0.1**	**0.2**	**0.2**	**0.2**	**0.2**	**0.2**	**0.2**

Source: "Advertising expenditures in Japan during 1992," Dentsu.

which are usually carried out through leaflets and inserts using discounts instead of coupons.)

There has been little interest in coupons. A report from Nikkei Advertising Research Center found that in 1993 less than 1 percent of agencies "definitely wish to use" coupon advertising and 11 percent "do not want to use them under any conditions." Advertising agencies tend to stress communication prior to purchase rather than point-of-sale communications.

Consumers also are not accustomed to coupon clipping. Although Japanese consumers are price sensitive, they are less price sensitive overall than their Western peers.

Growing Interest in Promotions

Sales promotion is catching on in Japan, as shown by the steadily rising expenditures in Exhibit 8.4, although the growth is still slow. Promotions can be expected to play an increasingly important role in marketing in Japan, as customers shop around more and become more price sensitive. Japanese consumers are increasingly engaging in impulse buying rather than deciding on a brand before going to the store. This increase, along with relaxed regulations, is expected to lead to an increase in trade promotions.

Implications: Using Pricing Strategically

There have never been greater opportunities to use pricing strategically in Japanese markets. Companies that are aware of the rising price sensitivity of Japanese consumers, as well as their continued demands for high quality, have an opportunity to use pricing as a creative tool for market entry and growth.

Among the implications of the rising importance of pricing:

• Look for opportunities to use pricing strategically. Creative pricing strategies can provide significant advantages. Given the interest in value, companies that can deliver high quality for a lower price have greater advantages in Japan today than in the past.

• Use discounting and other low-price retailing formats. Outlet malls, discount stores, buying clubs and other low-priced formats provide the means for your company to grow rapidly in Japan. Look to these channels for your products or to develop these channels as a retail entry strategy.

• Don't sacrifice quality. In developing pricing strategies, be cautious about what is sacrificed. Japanese customers are less forgiving about lapses in quality, even for low-priced products. They also have distinct standards for packaging and perfection.

• Use promotions. Just because promotions have not been used regularly in Japan in the past doesn't mean they won't be effective in the future. Innovative companies are now generating individualized promotions. For example, a Domino's Pizza customer who orders one type of pizza fairly regularly might receive a coupon in a week when the order fails to come in.

• Look for similar pricing shifts in other parts of Asia. The shift from relative indifference to pricing in tightly regulated markets to increased consumer sensitivity can be expected in other Asian markets. The Japanese attitudes toward quality, because Japanese firms were central in building these markets, may also be expected to occur in many Asian markets. Because these markets are not as far along on the move to consumer-driven markets, expect pricing to become more important in the future.

Previously in Japan, "price" was removed from the *domestic* competitive mix by national policy, which meant intense competition on "quality" and "service." This competition raised standards, and Japan benefitted immensely in international competition, especially when it had a cost advantage in yen/dollar terms. Thus, a quality product was produced. For the *domestic market*, a margin was added to arrive at the market price. In the days of rapid economic growth,

Signs of Change

Prescription for Success

When Smith, Kline & French launched its new multisymptom cold remedy, Contac, in Japan in 1987, it used a series of promotions that were unheard of in pharmaceuticals. First, it offered newspaper and magazine sample coupons. To meet Ministry of Health restrictions that allow only authorized drug stores to offer product samples, Smith, Kline & French set up its own drug store in its Japanese headquarters. The company also used trucks decorated as packages and featured a team of hundreds of yellow-clad women who handed out giveaways and sample cards to consumers. The samples not only encouraged trials but also gave the company a list of names and addresses. The new Contac halted the decline of the original remedy and led to 20-percent sales growth for both products in its first year.[20]

consumers snapped up these products that signified an improvement in the quality of life.

Today, macroeconomic forces have triggered changes in corporate behavior. Consumers have new choices. It is uncertain what effect these changes will have on pricing and promotions, but it seems clear that both will become increasingly important to Japanese marketing. Approaches to pricing are becoming more consumer driven. As pricing becomes a more defined arena of competition, the use of promotions to draw customers in is a natural progression. It is evident that now, more than ever, the consumers are calling the shots.

Points of Leverage

- How important is price to your customers?
- To what extent and along what dimensions are customers willing to trade quality for lower prices?

- Will customers accept self-service or other cost-cutting approaches for lower prices? On which dimensions will they be unwilling to sacrifice quality for a lower price?

- Are there new ways to use promotions that have not been tried in your home markets? How do changes in regulations and customer attitudes create opportunities?

- Are you capitalizing on the opportunities for value-based pricing?

- How creative have you been in your pricing strategies?

- What are you doing to prepare yourself for a market in which customers can determine the price (as with www.priceline.com)?

9

Goodbye to Greetings—
New Rules of Communications,
Advertising, and Public Relations

*"If I knew anything about advertising in Japan, I
would tell you. But I don't—yet."*[1]
David Ogilvy, co-founder of Ogilvy & Mather
advertising agency

Japanese advertising has typically puzzled Western observers. For
example, one advertisement for Mita copiers featured an image
of a building being demolished, mentioning Mita only at the end.
Another ad that was very effective featured a moving solo by American soprano Katherine Battle. It ended with the line, "I know good
whiskey," and the name Nikka Whiskey, almost as an afterthought.
This commercial not only boosted Nikka sales by 20 percent, it
helped sell more than 250,000 of the singer's records in Japan and
it made her recital tour an overwhelming success. What's more, it
was selected Best Television Commercial Film at the 1987 Dentsu
Awards, Japan's most prestigious advertising honors.

Tamotsu Kishii, dentsu senior creative director, notes, "Although
it's not easy to find a connection between a copy machine and a
building being demolished—since there is none—it is precisely this
great disparity that, to the Japanese, imbues this commercial with
impact and, to Westerners, makes it so difficult to appreciate."[2]

Changes in advertising create opportunities for more Western-
style advertising to be successful in Japan, allowing more content and

a stronger message to be added. While some advertising from other parts of the world may work well in Japan (for example, Nike ads featuring Michael Jordan were brought over virtually unchanged), many other ads would be totally out of place in the West. This chapter explores some of these differences and the ways advertising in Japan is adopting more Western approaches, even as the West moves closer to a Japanese approach.

The restructuring of the Japanese advertising industry also has affected traditional advertising practices. The concentration of media access in the hands of a few powerful agencies tended to make this access more important than creative content. The traditional practice of agencies representing multiple clients in the same industry tended to dampen the practice of comparative advertising. This structure is changing with a wave of firm restructurings and an influx of investment by foreign advertising agencies.

Shakespeare and Kabuki: Japanese Styles of Communication

Traditional Japanese advertising focused on conveying a mood rather than detailing product benefits. With a focus on corporate brands, advertising is designed to keep the company name in front of the consumer. This led to "hello advertising," in which the manufacturer essentially said "Hello, how are you?" to its loyal customers. The product or service being promoted was almost incidental.

Although "mood versus message" has been a useful shorthand in describing differences between Japanese advertising, one way to gain a deeper understanding of the difference content plays in Japanese communications is to consider the distinction between Shakespearean theater and Japanese Kabuki theater. The actors' words in a Shakespearean production are of vital importance. In contrast, what the Shakespearean actor communicates through words, the Kabuki player communicates through gesture. (This could also be true of a line delivered by a great Shakespearean actor, so it is still a matter of emphasis.) For the average Kabuki viewer, the pleasure is in seeing the stylistic flourishes handed down within the great Kabuki families. More often than not, the delivery generates more enthusiasm than the message.

Similarly, the Japanese *itamae*—the rough equivalent of the Western chef—is applauded for the visual pleasure his preparation gives, for the way the food is presented, and for his attention to minor details. The Western chef is judged less on the visual appeal than on the content.

This duality is also seen in the depiction of Japanese language as *kanji* (ideographic characters) or *katakana* (the phonetic symbols). There is some evidence that the different communications styles use different parts of the brain. In the 1960s, Shigeru Yamadori, a young doctor at the Kobe University Hospital, published an unusual thesis proposing that *kanji* and *katakana* "were memorized in different parts of the brain." He based his conclusion on a case study of a patient who had been hospitalized after cerebral apoplexy. Incredibly, as an aftereffect, this patient had completely forgotten *katakana* and *hiragana*, both Japanese-developed phonetic symbols, as opposed to the Chinese ideographs, which he retained his ability to read.

As the Japanese communicate by using both methods of writing, it meant that the patient could no longer read the newspaper as the phonetic portion was blocked out. He could write his name and address, which were all in *kanji*, but he could not decipher sentences. As such a "pure case" was rare, checks were repeated over two years before the conclusion was reached that "unlike phonetic symbols, which are stored in the left sphere of the brain, *kanji* are stored in the right sphere, like pictures." Our own data, taken together with this finding, suggests that the Japanese ability to perceive symbols is greater than that of the Westerner, perhaps due to the long conditioning received in learning *kanji*. In another example, the Oriental art of calligraphy is far removed from penmanship of the West.

Senators and Samurai

There is another difference in Japanese communication that may have a historical source. The Western foundation of "intellectual or cognitive" communication is said to have been established by the Greeks and is essentially a culture of debate. The Western businessman states his position at a meeting—the thesis—and this is taken up by a counter point of view—the antithesis. After further debate, the meeting participants arrive at a decision or resolution—the synthesis. The process is based on an aural system of communication.

The Japanese, on the other hand, have no such historical tradition of verbal debate. In the highly structured Tokugawa-era society of the samurai, the farmer, the artisan, and the merchant—in that order of social ranking—free and direct verbal communication was quite risky. The samurai had absolute rights over the rest of the community, described as *kirisute gomen*, literally translated as, "I can chop off your head and you have no recourse in the courts." In general, the samurai did not abuse this right, to avoid the social upheaval that would result from total oppression. The fact remains that such a right existed, and thus there emerged a very cautious form of verbal response within the community. Obviously, one should not offend by giving the wrong answer. But if you could not be certain of the right answer, it was better for everybody if you answered in a way that could be interpreted as either "yes" or "no."

In modern-day Japan, such an illustration seems exaggerated. Certainly the legacy of the Tokugawa samurai era is fading, although it still remains to some extent in the administrative infrastructure of the government and in many of the larger corporations. The point is, however, that given these very different historical backgrounds to the process of communication, the way in which an advertising message is conveyed in Japan is quite different from that in Western cultures.

A word of caution: Just as in the United States or elsewhere, there is simply no absolute rule for good advertising. There are many examples of successful Japanese advertising that are not based on mood. Equally, there are many that are based on mood and are typically Japanese. This does not prove anything, because one could produce an equal batch of *both* that were not successful. What should be recognized is that the "cultural mode" is different from Western modes and that advertisers may have to formulate and judge their advertising differently from how they normally would. The "mood" versus "logic" issue can be a red herring.

Besides the Shakespeare and Kabuki difference, there is a wide range of cultural, demographic, and structural dissimilarities that affect Japanese marketing and advertising.

Cultural Differences

Among the key cultural differences that are reflected in Japanese advertising are:

Respect for Tradition

The Japanese value of stability in their social system leads to an emphasis on tradition in advertising. Citizen watches, for example, used an unlikely set of models for its advertising campaign. The ads, shown in Exhibit 9.1, depict "centenarians" with captions such as, "100 years old; active at work." The ad's message was that Citizen watches "run the distance of your life. Prepared for lifetime maintenance." Similarly, a recent Mercedes ad stressed that while it was "reinventing the car," the company was the first to manufacture a passenger car. Shiseido, in launching its new cosmetic lotion Eudermine, stressed its "century's progress toward better skin."

Mutual Dependence

In contrast to the marketing of Western cosmetics, where the product is an expression of individuality, Japanese companies stress the partnership involved in achieving beauty. Company beauty consultants offer individual consultations with customers. A Shiseido

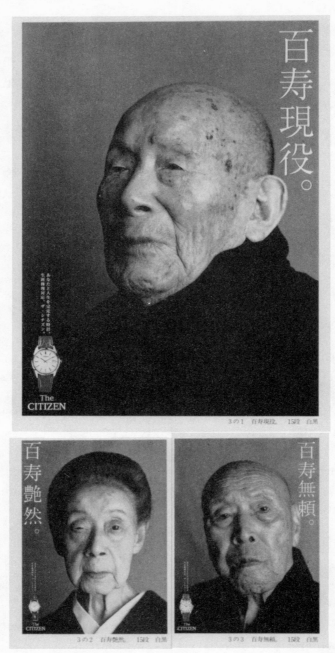

Exhibit 9.1. Citizen uses respect for tradition to advertise watches.

campaign, instead of focusing on the cosmetics for personal expression, created an ad with a large and simple message, "Together, we will be Beautiful—Shiseido." Similarly, how many Western computer companies would run an ad showing two cuddling rabbits, like the one used by NEC to stress support of its customer stores? The ad, shown in Exhibit 9.2, reads "snuggled against, but not leaning on each other."

Harmony With Nature

Mercedes showed its cars blending into the natural landscape with a theme of "Mercedes of the Beautiful Country," and Toyota showed its Crown Majesta model parked in front of Mount Fuji. Citizen displayed its watches engulfed by flowers or ivy leaves. Panasonic's ad for its digitally controlled audio system, produced during the Nagano Olympics, is illustrated with a tranquil snowscape, as shown in Exhibit 9.3. Two bird feathers transformed the word "voice" into "noise" and the copy stressed how the audio system can preserve the tranquility of Nagano—demonstrating that the companies that do not disturb nature are to be respected. Finally, this concern for the environment is seen in the blockbuster hit animated film *Princess Momonoke*. The film, which in Japan surpassed *E.T.*, *Jurassic Park*, and *Star Wars* in box office receipts, features the theme of conflict between industrialization and nature.

Use of Seasons

A related feature of Japanese advertising is the use of seasons. Commercials are often set within a specific season and then they are pulled when the season passes. At the extreme are products designed for a certain season such as Sapporo Beer's Winter's Tale. This product, named after Shakespeare's play and featuring excerpts from the Bard appearing on the label in English, is only marketed in the winter. Faithful to its name, the product has a higher alcoholic content, presumably for its warming effect, and is off the shelf once the cooler months are over.[3]

Exhibit 9.2. High-tech firm C&C Intelligent Store uses soft touch to try to "snuggle" up to customers.

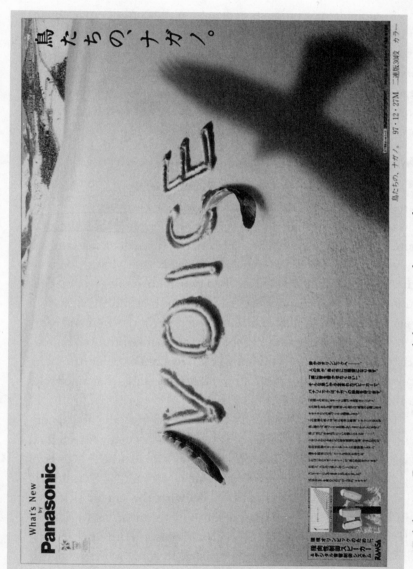

Exhibit 9.3. Panasonic uses a natural theme to market its audio systems.

Newness and Evolution

Acceptable new products evolve from the current environment gradually. Japanese advertising stresses this gentle process. For example, an ad for Tandem systems shows a green leaf with the caption "Wind" scrawled in one corner, seen in Exhibit 9.4. The copy read, "We are with the times," a line that is less shocking than a revolutionary message of change, particularly suited to the pre-bubble economy in which it was introduced.

Distinctive Use of Celebrities, Including Gaijin (Foreigners)

Some 63 percent of all Japanese commercials in 1997 featured hired celebrities. Foreign celebrities have long been used to increase interest in commercials and to convey an international sophistication. In the 1960s, anonymous foreigners were used to capitalize on the mystique of the West. For example, the Nissan Motor Company campaign to launch its Skyline used two anonymous *gaijin* models, dubbed "Ken and Mary," a typical clean-cut boy and girl next door from a U.S. suburb. Ten years later, the anonymous Ken and Mary were replaced by megastar Paul Newman. Charles Bronson, Sammy Davis, Jr., and Orson Welles are just a few of the celebrities who have helped to give products an international status that aided sales in the domestic market.[4]

These celebrities often had little connection to the actual content of the ad. For example, a Toyota advertisement featured an image of Alfred Hitchcock on a director's chair in the corner of the ad. He asks: "Have you tried the new Mark II? No? You should try it." Although he has little to do with the car or the text, Hitchcock's presence evokes a sense of tradition as well as an international flavor. Similarly, actor Harrison Ford appears in a Kirin ad carrying a large bottle of beer. In some advertisements, there is a closer connection to the product, as when supermodel Naomi Campbell was featured in an ad for Shiseido's Total Beauty Clinic.

Exhibit 9.4. Tandem emphasizes newness with a slogan: "We are with the times."

Demographic Differences

Demographic differences in the Japanese market have also changed approaches to advertising. Among these are:

Aging of Society

With a rapidly increasing elderly population, many Japanese ads feature seniors. For example, a Shiseido ad shows a gray-haired woman in a kimono. A series of ads for a skincare product were targeted toward women in their fifties, an audience that is typically ignored in cosmetics ads.

Changing Families

Public policymakers have run advertisements stressing that fathers need to take more responsibility for raising children, with the hope that mothers who receive more help will have more children. One ad features a popular modern dance performer holding his child, as shown in Exhibit 9.5. He had married a popular singing idol at the tender age of twenty and promptly had a child. Many other ads focus on parents with children, particularly the changing role of fathers in the family.

Generation Gaps and Individualism

The gap between the generations is often highlighted in commercials, particularly those pitched to youth. For example, an ad for a Kodak disposable camera shows a teenaged daughter returning home late. When her irate father asks her where she has been, she snaps his picture. The punchline is, "Let's talk through photographs." Youth-oriented advertising is increasingly revealing the in-your-face attitudes of the new Japanese consumer. These advertisements often are critical of tradition. An advertisement for Fuji Television shows a woman criticizing everything about a traditional wedding until she sees the Fuji television cameras. She then says, "Fuji Television's here. Oh." An ad for Boss coffee shows a young commuter who picks

Exhibit 9.5. Government ad emphasizes changing families.

up a can of coffee on the train and is told, "Don't forget to recycle."
He responds, "Get off my back. I'm the boss."

Structural Differences

The structure of the Japanese advertising industry and traditional approaches of agencies and clients also led to other distinctive features of Japanese advertising, including:

Shorter Spots

In part because of the control of airtime by a few agencies,
Japan is one of the few countries in which airtime for longer commercials carries a substantial premium over the fifteen-second
commercial, which accounted for more than two-thirds of all television advertising. The rules tend to force advertisers to purchase
the shorter commercials, even when it leads to such bizarre sights
as the same commercial running back-to-back.

Fewer Long-running Campaigns

There are far fewer long-running campaigns in Japan than in the
United States. For example, of the winning commercials from
the All Nippon Commercial Broadcasting Council in 1997, only
one (Nissin Cup-A-Noodles) was the continuation of a long-running campaign.

Importance of Word of Mouth

There is a much greater emphasis on word of mouth in launching
new products in Japan, particularly high-tech products. Manufacturers hand out samples of video games in neighborhoods where target
customers reside. There are a variety of trendy magazines that track
new product developments, and lead customers often read them.

Word of mouth is so important in selling video games Sega
Enterprises actually addresses it in its own advertising. When Sony
launched Playstation, Sega's sales slumped. One very unusual Sega
television ad showed the managing director of Sega walking down
the street past a child who screams "Sega is no good. Playstation is

much better." The advertisement is aimed deliberately at changing word of mouth, and goes on to say that Sega is coming back. Although it is a bit unusual, even with the Japanese sense of humor, to show your own managing director being taunted by customers, the ad had the desired effect. It became one of the most talked-about advertisements of the season. That meant it generated the world-of-mouth interest Sega was seeking and Sega's sales improved.

Toyota created a new showroom and entertainment center outside Tokyo that includes a two-kilometer test track. Car shoppers can drive not only Toyota models but also other popular models on the test track. As soon as new Toyota models are introduced, they are taken to the track and the word of mouth begins.

Self-effacing Humor

While the head of Pepsi Japan didn't take a beating like the Sega managing director, the company's spokes-hero and soda can did. Pepsi, which trails Coca-Cola in Japan by nine to one, created an ad in which a futuristic "Pepsi-man" runs through the streets, only to be met with a punch from a boxer. The spot closes with a dented can, as shown in Exhibit 9.6. And this is an ad designed to sell Pepsi. (Why wait for rivals to beat you up when you can do it yourself?) So much for the Pepsi challenge.

Moving to Message

The communications divide between Japan and the West is not as great as it once was. On the one hand, Western advertisers are beginning to pick up more of an emphasis on mood, with the use of emotional advertising on the rise. At the same time, Japanese advertisers are adopting more Western approaches to touting product benefits. The differences now are not huge cultural chasms, but rather a question of degree of difference.

Today, mood and message (touting features and benefits) exist side by side. For example, an ad for Honda's Inspire takes a more traditionally Japanese approach. The copy reads, "For me, Inspire.

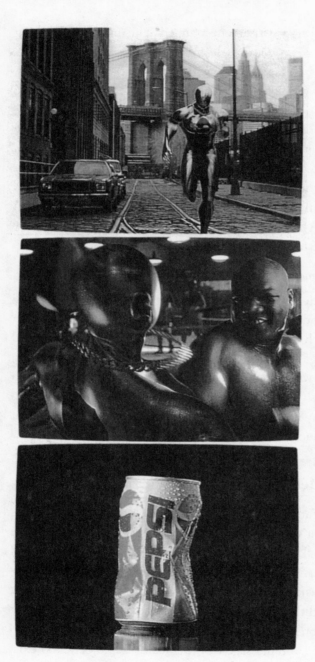

Exhibit 9.6. Pepsi ad uses self-effacing humor, including denting its own can.

Inspire, for me." This is a soft approach that is characteristic of traditional Japanese advertising. The price and descriptions of the car's features are noticeably absent. A second advertisement that appeared about the same time, for Toyota, is virtually the same as its Western counterparts. It describes product features and clearly states the price.

A Little Humor Sweetens the Message

Viewers may still be a bit uncomfortable with this content-laden approach, and it sometimes sneaks in by the back door. Product benefits are often delivered with a large dose of humor. Advertisers almost poke fun at themselves for focusing so much on content.

For example, a Sony Playstation advertisement begins with a serious press conference at which an executive discusses the features of the product, but then the spokesman puts on a mask of a Playstation character. The advertisement discusses product benefits but in a humorous way. In another example, a t-shirt commercial features a young woman with a pointer discussing the benefits of the cotton t-shirts as an older gentleman stands smiling in one of the shirts. The man says, "It's a little difficult to understand, but I feel good." This self-deprecating humor offers the information about product benefits while poking fun at the idea of a content-oriented ad.

In a culture in which modesty is still one of the prime virtues—"the riper the rice, the deeper it bows its head"—some straight pitches are considered "too pushy." However, a pair of slapstick comedians can put the point across very effectively. Because they are making idiots of themselves, they are not offensive and yet the point they are making sinks in.

The Structure of the Industry and the Rise of Comparative Advertising

Until 1990, advertisers in Japan believed that the market, with its emphasis on harmony, couldn't stomach comparative advertising.

In that year, Pepsi-Cola aired a television commercial that directly challenged Coca-Cola. Another Japanese advertising taboo had fallen. Viewers not only found no offense in the advertising, but they thought it was highly entertaining. The first ad left open the question of whether it was accepted because the comparison was between two U.S. firms. But then further comparative ads appeared. Cadillac compared its warranty of three years and 100,000 miles to the three-year, 60,000-mile warranty offered by Lexus. Proving that Japanese companies can also play at this game, NEC also took on IBM in an ad campaign.

A direct comparison between two Japanese firms has yet to happen, but it is getting closer. For example, a video game commercial features a Mr. Cigar and a Mr. Anthony (a very thinly veiled reference to Sega and Sony). A credit card advertisement compares features for a new card with those of existing cards, without mentioning them by name. Japanese firms are a bit more circumspect than their U.S. counterparts.

There has been no public outcry against this assault on harmony. In fact, a survey of more than 800 Tokyo women found that two-thirds said they had no objection to comparative advertising. So why was it so uncommon? Much of the reluctance to directly challenge competing products may be a result of the structure of Japanese advertising. Major Japanese agencies often represent competing clients. Thus, the reluctance to launch a direct assault on a competitor through advertising very likely had more to do with the institutional structure of the advertising industry than Japanese culture.

The Concentration of the Japanese Ad Industry

In U.S. advertising, firms are hired for their creativity and ideas. In Japan, the emphasis is access—so firms are hired for their media. This makes it easier for a single agency to represent direct competitors in an industry. Dentsu, for example, handled ads for the competing parties in national elections, something that would have been unheard of in the United States.

The advertising industry in Japan is much more concentrated than in the United States. Familiar worldwide advertising agencies account for less than a 6-percent share of the Japanese advertising market—all totaled, about half as much as Hakuhodo, the second-largest domestic agency. Two superagencies, Hakuhodo and Dentsu, act as "wholesalers" of TV airtime.[5]

A Big Bang?

There is an increasing disconnect between advertisers and agencies in Japan. As noted in Chapter Six, a study sponsored by Ogilvy & Mather Asia Pacific found that advertising clients are far more interested in brand building than their agencies. The study also found that only 3 percent of clients rated agencies as being very or quite helpful, while 81 percent of the agencies themselves felt they were very or quite helpful. The reason for the disconnect may be seen in the differences in what the two sides cite as the reasons for a successful relationship. While agencies cite communications with the client and other administrative strengths, clients tend to value efficiency and effectiveness of their advertising and reaching a target audience with creative messages.

Mark Blair, regional planning director for Ogilvy & Mather Asia Pacific, suggests that this divide in perceptions may offer opportunities for outside advertising firms to enter Japan. "There is not a 'big bang' as such in Japanese advertising as yet. However, there are encouraging signs (if you are a Westerner dealing with Japan) that things are changing. Ominously, it is the clients who are taking the lead; and it is important for agencies to consider the implications of waiting in the wings too long.)"[6]

There has been a tremendous influx of foreign capital and a burgeoning of international alliances. Major world agencies such as Omnicom and British firm WPP Group have taken large stakes in Japanese agencies. Leo Burnett increased its investment in Kyodo to make it a 100-percent subsidiary to enhance its use of digital media and outdoor ads. Burnett also announced a capital alliance with Dentsu.[7] This influx of foreign capital and ideas, already underway with responses to the changes in the market, was accelerated with the rush of foreign companies into the financial sector. Japanese agencies were less prepared to meet the demands of these clients and present their new messages.

Domestic firms have launched major reorganizations to meet these changes and take advantage of new technology. Top advertising agency Dentsu announced plans in 1999 for the extensive reorganization of its business to establish better profit and loss management and to give greater decision-making power to its units. The move followed a similar restructuring by number-two domestic agency, Hakuhodo, in 1998.[8]

There also have been a number of prominent mergers among domestic firms. For example, on January 1, 1999, the third-largest agency, Asahi Tsushinsha (Asatsu), merged with number-seven firm Saiichi Kikaku to create "Atsatsu D.I.K." This powerful combination—backed by an investment by WPP (parent of J. Walter Thompson and Ogilvy & Mather)—gives the new firm powerful global resources and insight in competing with the top two firms, Dentsu and Hakuhodo.[9]

Diversity of Approaches

Whether or not the changes create opportunities for outside firms, they are leading to increasingly divergent views of what constitutes "good advertising" in Japan. A 1998 survey of 254 senior- and middle-ranking Japanese marketing and advertising professionals identified five primary approaches:

Connectors

The largest group of advertisers in the sample at 30 percent, the Connectors are most interested in how the ads foster personal bonds between brand and consumer. They are the closest to Western marketers and may be taking the lead in brand building in Japan.

Product Pushers

These advertisers (19 percent) focus on creating a short-term sales lift by portraying the product's strengths. At the same time, however, they have a greater focus on brand image and reject the more "frivolous" aspects such as entertainment, celebrities, newsworthiness, etc.

Ubiquity Seekers

Ubiquity Seekers (19 percent) are driven by a desire to win awards and popular acclaim. They use a broad range of integrated marketing activities, hoping to use this ever-presence to boost long-term and short-term sales.

Cut-throughs

Closest to the stereotypical view of Japanese advertisers, these professionals (18 percent) focus on drawing attention through famous celebrities, exaggerated product attributes, and other memorable associations. They are not interested in either short-term sales results or long-term brand building.

Entertainers

This group, comprising 14 percent of respondents, believes that advertising should be entertaining or newsworthy. They don't support the use of celebrities or showing the target audience. They are less concerned with brand building and more concerned with top-line results.

Growth of Advertising

It probably comes as no surprise, with the emergence of a more developed consumer market, that advertising has been recognized as crucial to the success of Japanese firms. Spending has risen sharply, as shown in Exhibit 9.7. Between 1960 and 1990, total advertising spending in Japan increased by more than thirty times, from

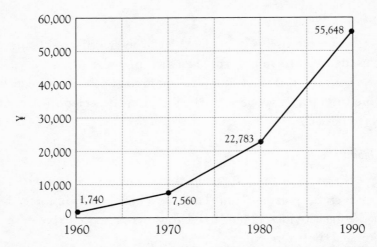

Exhibit 9.7. Change in Total Advertising Spending (¥100 million)
Source: Dentsu, in Japan Almanac, 1996.

¥174 billion to ¥5.6 trillion ($40 billion). Although Internet advertising continues to be a small fraction of the total market, it is growing rapidly in both Japan and other parts of Asia, as will be discussed in Chapter Ten.

Advertising can have a significant impact on Japanese consumers. In the 1960s, almost no diamonds were sold in Japan. But after three decades of DeBeers advertising, the Japanese diamond market equals the U.S. market, with the two countries accounting for 64 percent of the world's $49 billion (¥5.8 trillion) in diamond jewelry sales.[10] More than 70 percent of Japanese brides now go to the altar with a diamond ring. Unlike the U.S. diamond advertising, which focuses on diamonds as gifts, the Japanese ads more directly encourage young working women to buy diamonds for themselves.

Implications for Advertising in Japan and Asia

The Japanese market teaches important lessons about the interaction between culture and structure in the advertising business. The tradition and structure of the industry had a tremendous impact on the shape of the product. Managers need to be careful to discern how much of the peculiarities of the business are a result of structure and tradition instead of culture. Western approaches such as comparative advertising or benefits-focused ads might be effective even if they have not yet been tried.

At the same time, the greater emphasis on mood and images may be seen in other cultures that use ideographs in their communications. Similarities in language and therefore thinking may make the mood-focused or visually appealing Japanese ads better suited to Asia than the message- or content-focused Western ads.

These similarities may make Japanese style advertising more successful overall in these markets, although there are still important individual differences. Advertisers need to tailor messages and the medium to specific Asian markets. For example, to market monosodium glutamate (MSG) throughout Asia, Ajinomoto used variations on the same advertising to tailor its pitch to local markets. It used alliteration in its advertising that appeared as "Tak Tak" in the Philippines, "Chup Chup" in Indonesia, and "Thae Thae" in Thailand. The melody for its jingle also was modified market by market, adapted to local dialects and instruments without losing its basic form.

How can managers apply this insight on Japanese advertising in Japan and other parts of Asia? A few points to consider:

• Look for opportunities to apply Western approaches. Although Western advertisers sometimes feel they have to throw out the book to succeed in Japan, they still need to pay attention to advertising fundamentals. Lack of verbal content does not necessarily mean an absence of an advertising concept. Advertisements that fail probably do so for the same reason that some nonmood commercials fail—because of the lack of a meaningful concept or of improper product positioning. Traditional approaches and advertising expertise can be successfully applied in Japan, as long as the cultural differences are kept in mind. In Japan, as in any market, the key to successful advertising is to develop ads that appeal to the target audience.

- Break the fifteen-second barrier. While Japanese advertising rates make the fifteen-second spot much less expensive than longer ads, companies should consider whether the tradeoffs in less opportunity to build strong brand awareness are worth the savings. They should look for ways to create advertising that will do more than make a quick impression, but will actually help build a relationship between the viewer and the brand.

- Foreign agencies should look for opportunities for entry. Given the changes in Japanese advertising and the gap between the agencies and clients, foreign firms should look carefully at whether or not there are new opportunities to enter Japan. Many major global firms are already on the move. Domestic firms should look at ways to develop the capabilities to meet the new demands of clients. Advertisers should carefully consider where they can best find or develop the insight needed to succeed.

- Capitalize on the rise of Pan-Asian and global media. With increasing opportunities to buy advertising across the region and around the world, companies can build broader campaigns more efficiently and effectively. In orchestrating these campaigns, however, they need to pay even more attention to cultural differences and the different approaches required by different markets.

Points of Leverage

- To what extent does your current advertising rely upon mood over message? Do you need to rethink this balance, given the rising importance of cognitive messages?

- For non-Japanese firms, how can you better utilize "mood" in your advertising? Can your advertising address some of the other distinctive features of Japanese advertising?

- Who are your best advertising partners, given the changes in the structure of the Japanese advertising industry and new marketing challenges?

- How focused have you been in defining target segments for advertising communications? Have you changed your focus on segments in response to changes in the market?

- Have you developed integrated marketing communication? How do you balance and integrate mass advertising, sales promotion, and public relations? Do you need to change the balance in the light of changes in the market?

- How have you addressed the new communication paradigm of the Internet, including the links between communication, education, and entertainment, and the addition of increased interactivity?

- How can you best balance traditional Japanese approaches with more content-driven approaches?

- To what extent is top management in Japan committed to communications decisions? To what extent is top management conscious of employees as an audience in making advertising and public relations decisions?

The Rise of Cybermarketing

Japan, with its historical distribution and entry barriers, seems like a market made for the Internet. U.S. direct marketers have found that catalogs and phone lines offered new channels to directly reach customers in Japan—or for the customers themselves to seek out lower-priced foreign retailers. The Internet provides an even more direct and interactive marketplace, while at the same time short-circuiting the traditional middlemen and channel relationships that have made the Japanese market so difficult to penetrate. (Of course, this is changing due to innovations in distribution, as will be discussed in the next chapter.)

This potential was not initially realized because, early in the cyberage, Japan trailed not only the United States but also the Czech Republic in per capita Internet usage. The growth of electronic commerce (or "e-commerce") in Japan was initially slowed by a lack of infrastructure, language, and customer interest. But in the late 1990s, Japan finally connected.

A Three-Trillion-Yen Market

By the end of the decade, e-commerce had arrived. Personal computer penetration into the home, which had not made much progress in the early 1990s, skyrocketed at the end of the decade, as shown in Exhibit 10.1. By early 1999, an estimated ten to

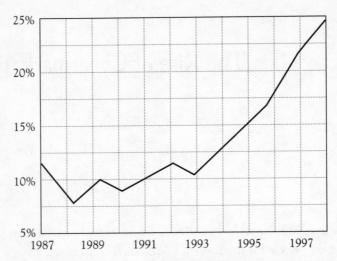

Exhibit 10.1. Penetration of Personal Computers in the Home
Source: Economic Planning Agency, 1998.

fourteen million Japanese were online and the population of cyber-Japan was expected to reach twenty million by 2000, as shown in Exhibit 10.2.[1] By early 1999, search engine Excite reported that users were arriving at its Japanese site at the rate of 200,000 per week, accessing two million pages per day.[2] A host of online services was growing rapidly.

By early 1999, 46.6 percent of Japanese Internet users had shopped online.[3] Nomura's think tank estimated that there were about 14,000 virtual stores. These stores were opening at a phenomenal rate, with the number of sales increasing rapidly. Domestic e-commerce was expected to exceed $1 billion (¥120 billion) in 1999. Online sales reached $695 million (¥85 billion) in 1997. The most popular products were computer hardware, software, books, and airline tickets.[4] Although home PC purchases fell due to the recession, the Internet continued to rise through increased use and multiple users within a single household.

Andersen Consulting projects that the e-commerce market in Japan will expand by about fifty times from 1998 to 2003, when it

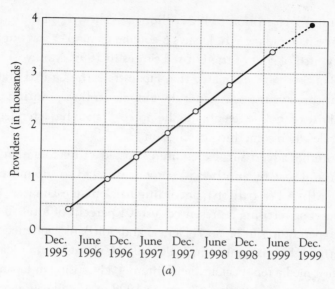

(a)

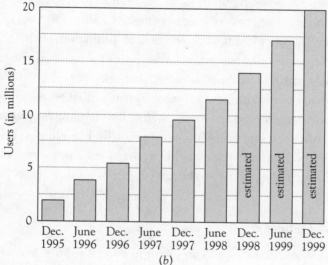

(b)

Exhibit 10.2. (a) Number of Internet Providers. (b) Number of Internet Users

Source: Postal Ministry, Japan Internet Association, 1998.

will top ¥3.16 trillion ($380 trillion) , as shown in Exhibit 10.3. Despite its rapid growth, Japan's e-commerce market was only one-thirty-fifth of that of the United States in 1999. Masayoshi Son, CEO of Softbank, estimated that Japan trails the United States by about three years in Internet development. But, pointing to the rapid rise of mobile telephones, he noted, "Japan has a tendency to explode when something catches on."[5]

Internet advertising expenditures posted a threefold increase in 1997 and rose by another 50 percent in 1998 to top more than $70 million (¥8 trillion), according to Dentsu estimates. (Still, Internet advertising represented just .01 percent of total advertising expenditures in Japan.)[6] Dentsu and SoftBank launched a new Internet advertising unit in 1996 called Cyber Communications, the first media rep specializing in Internet advertising in Japan. Several new firms sprang up in Japan in 1998 to provide audience ratings and other analysis of Internet sites, including LibArts, IST, and Nihon Research Center.[7] Sophisticated companies such as Sumitomo began to offer customized Web pages for users and began setting advertising fees based on effectiveness.

Japan's postal ministry announced plans in 1999 to join up with sixteen companies to establish a system for charging for products on the Internet. Companies, including Fujitsu, Dai Nippon Printing, and All Nippon Airways, would be part of the agreement, which is due to be launched in a trial involving 20,000 users in January 2000.[8]

Who's Online?

The average Internet user in Japan in the late 1990s is young and male. Some 60 percent of Internet users are twenty years old or younger.[9] Women, while accounting for about 23 percent of the online population in 1998, are coming online rapidly, as shown in Exhibit 10.4. Women accounted for more than 30 percent of *new* users in 1998, compared with just over 8 percent in 1993. These

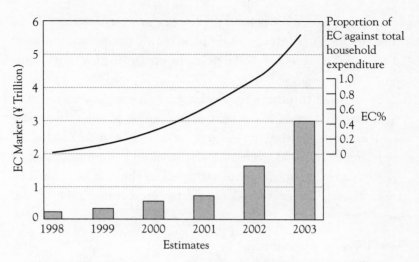

Exhibit 10.3. The Electronic Commerce (EC) Consumer Market
Source: MITI, Andersen Consulting, 1998.

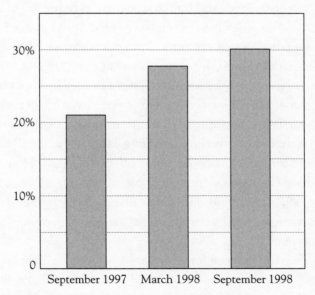

Exhibit 10.4. Proportion of Female Internet Users
Source: Fujitsu Soken, 1999.

women may have more potential for developing e-commerce. While Japanese men used the Internet primarily for work, the majority of the new women users (78 percent) went online for "entertainment."[10]

Specialized Internet services for women are gaining popularity among this growing segment of the online population. These services include Mail & Chat Club, with a membership of approximately 7,000 women, Lady First, and Woman (through AOL Japan). Participants are attracted to the site because they are restricted or protected, avoiding concerns about sexual harassment.[11]

New Cyber-Opportunities

If the rise of discounters created cracks in the Japanese distribution system, the advance of the Internet is shaking its foundations. Among the major areas of e-commerce are personal computers, travel, clothing, food, and books, as shown in Exhibit 10.5.

As the e-commerce market has unfolded, it has created intense interest among foreign entrants. Foreign companies often have an advantage over domestic rivals because they are not bound by current relationships with trading partners. Dell Computers, conducting half its sales over the Internet, saw a 33-percent sales growth in 1998, while many competitors saw declines. Search engine Yahoo! announced plans for a large virtual mall in Japan that could bring hundreds of online outlets together.[12] Home Corp., a U.S.-based high-speed Internet access provider, announced a venture in 1999 to join with Japanese cable operator Jupiter Telecommunications (owned by Sumitomo) to tap into the rapidly growing Japanese market.[13]

The online market for new cars is a prime example of how Japanese consumers, always attracted to the latest technology, are moving Japanese e-commerce into the fast lane. By early 1999, at least six Japanese sites were offering cars online, and Internet sales were expected to account for 50,000 sales or 1 percent of all new

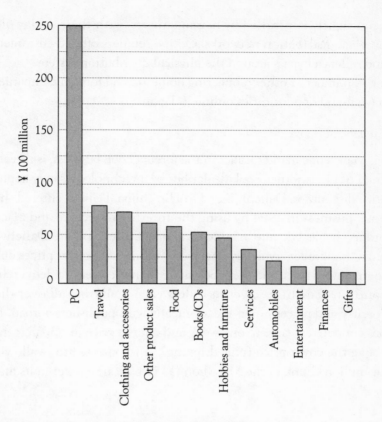

Exhibit 10.5. The Japanese E-Commerce Market
Source: MITI, Andersen Consulting, 1998.

cars sold that year. One domestic site, Quick-go.to, reported 50,000 hits on its first weekend of operation. In addition to the domestic competitors, foreign firms such as Autobytel.com and Microsoft's Carpoint were planning to move into the Japanese market. Other large Japanese firms, including employment magazine publisher Recruit, were also planning online car businesses.[14] In response, major automakers, such as Nissan Motors, began developing their own sites to link customers with dealers.

This growth of online car sales demonstrates the power of the Internet in reshaping Japanese markets. Automobile retailing had been tightly controlled by manufacturers, with their stodgy old physical distribution networks. Online retailers offered customers and sellers a bypass around the physical distribution system.

A number of other pioneering domestic and foreign companies have found opportunities online in Japan:

Broadband Books

Maruzen, a market leader in the foreign book business, is threatened not by another book dealer but by a technology-savvy appliance discounter, Daiichi. Based in Hiroshima, Daiichi entered the book business in 1994 by using the Internet to receive and place orders. It has become a fierce rival of Maruzen. Before Daiichi's entry, booksellers typically charged four times the cover prices due to inventory risks, and they took more than six weeks to deliver. In contrast, Daiichi receives its orders via e-mail from all over the country and places orders electronically with publishers abroad. It has cut delivery time to one week and offers a price just 30 percent above the cover price (plus shipping). It is expected to swallow a $4-million chunk of the $1-billion (¥120 billion) market in its first year.

Singing Wires

One profitable information technology-based businesses, unique to Japan, is an online karaoke service. Taito Company's online karaoke systems offers karaoke clubs access to download the latest songs, so customers can sing along to the current hits. With 60 percent of the population participating in karaoke, this is a $12-billion (¥1.4 trillion) market, requiring 60,000 to 100,000 replacement units each year. Taito, offering great speed and efficiency in delivery new song titles to the market, hopes to capture a good part of it. This is an example of the distinctively Japanese needs that can be met through the creative application of new technology.

World Wide Wine

Virtual Vineyards, a California-based Internet wine retailer, reports that 10 percent of its sales come from abroad, with the largest proportion from Japan. It has set up Japanese-language pages on its Web sites. And given the strict alcohol sales regulations of some U.S. states, "It is easier to ship to Japan than it is to Texas," says co-founder Peter Granoff.[15]

In-Store E-Commerce

Convenience stores are using e-commerce kiosks to offer a wide range of products, from concert tickets to software. The systems allow small stores to offer thousands of items and allow consumers to make "online" purchases without concern about security or a need for an Internet connection.[16]

Differences in Regulation, Culture, and Language

Although the spread of technology is a sign of the potential for e-commerce in Japan, technology may not be the most significant

---

Signs of Change

Camping Out On the Internet

One sign of the increasing penetration and usefulness of the Internet is the low-tech application in The Camping Forum. This online discussion and information site offers advice and tips on specific Japanese camping areas. In the summer of 1998, the forum used a laptop and video camera to stage a live broadcast of a camping event in Amori. More than 100 families gathered in real tents for the five-day event and another 600 visitors "camped out" online.[17]

factor in the widespread use of the Internet. Japan's xenophobia, language barrier, rigid social compartmentalization, and education system may all tend to affect the usefulness of the Internet. Japan needs to overhaul "anachronistic regulatory, educational, and business practices that were designed for the last wave."[18] These factors may tend to create a Japanese Internet that is distinct from other parts of the world.

Language

It is not technology, but language that may be the critical issue in shaping the future of the Internet in Japan. The most valuable resources on the Web will be in Japanese, so effective translation and interpretation capabilities will be important for the spread of the Internet. Technology may also make a huge difference as automatic language translators become more refined and effective.

Regulation and Financial Infrastructure

Regulation will also be a significant factor in the growth of e-commerce in Japan. Political parties were banned from using the Internet in 1996 and it was not until 1998 that the government ministries allowed online transactions. The slowness of regulators and investors to move on e-commerce in Japan may give foreign companies a greater opportunity to build their markets. Given the reluctance of Japanese banks to adopt standardized credit procedures for online sales, some Japanese e-commerce pioneers routed their transactions through U.S. banks.[19]

Security

More than half of Internet users cited security as the reason for not shopping online in a survey in late 1998. And even of those who did shop, more than 56 percent expressed concern about giving out credit card numbers and other personal information online.[20] Japan has begun to create the systems of certification and payment that are crucial to transactions online. Several certification companies, for example, were established to verify the identities of online purchasers for companies. These include firms such as Japan-Verisign Inc. and CyberTrust Japan Inc., created by foreign companies, and a domestic verification service called Japan Certification Services, created by Hitachi, Fujitsu, NEC, and other partners.

Privacy

Privacy, which is a concern around the world, may be even more of a significant factor in the development of the Internet in Japan. For example, online chat rooms have a different character in Japan than in other parts of the world. America Online (AOL) in Japan has found that Japanese Web surfers are more reticent about sharing their thoughts with strangers online. Japanese visitors to chat rooms are take aback by the directness of Western chat users and often observe rather than participate in the discussion. On the other hand, the anonymity of the chat room can be attractive to some users.[21]

Value-Added Networks

Companies are also using electronic data interchange (EDI) and other electronic connections between manufacturers and retailers to speed delivery and gain insight into customers. Taisho Pharmaceuticals became the market leader in over-the-counter drugs by creating a value-added network with retailers. Using a point-of-sale cash register connected to computers at the Taisho headquarters, the company sends out personalized newsletter to owners every week, giving feedback on sales trends, new product introduction news—also that of rivals—together with test results from labs. This gives Tashio competitive information so it can outsell and set margins in such a way that it exceeds that of rivals. As an added incentive, drug store owners have stock on Tashio. The company directly encourages their sales and introduction of new product through seminars broadcast around Japan via satellite. Discount drug stores are undermining this advantage.

Mass Customization

In addition to e-commerce, Japanese companies have used information technology in other ways to transform marketing. Japanese firms have been leaders in developing products customized to individual customers, from automobiles to bicycles to eyeglasses. For example, even before the support of more sophisticated technology, National Bicycle created a system for relaying measurements and color preferences of cyclists to an automated factory that could create custom Panasonic bicycles relatively quickly and cheaply. In addition to selling the customized bicycles themselves, the selections of frame sizes and colors offered valuable insight for the mass-produced retail versions of its product. Similarly, Toyota and Nissan developed the capabilities to offer customized automobiles, and Samsung developed the capabilities to offer made-to-order refrigerators.

Paris Miki, a Japanese eyewear retailer with the largest number of stores in the world, uses high-tech systems to match eyeglass frames to the face of an individual customer. The system takes digital pictures of the customer's face and uses the image, along with a survey of customer preferences, to suggest eyeglasses to fit. The system then shows the eyeglasses on the image of the consumer's face and the optician works with the customer to modify the design. The result is printed out and created in an in-store lab in as little as an hour.

Technology can also be used to customize more than products. Marketing communications, pricing, interactive advertising, and distribution can be facilitated through information technology. Given the increased heterogeneity and emphasis on individuality in Japanese markets, the ability offered by technology to inexpensively customize is expected to be even more valuable.

Asian Cybermarkets

Although Japan's Internet population (and e-commerce spending potential) is far greater than that of other parts of Asia, it is clear that other Asian markets will enter the cyberage at an even faster pace than Japan. By the end of 1998, there were an estimated 22 to 25 million people online in Asia.[22] Japan still accounted for nearly two-thirds of Asia's Internet traffic, but those proportions were expected to change, as shown in Exhibit 10.6. Bandwidth is being created rapidly across Asia, creating the foundation for an explosion of e-commerce. With submarine cables being run across the Pacific and around Asia, bandwidth is expected to increase sixfold, from twenty gigabits in 1998 to 140 gigabits in 2000. This increased bandwidth will mean not only faster speeds but the practical application of online videoconferencing, education, and seamless commerce. Advances in translation software will further facilitate cross-culture e-commerce. Finally, in addition to land-based cables, companies such as Intelsat, Teleglobe, and USAsia have developed satellite-based Internet services, limiting the infrastructure needed to reach Asian users.[23]

This has tremendous implications for marketing in China and in other parts of Asia, and it could accelerate the fall of entry barriers and increase access to global information and products. China, for example, has launched a "Three Golden Projects" ini-

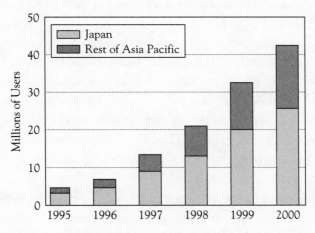

Exhibit 10.6. Internet Users In the Asia-Pacific Region
Source: AsiaWeek, April 17, 1998.

tiative to modernize its information technology infrastructure by 2003 to pave the way for e-commerce. The first project is the "Golden Bridge," to launch satellites and install fiber-optic cable networks throughout China. Building this bridge, China launched the China Wide Web project, the first nationwide intranet in 1997, with servers planned for more than fifty cities around China. The second project, "Golden Customs," will track quotas, foreign currency, and trade statistics. Finally, "Golden Card" is an initiative to replace cash transactions with electronic transactions.[24] By early 1999, the official Chinese news agency estimated that there were 1.5 million Internet users in China, although others estimate the actual number was in excess of two million (officially, shared Internet accounts are illegal, so the government doesn't count them).[25] The Chinese online population is projected to reach more than nine million by 2002. Despite the rapid growth of the Internet, potential for e-commerce in China is limited by lack of users' credit and spending power.

In Taiwan, Internet use reached 2.7 million at the end of 1998 and was expected to rise by another 30 percent to reach 3.5 million by the end of the millennium.[26] Online advertising was expected to reach $28 million in 2000.[27] Internet users in Korea crossed three million and e-commerce reached $240 million in 1998.[28]

A 1997 study of 3.1 million affluent consumers in seven Asian capital cities (Bangkok, Hong Kong, Jakarta, Kuala Lumpur, Manila, Singapore, and Taipei) found that 1.6 million owned personal computers. This was almost as many as owned automobiles. The survey found that 37 percent of the affluent consumers (the top 10 percent of the population in the cities) had Internet experience. This varied widely by city, with the most users in Singapore and the least in Manila, as shown in Exhibit 10.7.

The highest use of the Internet was among younger consumers and usage increased with personal income, from a low of 23 percent for those earning below $10,000 to a high of 54 percent for those earning above $50,000. The highest percentage used the Internet for leisure and entertainment (42 percent), but a third used it for business or research. Significantly, nearly a third (29 percent) used it for shopping or to obtain product information.[29]

The spread of technology will enable more electronic transactions, perhaps in ways that are unanticipated by the bureaucrats with their major infrastructure projects. Computer sales are already taking off in China, particularly in the higher-income cities. In wealthy coastal cities, there are now five computers for every 100 families, and this is rising rapidly. Sales of personal computers in China rose 30 percent in 1996 to 1.8 million, and were expected to grow by 60 percent the following year. In Beijing, 23 percent of secondary school students reported reading Bill Gates's book *The Road Ahead,* making it one of the most popular books in the city.[30]

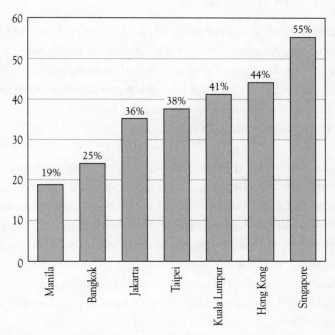

Exhibit 10.7. Internet Use by Affluent Consumers (%)
Source: Asian Target Markets Survey, 1997.

There are some initiatives for Asian cooperation on the Internet. For example, Japan and China announced plans at the end of 1998 to start a joint think tank on the Internet. The Asian Internet Research Foundation, a cooperative venture between Japan's Nihon Net Research and China Internet Research Foundation, was expected to create a center to challenge U.S. dominance as a technology provider in the region.[31] It may make Japan an even more important center for e-commerce in the region.

There is wide variation in Internet penetration among Asian nations. An AC Nielsen survey found that Singapore posted a 25-percent rate, similar to that of the United States and ahead of Germany, while Indonesia and Thailand were at less than 2 percent.[32]

Management Implications

The growth of e-commerce in Japan, as in other parts of the world, is somewhat unpredictable. But it offers an unprecedented opportunity for market entry for companies that have been unable or unwilling to invest in physical marketing and distribution in Japan. In an instant, companies can tap into the Japanese market.

A few caveats to keep in mind:

• Build awareness. Much of the past success of online retail sites has been by word-of-mouth. Foreign companies offering quality products and reasonable prices had customers beating a path to their doors. As the field becomes more crowded, the use of online advertising, as well as advertising in other media, will be crucial in driving traffic to the site.

• Japanese consumers behave differently. Pay attention to cultural differences such as increased concerns for privacy and security, and develop online sites that meet these concerns.

• Use Japanese language. Although U.S. retailers have been able to make tremendous progress with English-only sites, a Japanese site creates greater opportunities and opens sales to a broader market. While very successful retailers such as clothing retailer Hanna Andersson have not translated their sites, most companies that do not currently have Japanese-language sites are considering creating them.

• Carefully experiment with site design. The design of online retail sites has a tremendous impact on whether browsers become buyers. Given the different logic of the Japanese language and advertising, it is important to experiment with different site designs—including testing the impact of colors and images—to find the formula that works best in Japan. Don't assume the same structure and feel of the site will work just as well in Japan.

• Use customization. Developing customized products and advertising can help to connect with specific segments of the market. Examine ways to use existing capabilities for customization and opportunities to develop new relationships with customers.

• Keep an eye on those mobile phones and videogames. With 40 million mobile phone customers in Japan—and cell phone use almost universal among teenagers—wireless communications can be expected to play an even greater role in the spread of the Japanese Internet than in other parts of the world. Already companies are offering services that link customers to retailers through their mobile phones to make restaurant reservations or check bank balances. The widespread popularity of videogames in Japan is another electronic avenue to customers, as Sony and other manufacturers add the power and features to make their machines portals to the Web.

At this point, as Japanese e-commerce becomes increasingly popular, there will be intense competition for the ever-growing cyber-market in Japan. While companies may have been able to succeed despite sub-optimal site and online strategies, the market will now be much less forgiving. It is important to experiment with what works best in Japan and then use these lessons to conduct further experiments in Asia. Because of some language similarities, for example, lessons learned in Japan may help in Asian electronic markets. The advantage of the Internet is that it makes these kinds of direct experiments relatively simple and inexpensive to conduct.

Points of Leverage

- How can you use cybermarketing to sell your products and services or to provide information and support to customers?

- To what extent can your product or service be made "digital" so it can be conveyed online?

- What potential threats to your existing markets and distribution channels might arise with the development of the Internet? How can you preempt these moves?

- How can you best develop online communities around your products and markets? How do these communities in Japan need to be different from those in the West?

- Do you understand the emerging cyberconsumers (consumers who can customize their own products, select their own information, set their own prices, and buy anytime and anyplace)?

- Have you reexamined your business models to ensure they are consistent with the new opportunities offered by the revolutions in information technology?

- Have you utilized advances in information technology, not only to increase the speed and efficiency of your operations, but to capture new clients?

- What has been the impact of the information revolution on logistics, buying, and other related areas in your operations? Are you as advanced in using ECR, EDI and supply chain management in Japan as you are in other parts of the world? If no, what factors are responsible for the differences?

11

Breaking the Labyrinth—New Rules of Distribution

"Even when its economy was booming, Japan had one glaring problem: a distribution system as labyrinthine as a shogun's palace."

Emily Thornton, Fortune[1]

Clothing retailer Hanna Andersson has no retail outlets in Japan, yet Japanese purchases accounted for about 20 percent of worldwide sales of the Portland, Oregon-based direct marketer in 1998. When Hanna Andersson moved into Japan in 1995, it rode the wave of direct marketing growth that propelled the expansion of Lands' End, L.L. Bean, REI, and other retailers. From 1995 to 1997, the company posted triple-digit growth rates in Japan. Its high-quality and colorful Swedish products and superior customer service won the hearts of Japanese customers.

The company established a call center in Tokyo, in partnership with Prestige International, to provide Japanese-language customer service. Hanna Andersson translated its catalogs into Japanese without major changes in the layout. All the orders are still fulfilled from its U.S. warehouses, with an average lead time of eight days.[2]

The arrival of direct marketers such as Hanna Andersson was one of the first waves of a series of retailing revolutions that have cracked open the impenetrable Japanese distribution system. The "air" attack by the direct marketers bypassed the physical retail outlets completely. But the distribution revolution continued with "ground" offenses, including the arrival of foreign retailers such as the Gap in the downtown areas, the creation of category killers and other superstores, and the rise of shopping malls and discount outlets in the suburbs. These newcomers took advantage of changing Japanese regulations and consumer demands. The "labyrinthine" Japanese distribution system, which had been a closed and inefficient network of tiny mom-and-pop stores fed by a complex network of middlemen, is breaking wide open.

Trouble in the Nintendo Kingdom

A decade ago, a company had little chance of selling to Japanese consumers without a partner with the relationships to gain access to the Japanese distribution system. From car dealers to consumer goods, this relatively impermeable system was a significant barrier to entry in Japanese markets. Some trailblazing companies such as Coca-Cola and BMW had the creativity and perseverance to build their own distribution networks in Japan, but many others were shut out because they didn't have the relationships needed to penetrate the market.

The strength of the relationships in this traditional distribution system can be seen in the controversy that surrounded the decision by Nintendo Company to bypass its distribution network and distribute games directly to Toys "R" Us in 1991. This wholesale network was often referred to as the Nintendo "kingdom." But Toys "R" Us recognized it needed to find a way around this notoriously inefficient distribution system, which operated under tight guidelines of inventory control that precluded discounting.

In announcing the decision, a cautious Nintendo President Hiroshi Yamauchi tried to soften the blow by saying that the deal "depends on existing wholesalers not being too upset." But, in the end, the power of Toys "R" Us, a major customer of Nintendo in

Japan and in the United States, won over objections of the traditional distribution network.[3] And Toys "R" Us was concerned about offering the best value to customers. It was clear it was not the wholesalers but the customer who was king.

New Opportunities for Distribution

Distribution in Japan has moved from diffused small stores to larger outlets, from dominant manufacturers pushing products through dedicated pipelines to open systems driven by consumer demand. Convenience stores, discount outlets, and mail order all have experienced double-digit growth rates in recent years. Laws prohibiting large stores are starting to relax, making entry even easier.

While sales of department stores and small specialty stores declined, large superstores and convenience stores continued to expand their numbers, as shown in Exhibit 11.1.

For the marketer, there is now a wide range of distribution channels that have emerged. In addition to cybermarketing (dis-

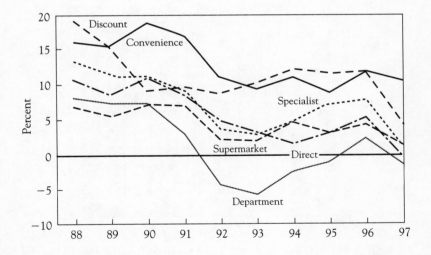

Exhibit 11.1. Sales By Retail Types
Source: Nikkei Ryutsu Shinbun's surveys of respective retail types, 1998.

cussed in the preceding chapter), companies can link to customers through:

Direct Marketing

Direct marketing sales in Japan grew from just over ¥1 trillion ($7.8 billion) to ¥2.2 trillion ($17 billion) between 1987 and 1997, as shown in Exhibit 11.2. While sales tapered off slightly in 1997, the market remained strong. (While the Japan Direct Mail Association does not beak out foreign direct-mail sales, it does attribute the overall decline in part to the rise of discounters and aggressive entry by foreign direct mail firms.[4]) International direct mail has flourished as Japanese customers realize that U.S. prices are only a phone call away. Mail order sales from the United States totaled $750 million (¥71 billion) in 1995, and Japan rapidly became L.L. Bean's largest foreign market.[5] It is not just foreign retailers who have used this route to circumvent traditional distribution systems.

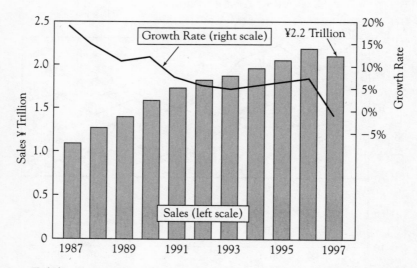

Exhibit 11.2. Direct Mail Sales and Growth Rate (Estimate For the Total Industry)

Source: Japan Direct Mail Association, 1998.

Japanese retailer Cecile used direct mail to build a $2-million (¥240 million) clothing business from a small island off the coast of Hiroshima. Direct mail catalogs offered a way for companies to go directly to customers rather than through the winding Japanese distribution system. The primary products sold this way were apparel, furniture, home electronics, and other household goods, although purchases of travel, insurance, finance, and other services continued to grow.

Category Killers

Led by Toys "R" Us, a whole host of other category killers, such as OfficeMax and Sports Authority, have moved into Japan. To drive down costs, discounters have been creative in bypassing traditional convoluted distribution channels, creating their own distribution systems to beat their own pathways from manufacturer to retail shelves. By 1999, top Japanese office supply company Kokuyo found itself battered by intense competition from Office Depot and OfficeMax in the Japanese market. *Nikkei Ryutsu Shimbun* notes that the firm's "binding distribution channel is now becoming a burden," with increased competition from overseas retailers, convenience stores, supermarkets, and catalogs.[6]

Large-scale American-style Shopping Centers

Department stores used to have to be in the center of the population to be successful. But now, as consumers are willing to drive to find selection and value outside of their local neighborhoods, the emergence of American-style shopping centers and malls is increasing. These new shopping centers are beginning to encircle Tokyo. Jusco, for example, opened a new center in an isolated field twenty to thirty minutes from two rural towns, and the store is flourishing.

Door-to-door

Amway took advantage of changing shopping patterns to establish a strong position in Japan. Traditional door-to-door salespeople were expert consultants. This approach was expensive and products were higher-priced than those in stores. Amway hit at a time of an increase in working women and a corresponding decline in time for shopping. It offered greater incentives to its salespeople and offered a variety of products that made the company very successful in Japan.

New Relationships Between Retailers and Manufacturers

The entry of SPA (specialty store retailer of private-label apparel) has shaken up Japanese apparel retailing. This system links information on sales trends in private-label stores directly to manufacturers, increasing efficiency and inventory control. The success of SPA in Japan was led by foreign companies, but it is not being adopted by Japanese firms.

Convenience Stores

Convenience stores were small enough to fly under the radar of Japan's tough restrictions, but they collectively had enough buying power and sophistication to transform retailing and reduce the dominance of manufacturers. Their sophisticated use of purchasing and information systems created a much more customer-focused product replenishment and selection process.

Vending Machines

Japan is the world leader in vending machines. Its sales in 1992 were equivalent to about twice the entire GNP of New Zealand. Turnover in Japanese vending machines is the highest in the world, about twice that of the United States. Vending machines have been called "Japan's Ultimate Convenience Stores." They are everywhere on the streets of Tokyo, offering products ranging from beverages and tobacco to safety razors, dry cell batteries, toys, tickets, flowers, motor oil, meat pies, CDs, school transcripts, life insurance, fresh eggs, pornographic videos, and handmade noodles.[7] There are few products that could *not* be sold in vending machines. One of the keys to Coca-Cola's ability to build a dominant position in the Japanese markets was its control of more than 870,000 of the two million vending machines in Japan.[8]

Franchising

Franchise stores have experienced rapid growth, particularly in convenience stores, with the addition of more than 12,000 stores between 1986 and 1997. The number of franchise chains expanded from 626 in 1987 to 890 in 1997. Between 1996 and 1997, eighty-seven new chains were launched in Japan. Although most of this growth is concentrated in convenience stores, other categories such as books, cameras, glasses, discount stores, jewelry, toys, and restaurants, have seen an increase in franchising.[9]

Racing into Retail

Given these new opportunities in distribution, foreign retailers are racing into Japan. A survey of 300 Japanese firms in the distribution sector, conducted in January/February 1998 by the Japan Productivity Center for Socio-Economic Development, found that more than 90 percent expected that the entry of foreign retailers would increase. Some 42 percent of retailers felt entry would increase "greatly" and 50 percent felt it would increase "somewhat." The companies, however, were divided on how much of a threat these new entrants pose, as shown in Exhibit 11.3.

The increasing interest of foreign retailers in Japan is an indication of the structural changes afoot. These changes have been driven forward by evolving consumer attitudes and the rise of entrepreneurial firms as discussed in Chapter Two. The modifications in distribution are also result of other forces, including the declining power of manufacturers and the relaxation of formerly stringent regulations. Manufacturers once took most of the risks of retailing and reaped most of the rewards. The rise of independent retailers has shifted power away from manufacturers. Japan's emphasis on small stores was codified in laws such as the Large-Scale Retail Store Law

Our company is:

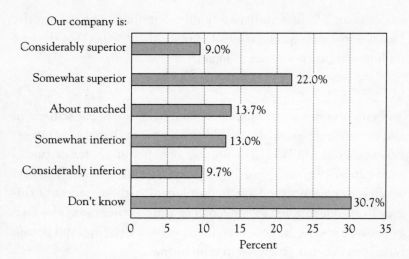

Exhibit 11.3. Japanese Distribution Firms' Perceptions of the Competitive Threat of Foreign Retailers
Source: Japan Productivity Center for Socio-Economic Development, Survey of 300 firms in the distribution sector, Jan.–Feb. 1998.

(*Daiten-ho*), which makes it difficult to establish a large retail store in Japan. However, this regulation is beginning to be relaxed.

Decline of Dominant Manufacturers

To understand the radical nature of the changes in Japanese retailing, one must first understand how manufacturers dominated the traditional marketplace. Japanese department stores, in effect, merely "rented space" to manufacturers. An average of 80 percent of salesclerks at large department stores were employees of the manufacturers, not the retailers.

The largest department stores in Japan, the Ikebukuro Branch of Tobu, had 8,700 shopkeepers, only 2,700 of which were actually full-time employees of the department store. All but 10 to 25 percent of its goods were under consignment from the manufacturer. In men's suits, the store's own employees handled just 25 percent of sales, with the remaining 75 percent sold by manufacturer and retailer representatives.[10]

The retailer, in effect, merely supplied the space for the manufacturer to set up shop, with its own goods and its own salespeople. The retailer understandably had a very minor role in the process. Further, there was little incentive for the retailer to capture information about customers, given its hands-off approach. The stores, with little value-added, had very small margins. The suppliers, on the other hand, given the risk of an average of 40-percent returns of merchandise, had to keep prices high.

New retailers saw opportunities in these inefficient systems. Discounters like Kojima and direct marketers challenged the department stores. They were willing to take their own risks and reap the rewards. They bought their goods from suppliers and sold them. With their lower risk, manufacturers were willing to offer steep discounts. Spurred by the attacks of the discounters and direct marketers, large retailers are changing their purchasing patterns. Supermarkets, in particular, are abandoning their consignment purchasing from wholesalers to buy directly from the source and take the risk on the purchase. This counteroffensive has led to a shakeout among the discounters, who are often no match for the purchasing power of large supermarket chains. But the net result for Japanese consumers is that more stores are operating like discounters, resulting in lower prices.

Manufacturers also tightly controlled networks of small *keiretsu* stores. These exclusive networks were once a source of strength for major manufacturers such as Matsushita and Shiseido. In the 1990s, however, faced with new competition from larger channels, these inefficient *keiretsu* stores became a burden. Manufacturers rapidly began routing their products around the *keiretsu* stores.

As one sign of the system cracking, Shiseido announced that not all of its *keiretsu* stores would be supplied with its new brand. Instead, the brand would be sold through department stores and other channels. There is bound to be some fallout from actions such as this, as well as a reduction in the 25,000 cosmetic stores in Japan. The auto parts network, once an impenetrable fortress of *keiretsu* relationships between Japanese partmakers and automakers, is also becoming more open. One indication is the rise in sales of American-made parts, which expanded by eightfold between fiscal years 1986 to 1994, from $2.94 billion (¥500 billion) to $19.86 billion (¥2 trillion).[11]

The shift in power from manufacturers could be seen in a showdown between Daiei, Japan's largest retailer, and Matsushita. When Daiei launched its own private label television, Matsushita refused to supply Daiei with its products now that the retailer had become a competitor. At the end of 1995, under increasing pressure from discounters and large retailers, Matsushita relented. Its decision to sell its products to Daiei was hailed as the end of distribution dominated by the manufacturer.

Improved Regulation

Even before substantial changes to the Large-Scale Retail Store Law (*Daiten-ho*) were made, convenience stores were small enough to be exempt from it. They were able to benefit from the efficiencies of scale spread across large chains, while avoiding the burden of the *Daiten-ho*.

Discount clubs and wholesale clubs also escape the law because they are not traditional retailers. An irony is that Toys "R" Us, which has been a vocal opponent of the *Daiten-ho*, now finds itself in the position of calling for it to be more strictly enforced because it faces competition from a toy wholesale club Akachan Tempo (Baby Store), which is exempt. Toys "R" Us has protested that the club should come under the law, drawing attention to the inability of the old regulations to handle the complexity of modern markets.

Increasing Automobile Ownership

The traditional Japanese retailing network, dominated by small, local stores, made more sense in a nation with high population density and low rates of motor vehicle ownership in the city centers. The inefficiency of small- and medium-size retailers was offset by the convenience of stores close to home. Increased car ownership has helped promote the development of suburban retailing, allowing Japanese consumers to more easily leave the local store and move to the larger, regional retailers.

Rethinking Distribution Relationships

In the traditional Japanese market, channel equity—access to distribution—was more important than brand equity. The challenge was to get a product into the *keiretsu* store or onto the supermarket shelf. Then, customers would buy it.

The most successful marketers in Japan were generally powerful manufacturers that controlled distribution channels: Matsushita (appliances) and Shiseido (cosmetics) relied upon their network of *keiretsu* stores to outsell rivals. Nisseki (gasoline) relied upon more outlets. Nissei (insurance) and Takeda (pharmaceuticals) relied upon a large salesforce. Ajinomoto (food) had more products to fill the shelves. It was this dominance of the retail channels that made these companies successful, not primarily through their brand equity or quality, but their ability to reach the consumers.

The distribution opportunities opening up have shifted the emphasis from channel equity to brand equity. It has led some retailers to rethink the value of relationships with Japanese partners. Monsanto broke its relationship with its distributors to ally itself to a stronger partner. This reduced its distribution costs and was expected to boost its market share because of direct contact with end customers.[12]

Mercedes-Benz Japan also rethought its distribution networks. "Until the 1960s the market really was closed, although of course one can argue about the legitimacy of that," said Rainer Jahn, president of Mercedes-Benz Japan Co., Ltd. "Japanese automakers developed their own distribution networks. Under such circumstances, any foreign manufacturer who wanted to establish a vehicle distributorship here found the going very tough. All the strategic locations were already occupied."[13]

Accepting this reality, Mercedes-Benz realized it needed a Japanese partner to make headway in Japan. It made Yanase, a nationwide Japanese automotive chain, the sole distributor of Mercedes products in Japan in 1954.

These realities have changed. When Mercedes decided to set up an independent network of exclusive dealers in 1989 (Yanase sold other cars as well), it was clear the situation was quite different. Mercedes had no trouble finding independent dealers. "In early 1989, we ran a big advertisement saying that we were deploying a new dealer network and inviting interested people to come to us," explains Hajime Saburi, general manager of the executive office of Mercedes-Benz Japan Co. Ltd. "We had a very positive response. We selected the dealers out of the candidates. We didn't really have to go out to find dealers. They came to us. Of course, we are in a good position because we have a good product, but it's not the product only. It's the product, the network, and the continuity of presence."

The new dealers included owners of domestic auto dealerships, but also owners of warehousing, petroleum distribution, and textile companies. By 1996, this network accounted for 20 percent of the company's sales in Japan. Mercedes also developed dual dealerships with Mitsubishi Galant dealers.

For Mercedes, it was the power of its brand that facilitated the creation of the new distribution channel. This reputation was hard won. When the Japanese government raised automotive standards in the early-1970s, many European automakers withdrew from the market, but Mercedes, BMW, Porsche, and Volvo made large investments to clear the new hurdles and remain in the market. They suffered losses in the short run, however. "Their determination to stay in the market is the basis for their present success," Saburi said. "There are many European makes that just disappeared for eight or ten years. By the time they came back, the manufacturers who stayed, painstakingly, were much more advanced."

It is not the power of distribution channels that makes an automaker successful. It is the power of brand that creates the distribution channel. Thus, brand equity is becoming more important than channel equity.

Implications of Distribution Changes

The process of transition from traditional retailing to modern retailing is likely to be much more rapid in other parts of Asia than in Japan. It took Japan about fifty years to make the transition. Japan spent about twenty-five years to move from the dominance of mom-and-pop stores to supermarkets, then another fifteen years to accept convenience stores, and another ten to adopt commerce. Asia is moving more quickly, thanks to technology, communications, and aggressive competitors. Shopping centers and convenience stores are already popular in Bangkok, Thailand. The old, humble, mom-and-pop stores continue to exist side by side with the new retailers, as in Japan, but new retail models are appearing rapidly. Experience in Japan offers insight into these developments.

Many Asian nations are also experiencing a move from personal touch to more professional relationships with companies. This trend will speed the decline of the traditional mom-and-pop stores.

Shifts in distribution can also accelerate if outsiders recognize the inherent opportunities and capitalize on them. Many of the distribution innovations in Japanese markets were not triggered by a certain event but rather by the recognition of the opportunity. What opportunities for changing distribution in Japan and other parts of Asia are there today, but have not yet been recognized?

The rise of larger retailers has not eliminated the smaller Japanese retailer. For some products, the traditional distribution system will continue to be the most efficient route. For small, frequently purchased items, local stores will continue to be important, but these are increasingly convenience chains rather than individually owned shops. There will be a mix of both, with an overall tendency toward increased size of retailers and decreased concentration of wholesalers.

These changes in distribution mean that marketers have more channels than ever for moving their products to market. Those who already have investments in the old distribution channels will often face difficult organizational challenges in managing the transition to new distribution structures. Because of these challenges, newcomers sometimes have an advantage.

Points of Leverage

For all companies using distribution channels:

- How can you use direct mail, e-commerce, and other channels to reach customers without going through local distribution networks? How does the approach need to be tailored to the local area (through local-language translations)?

- How effective are your distribution partnerships, in meeting the needs of the current market?

- How can shifts in regulation be used or encouraged to establish new distribution channels?

- How will demographic shifts in other Asian nations (such as rising automobile ownership, changing customer demands, and new regulations) create opportunities for new distribution channels?

For retailers and other members of the distribution channel:

- How can you take advantage of changes in distribution to offer faster, cheaper, or better products and services to customers?

- How can you increase scale by establishing larger retail stores or using these channels? Are there opportunities to develop malls, superstores, and other outlets? Are there opportunities to move your store into one of these formats?

- What opportunities do these changes create for entry into Japan?

- Do you have difficulty hiring good salespeople who undersand the need for superior service quality? Do you see any changes in the availability of such good people due to shifts in employee attitudes?

12

Beyond Bowing—New Rules of Customer Satisfaction and Value Creation

"You said the consumers should complain more, but I couldn't do that. When I buy things, I'm happy I could buy it. I feel they are happy with my purchase. I have never made a complaint, even if I have found some problem with my purchase."

Male student at the University of Tokyo

One of the Japanese authors went into a U.S. department store to purchase a VCR shortly after the holiday season. He saw a long line of people waiting for service at a counter and he assumed it was the checkout. He was shocked to discover that it was the line for returns—not just because of its length, but because in Japan there is no line for returns. Japanese consumers do not return merchandise and they do not complain.

This reluctance to complain is puzzling in a nation with a reputation for having the toughest customers in the world. Japanese customers *are* demanding. They are known to refuse cars with tiny scratches and spurn products with dented or torn packaging. How can these two images of Japan be reconciled? And how is the Japanese approach to customer satisfaction and service changing?

Customer as God

A major Japanese automaker's sales manual called for dealers to welcome customers at the gate with at least one employee bowing to the oncoming car. When the customer leaves, at least three people should be bowing goodbye to the customer. This is extraordinary customer attention by U.S. standards, but it doesn't really serve the customer. It is a gesture of subservience to the customer "as god."

When Japanese firms speak of customer satisfaction, it has a different meaning than in the United States. It is personal rather than professional. It is focused on ensuring harmony in the relationship rather than ensuring customer benefits.

Although this stature as "god" means customers are *worshipped*, they are sometimes not well *served*, nor are they necessarily happy. For example, the driver manual of the Nagoya taxi company instructs them to use the following script for greeting and addressing customers, translated for emphasis into the words of a New York cabbie:

> *Greetings*—"Thank you for riding with us."
>
> *Confirmation*—"Where shall we go? That's the South Bronx, isn't it?"
>
> *Self-Introduction*—"I'm Archie Bunks of the Brooklyn Taxi Company. Hope you will bear with me for awhile."

Then, on arrival:

> *Report*—"Here we are."
>
> *Report*—"The fare comes to fifteen bucks."
>
> *Greetings*—"Thank you very much."
>
> *Confirmation*—"Please make sure that you haven't forgotten anything."
>
> *Request*—"Please ride with Brooklyn Taxi Company again."

Most New Yorkers would be dazzled (if a bit puzzled) by a cab driver who spoke like this, yet Japanese consumers ranked taxi cabs among the lowest in customer satisfaction. The taxi industry was second to last, just above government offices, in providing customer satisfaction. This taxi cab driver is the picture of servitude, but this posture of servitude does not ensure that the customer will be satisfied.

No Complaints

As indicated by the student comment that opened the chapter, complaining outside the channels of relationships is not a part of the culture. Japanese customers might be very picky when it comes to the finish of their automobiles and they wouldn't hesitate to call their local sales representative to ask him to set it right, but returning a product to a department store is not even a consideration for most Japanese consumers. The first action is based on a personal relationship with a salesperson. The second is based on an explicit or implied guarantee. Complaining in this context would not be appropriate in a country that values maintaining dignity. The best course of action is to keep quiet.

A survey of consumers in Tokyo, New York, and London asked participants if they complain when they purchase a product that is not up to expectations. Across the board, Tokyo customers were far less likely to speak up, as shown in Exhibit 12.1.

As an indication of the lack of experience in complaining, one of the early articles of the Japanese-language *Good Housekeeping* was on customer complaints. The magazine published a sample of product-complaint letters in English to companies abroad, providing readers with practical examples of how to express dissatisfaction.[1]

Universities are beginning to be more concerned about student satisfaction, as evidenced by surveys that began appearing in the early 1990s. Some top universities scored very low in student satisfaction. Before that time, universities were uniformly concerned

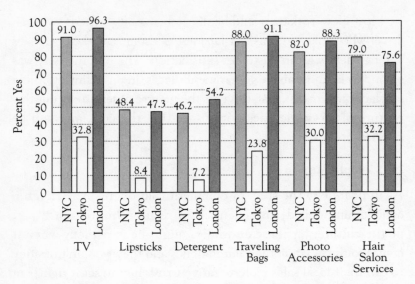

Exhibit 12.1. Customer Satisfaction: Do You Complain If a Product Is Not Up to Your Expectations?
Source: International Research Institute, MITI, 1996.

only with pleasing parents through strong test performance. But as competition for students intensified, interest in satisfaction here, as in other areas, has increased.

One enterprising Panasonic marketing manager used the Internet to help tap into sources of customer satisfaction. The manager, working on the development of a notebook PC called "Let's Note," came across an online forum on the product. He monitored the forum every day and passed along suggestions to the 100 people involved in the project. By the next day, solutions to many of the laptop's problems were developed and implemented. When the company developed a new model in June 1997, it invited fifteen members of the forum to join the development team to offer tips for improvements. By actively tracking complaints and identifying sources of dissatisfaction—even if customers were unwilling to complain themselves—the team was able to respond and improve satisfaction.

Professional Service

The model for service in Japan was one similar to servitude. Service was individualized and personalized. It was emotional and relied upon respect. The shop owner or retail representative was the customer's servant, helping him in any way, apologizing profusely if there were problems. There are many examples of the extreme lengths companies would go to satisfy their customers. But, in general, it was not the quality of the service that counted but rather the quality of the relationship. The relationship was based on courtesy rather than formal contracts. The expectation for a personal response is very different than a money-back guarantee, the right to return merchandise, and the right to complain.

Delivery service DHL's experience in Japan shows the difference between personal relationship and professional service. As the first international air-express service in Japan, DHL built its reputation through extraordinary acts of personal service. Early leaders of the firm personally picked up packages and delivered them to customers to meet seemingly impossible deadlines. In one case, a Japanese manager came to DHL on Saturday to request that a package be delivered from Seattle for a Monday meeting. DHL made the arrangements, picked up the package from the airport, and delivered it to the manager's home on Sunday evening.

These extraordinary tales of personal service helped build DHL's Japanese business rapidly. The company was ranked number one, and despite rising competition from Federal Express and other rivals, DHL employees felt that based on their strong relationships with customers, their company would continue to lead, even in the face of new competition.

But in 1985, there were rising signs of trouble, including increased customer complaints and some defections to rivals. Newly hired Sales Manager Shinichi Momose decided to put the company's service to a formal test. He shipped the same packages by different carriers and then compared speed, price, service levels, and

other factors. The tests revealed that DHL provided the lowest levels of service at the highest price. Clearly its number-one position—
sustained only by its relationships and reputation—would not last
very long with these levels of professional service.

Momose presented the results to the shocked managers of the
firm. This objective information about service motivated the group
to develop radically new strategies for improving cost and service.
DHL added a second daily pickup, rolled back a planned price
increase, boosted the size of its sales staff, and found ways to stream-
line costs.

The results of the service test encouraged a shift in focus from
relying upon past relationships with customers to focusing on real,
value-added service that would stand up to intense international
competition. The shift moved service from a vaguely defined sense
of leadership to a clearly articulated and measurable quantity. This
new view of the world helped revive DHL's Japanese sales, leading
to a 20-percent annual growth from the mid-1980s to 1990. DHL
retained its market leadership in Japan, with a 30-percent share.
The Japanese office made the largest contribution to corporate profits of any of the 210-plus countries where DHL operated. Although
the high growth was dampened by the recession, DHL continues to
outpace rivals.[2]

From Bowing Servitude to Value-Added Service

The rising model for customer service is closer to the Western concept. It is not dependent on the strength or length of the relationship between the customer and firm, but rather on the value-added
by the relationship. This value is formalized through money-back
guarantees and other commitments. Because there was no contract
under the old model, service was loosely defined. It depended on
the strength of the relationship between the buyer and the seller.

Servitude was an expected part of the Japanese customer-com-
pany relationship; therefore, it had no value in the mind of the customer. Service in Japan was considered free, like air, something that

was just naturally added to the product. As a result, there were very few service contracts or other service agreements. It became a cost of doing business for the company, but customers were not willing to pay for it. The rise of guarantees and the emergence of self-service operations is beginning to give service and satisfaction more of a tangible value. Companies in Japan are finding ways to value service, or lack of service, and increase their emphasis on professional, arms-length relationships.

No More Bowing Salespeople

In contrast to the three bowing salespeople at the old Japanese auto dealer, Ishi Maru, a new discount drug store, trains store consultants to avoid the personal contact that was the hallmark of service in the past. The retailer has a policy for consultants never to speak to customers until asked, to look at the floor, and to avoid eye contact. Customers would like to remain anonymous. Looking them in the eye would make the customer feel obliged to buy. The emphasis is on efficiency and low-cost operations rather than personal touch. Another example of the new, less personal marketing can be seen in the large theater and automotive showroom established by Toyota in Tokyo. Customers can enjoy looking at the latest models and also see free movies in the theater, but it is not the old-style personal relationship with a bowing salesperson.

Measuring Customer Satisfaction

Another sign of the rising interest in professional customer satisfaction is the arrival of J.D. Powers, which entered the Japanese market in 1995 through a venture with a Japanese marketing research firm. Its arrival in Japan shows that companies are increasingly concerned about customer satisfaction and they are paying to measure it.

All Nippon Airways (ANA) paid increasing attention to customer satisfaction after new competition came to the industry.

ANA had cut fringe benefits for flight attendants and the cost of service to customers. These cost-cutting measures resulted in a sharp decline in employees' motivation and a deterioration of service at the ticket counters and in the cabin. The company had a toll free 800 number and a customer center, but the feedback never made it back to employees.

ANA recognized the need for an enthusiastic revolution to become more customer-oriented. They brought in speakers such as the president of successful fast-food chain MosBurger to address employees. Senior managers are now exposed directly to the voices of customers. ANA is aiming at creating a truly customer-oriented company for the twenty-first century.

Service Packages

Mercedes-Benz Japan began offering a free after-sale service, "Mercedes Care," in 1998, which included regular maintenance and follow-ups after an accident. The goal was to attract new customers by achieving higher levels of customer satisfaction. The move was also designed to counter the perception of higher maintenance costs for foreign cars that has discouraged some buyers.[3]

Increased Training

Companies are giving employees the training to provide professional customer service. For example, Eddie Bauer set up its Eddie Bauer College in February 1998 to train store managers in customer satisfaction and other issues.[4]

Money-back Guarantees

The Gap and other retailers have been very successful with money-back guarantees, merchandise return policies, and other professional service benefits. Japanese department stores were reluctant to adopt these strategies at first, but are now following the lead of Western retailers.

Self-Service

If service has a value, then self-service becomes an acceptable tradeoff for lower costs and increased availability. Kinko's set up several stores in Japan, featuring self-service copiers and twenty-four-hour service. The 100-yen stores that are becoming popular in Japan are also self-service operations, sacrificing service for lower cost. Cosmetics in Japan have traditionally been sold through *keiretsu* stores that emphasized personalized, individual attention. In the mid-1990s, the rise of *serufu-sabisu* (self-service) products showed that customers were willing to sacrifice service for price. This led to a separation between high-end quality brands and the inexpensive utilitarian products.

Shiseido once relied upon *taimen hanbai* (face-to-face, personal selling), as the core of its marketing strategy. The company believed consumers needed counseling before purchasing cosmetics. In June 1994, Shiseido made a radical shift, moving forty-one brands into the self-service category, followed by another sixty-five products in the fall. By 1995, about 42 percent of the company's products were sold through self service. Akira Tsuruma, managing director of Shiseido, estimates that half of the company's sales will come from the *serufu* category in the future.[5]

Florists also used to be very expensive, full-service operations. But the Best discount flower chain and other discounters have offered products at half the market price to customer who are willing to select flowers themselves and take them to the register.

Liability Laws

One sign of a more professional, arm's-length relationship between customers and companies is the rise of product liability laws. The introduction of new product liability regulations has been a signal to consumers that their complaints will be recognized. *Tokyo Shimbun* reports that in the first six months after the introduction of the product liability law, approximately 1,500 complaints were filed, double the number for the same period before the law. Before the new law, it was difficult for the consumer to obtain enough information to prove producer negligence. The manufacturers had a moral obligation not to harm customers but there was little legal recourse for the customers.[6] (The Japanese government did step in with strict regulations on standards, testing, and licensing.[7])

Implications of Changes in Customer Satisfaction and Service

In the United States, the service sector is the largest and fastest-growing segment of the economy. In contrast, Japan's service sector, aside from restaurants and home delivery services, is under-developed in relation to the size of the market. For example, only 4.8 percent of transactions are handled by credit card, only about a third as many as in the United States. Credit card usage is increasing, however. The total number of credit cards issued in Japan grew by 287 percent between 1983 and 1993.[8]

The changing definition of service and the small size of the service sector in Japan represents an opportunity for new firms to create businesses or enhance existing offerings by bundling in a service component. Professional and contractual relationships now have greater value, so there are opportunities for companies to capture that value or distinguish themselves based on service. At the same time, the old relationship-focused market remains strong. Some customers will value and demand these relationships more than detached, professional service.

A similar shift can be expected in many Asian markets, from a traditional focus on personal relationships to value-added, professional relationship with companies. As these shifts occur—through increased competition, market development, and education of consumers—customer satisfaction and service become more important. Japan could be a good place to balance a tradition of servitude and dignity with the emergence of modern definitions of professional service and customer satisfaction. In particular, companies can take advantage of these changes by:

Moving From Personal to Professional Relationships

Managers should look for opportunities to move from traditional personal relationships to more professional relationships. What segments of the market would be most open to this?

Valuing Service

If customers value service, the company can begin to derive value from adding formal service contracts or guarantees. What value-added services can be sold at extra charge to customers?

Exploring Self Service

The alternative is to strip away service to offer a lower-cost product to customers. Where can self-service products be introduced at lower prices?

Points of Leverage

- To what extent is your customer satisfaction based on "bowing" and to what extent is it based on professional customer service?

- How satisfied are your customers? How can you better measure and improve customer satisfaction? How can you encourage customers to provide feedback and make complaints?

- Is your organization truly customer-focused? What is the internal status of the customer service department in your organization?

- How empowered are your employees to satisfy your key customers? Can your sales representatives make spontaneous judgements to meet the requests of your customers? How can you educate your employees to increase their customer focus?

- How can you use customer service to distinguish your products and services?

- What is the value of service to your customers and how can you better capitalize on this value?

- Are you effective in building customer retention and loyalty?

- Have you been able to capitalize on consumer word-of-mouth and endorsement for your product? How can you create communities around your products?

13

New Rules of Marketing Research

Three times a week, senior executives of Ito-Yokado's 7-Eleven Japan Company lunch on products that are under consideration or on the shelves of the chain's 4,800 stores. President Toshifumi Suzuki slips into stores unannounced and also has a team of 200 full-time testers spot-checking stores. The company invested in a $200 million (¥24 trillion) system to monitor inventory and customer preferences. Clerks even punch in the sex and approximate age of each customer to monitor buying patterns. If customers don't buy an item, it is pulled; 70 percent of the 3,000 items carried by each store are replaced annually. In 1985, third-ranked retailer Ito-Yokado stormed past first-ranked Daiei in profits. While other Japanese retailers were losing money during the recession in 1992, 7-Eleven posted a 42-percent operating margin and a 10-percent increase in sales. There was little doubt about the value of marketing information. (In fact, Ito-Yokado did so well it purchased a majority share in 7-Eleven's U.S. parent, Southland Corporation in 1990.)[1]

Ito-Yokado established a complete item-by-item control system based on consumer needs. The company also shifted from centrally planned merchandising to a store-led strategy. The results were remarkable. Between 1981 and 1989, the turnover period for merchandise fell from 25.7 days to just fifteen days, gross margins increased from 25.1 percent to 29.8 percent, and pre-tax profits increased from 3.3 percent to 6.3 percent.[2] The new system increased the frequency of deliveries and the turnover of merchandise. This system, however, created new problems for manufacturers as distribution and logistics costs skyrocketed.

Although the power of this information was demonstrated by Ito-Yokado, the emphasis was still on tracking movement of sales and products rather than on gaining information about customers. Japanese firms have been slow to do research in the pre-launch phase.

Traditional Japanese Approaches to Marketing Research

The whole concept of marketing information in Japan was related to forming and maintaining relationships, not on collecting data about customers. The word for information, *jyoho*, is composed of Chinese characters that mean "repaying an obligation." Information is related to repaying an obligation to those with whom one has a fixed relationship. There is, therefore, no market value to it.

Sony, Matsushita, Toyota, and other companies, which all conduct consumer attitude surveys, have not put much faith in scientific marketing research. As the head of Matsushita's videocassette recorder division once said, "Why do Americans do so much marketing research? You can find out what you need by traveling around and visiting the retailers who carry your product."[3]

Japanese market research traditionally combined "soft data" from visits to dealers and other channel members with "hard data" about shipments, inventory levels, and sales. When Japanese firms did survey customers, they interviewed those who had bought or used the product rather than looking for broader attitudes and trends. When Canon shifted its U.S. distribution strategy to bolster flagging sales in the early-1970s, it surveyed neither consumers nor retailers. Instead, Canon sent three managers to the United States to talk to camera shop owners.[4]

Instead of directly trying to understand customers before launching products, Japanese marketers have tended to implement many small changes and then monitor reaction by collecting data on distribution channels. Strong vertical integration of manufacturing and retailing has made this process easier.

Japanese companies traditionally collected information through such means as:

- Continuously monitoring brand sales and shares movement

- Tracking new brand shares

- Tracking the incumbents' shares after a new brand introduction

- Measuring the effects of in-store promotions

Because Japanese managers rarely received formal business training, there was little opportunity to be trained in Western marketing techniques. Some of the Japanese strategies for getting close to the customer and collecting soft data have be adopted by Western marketers. At the same time, Japanese companies are becoming increasingly interested in formal research, particularly as companies diversify their product lines and distribution channels.

Japanese companies are much more likely to rely upon a strategy of rapid experimentation than formal pretesting and other research. This may lead to a higher failure rate than more carefully launched products or advertising campaigns, but it also reduces what is often a much greater risk—that the move will be preempted by a rival. Seiko, for example, develops thousands of new watch designs every year and then produces those with promising sales.

Similarly, while some Japanese companies measure the impact and customer interest in commercials, very few pre-test commercials, as is generally the practice in the United States. This can lead to more rapid advertising launches, but also to a greater likelihood that the campaign will fail. For example, one senior executive ordered an advertising campaign pulled after he saw it for the first time on television.

Lack of Attention to Marketing Research

Traditionally, Japanese companies have watched the Neilsen Retail Index to understand their market share versus rivals. They spoke with retailers and looked at inventory, sales, and other information that show the items' actual movement through the channels. Individual purchasing patterns were not of much interest. Instead, companies examined their weekly sales.

Just-in-time delivery, or *kanban*, also affected the Japanese approach to marketing information. Just-in-time systems began in U.S. supermarkets, were popularized by Toyota, and then expanded to convenience stores, supermarkets, and other retailers in Japan in the 1980s. These systems relied upon accurate, on-going information about purchases and inventory, but not necessarily proactive information about customers.

Japan had been far behind the United States in collecting and using marketing information. In a 1980s article in *Journal of Advertising Research*, the Association of Market Research Firms estimated that the size of marketing research in Japan was about the same as in the United Kingdom, even though the GNP of Japan was about four times as large as that of the United Kingdom.

Research was focused on share rather than on understanding the market. Similarly, advertising was rarely tested. The media was treated like a shelf in the store. The presence of a product on the shelf is what is most important. The manufacturer with shelf space and media space moved product. Share of voice was what mattered, not share of mind.

These approaches were most effective in a market in which customers were relatively undifferentiated and predictable. Now, as Japanese consumers have become increasingly differentiated and unpredictable, and as they are increasingly making their needs known, conducting this kind of formal marketing research is extremely important.

Information Explosion

The rapid growth of point-of-sale information systems in Japan, increasing at an annual rate of 100 percent per year, is fundamentally changing the availability and use of marketing information.[5]

Japanese Article Number (JAN) barcodes now grace virtually every Japanese product. One sign of the pervasiveness of the barcode was an unusual children's toy launched in Japan in the early 1990s. The Bar Code Butler allowed children to scan in codes from different products from their cupboards. The pervasiveness of barcodes has not only transformed children's play in Japan, it has transformed retailing.

Initially, stores collected POS data on their own chains. In 1985, the first large-scale interorganizational database was developed by the Distribution Code Center Japan, a subsidiary of the Ministry of International Trade and Industry (MITI). It collected data from more than 100 supermarkets around the nation and supplied the information to its member companies, including major retailers and manufacturers.

Since then, several private data suppliers have emerged. They include marketing research firms, newspaper publishers, trading houses, and computer hardware manufacturers. They offer the service either on a commercial basis or as a complimentary benefit to their customers.

Manufacturers are using information technology to directly partner with retailers. For example, Tashio Pharmaceuticals used an extensive system of information technology to market and distribute its products to drug stores throughout Japan. It created and installed a point-of-sale system connected to 6,000 drug stores, about a quarter of all stores in Japan. The stores receive benefits from having the terminals. In addition to product discounts, the drug store receives daily reports on margins and pricing of Tashio products and those of competitors, new product announcements and tests, including those of Tashio's competitors, and advice on managing its product line to increase profits. Thus, a small store receives valuable advice that it could not afford to develop or purchase on its own.

The system also offers tremendous advantages to Tashio. The company can use the system to monitor sales of its products and those of its competitors on a daily basis. It can adjust its pricing and margins to outperform its competitors. The system also gives Tashio a window on the margins, sales, and new products of its rivals.

Scanner Panels

The first scanner panel started in Japan in 1983. By the start of 1992, there were six major panels, evenly divided between store scanning and home scanning. Store scanning uses a typical U.S. approach of issuing an ID card that customers use when checking out at the store POS register. In-home scanning, which is specifically designed for the Japanese environment, uses information scanned by customers through a scanner installed in the home.

Several factors make it difficult to use in-store scanning in Japan. The high density of retail stores and patterns of patronizing diverse stores make it harder to track purchases. Shoppers are very mobile, making a substantial portion of their purchases at stores outside their neighborhood. Finally, supermarket chains are not cooperative in the installation of external scanner terminals. Thus, in-store scanning works only if the target area is geographically and commercially isolated and the scanners are installed in the majority of stores in the area.

In-home scanning allows for more complete coverage of purchases, but it suffers from several drawbacks. The causal data related to purchases must be collected from the majority of the stores patronized by the panel members. Also, the task of inputting purchases at home is by no means easy, so there may be significant errors of omission as well as input errors. Great strides have been made in collecting the causal data, and validation studies have shown the measurement errors to be surprisingly small. Despite its drawbacks, in-home scanning seems to be more effective than store scanning.

The cutting-edge of Japanese marketing technology is a home scanning panel coupled with a television audience research system. VR Home Scan System, run by Video Research Ltd., created the first such system in Japan in 1987. Its sample of 1,000 households in a 1.3-mile radius of a typical Tokyo suburban residential area represents a relatively young white-collar household. It is used to track the impact of advertising and promotions by monitoring household purchases. Although this sample is by no means representative of the "mass" market in Japan, it fits nicely with manufacturers' concept of a lead market.

Rise of Marketing Research

Marketing research has gone from being a side dish to the main course. It was once used to confirm intuitive propositions of managers or executives, but it is now used to generate market insight. Marketing science and modeling are being employed more frequently in Japan. There has been a rise in membership in the Institute of Marketing Science and an increasing number of university courses in marketing science.

Ajinomoto, a major food manufacturer, launched a project to collect menus of lunches and dinners from 4,000 households across the country to understand what consumers are eating and how they are preparing it.

Ajinomoto also developed a system of identifying independent sub-markets out of a market of more than 200 items. These markets can be analyzed from PC terminals throughout the organization. If a sales person in the field is facing a problem of proposing shelf-space planning to a retailer, it could easily get a picture of sub-markets defined by items carried by that specific retailer. All individual household records are already stocked in the system. The salesperson could do the market definition exercise for any of the stores the company has relations with and provide the analysis to the store manager. The distance between the data and analysis, the analysis and results, and the decision maker is shortened.

This marketing information makes the old focus on share of retail shelf space almost irrelevant. The emphasis is now on the movement of individual products—which can now be tracked by sales information—rather than on the amount of shelf space held by a single corporation. The information that is needed is not merely about market share but about what individual customers and specific segments are seeking.

This information, and its proven value, is changing the way manufacturers and retailers approach the market. Retailers are using this information to take control of their businesses, which have long been dominated by the manufacturers.

Japanese marketers still use research more as a reference point rather than a decision point. Although the use of research is increasing, Japanese managers still usually feel their Western peers place to much emphasis on formal research.

Cultural Effects on Qualitative Research

Great care needs to be used in interpreting the marketing research. The marketing data may look the same as in the United States, but could mean something very different. Comparisons between similar numbers in Japan and other global markets may not always be meaningful. Researchers need to think carefully about the dynamics underlying the numbers and make modifications to the techniques to reflect the different culture and market of Japan.

While quantitative research drawn from POS data and other sources has increased, so have other research methods such as focus groups and surveys. But these research techniques have a distinct character in Japan because of cultural differences.

Middle of the Road

Japanese survey respondents tend to answer in a narrower range than their Western peers. Early in his career in Japan, one of the authors was involved in a project in which over thirty concepts were to be screened, using the same techniques that were used in the United States, the United Kingdom, Germany, and Australia. In each case, the most critical measure was a "top-of-the-box" rating on a certain scale.

On this basis, all concepts failed in Japan. Worse yet, the data were nondiscriminating—that is, the figures were similar for all concepts. The client was warned of this possibility. However, the experience of all the other countries could not be ignored, and the client had the prerogative to conduct the exercise. The data were discriminating to some extent when the top two boxes were combined, but this raised a quandary in that one could not be sure whether the discrimination simply indicated differences between mediocrities—some are not as bad as others—or the superiority of some over others.

The "theory," simply stated, is that when confronted with a verbal seven-point scale, or a range from "excellent" to "terrible," Westerners tend to start from the extremes. They consider a position quickly and then perhaps modify it, which means working from both ends and moving toward the center. The Japanese, on the other hand, tend to take a neutral position or start from the midpoint and move outward, seldom reaching the extremes, hence the low "top-of-the-box" ratings.

A company that screened advertising concepts in both Japan and the United States found marked differences in responses to the survey. The verbal scale was far less sensitive in Japan. Far fewer said, "I like it very much," or "I dislike it very much." They clung to the middle. About 20 percent of the U.S. respondents chose the highest box compared with just 7 percent of Japanese.

Using even number scales, or those without a strict midpoint, doesn't really resolve the issue. While this explanation is a little pat, it fits our usual observations of the Japanese being very cautious to take up a fixed position before all known facts and consequences are weighed. How, then, can one give a clear opinion on a product or an advertisement in a single-shot or short-term exposure? Here, *time* is the substance rather than the number of exposures.

Reticent Focus Groups

Focus groups in Japan are run differently because the Japanese are still uncomfortable being a complete minority. Traditional focus groups tend not to get strong impressions of individual opinions. U.S. focus groups tend to take a position early in the discussions, starting with the two extremes and moving in a bit. Japanese group members tend to evolve a position rather than start with a position.

There is not the need for the kind of closure typically sought in the United States. These differences can be seen in the music of Japan and the West. Western music is formally structured into sonatas. There is development of a theme and recapitulation. Japanese is not structured that way. There are no bars. They represent a continuous flow rather than a beginning or an end. Similarly, market research is a continuous revolving process in Japan. There is no beginning or end. The West has a concept, test marketing, and rollout in a fairly linear process.

First-time American visitors to these focus groups usually become frustrated. The focus group members spend a lot of time developing consensus. Mixed age groups do not work well because young people don't express their opinions in front of their elders. Homogeneous groups tend to work best.

Clothing retailer REI gave up on its formal focus groups in Japan in the light of these challenges. Instead, it worked to cultivate relationships with long-time Japanese customers and encourage them to be open in their feedback on products. Once they built this trust, they received useful comments.

Japanese consumers were also not used to the polling process, and they were not very responsive to telephone interviews when they were attempted twenty years ago. Mall interviews are also not possible because there were no malls. Political and other types of polling on television have acclimated Japanese respondents to the idea, making it easier to conduct polls. (This is the opposite of the United States, where telephone interviewing is acceptable, but face-to-face surveys are harder to conduct.)

The point is that measurement must be done with an understanding of the cultural environment. While approaches from other countries can be applied, they may need to be tailored to the unique demands of the local culture. Clearly, norms that have been developed within the culture must be applied.

Implications of Changes in Market Research

Some of the cultural effects seen in Japan will also have an impact on other Asian markets. The Japanese combination of hands-on soft data with formal hard data will be very useful in Asia, particularly when the formal data is not widely available.

The data infrastructure in Japan is far more developed than in other parts of Asia. Japan offers a model for the relatively rapid spread of marketing information. The Asian research infrastructure and understanding of the process of survey collection are not as well developed. Telephone directories are not available in many areas, and the penetration of phones is not complete. Customers are also not used to answering surveys. One company, for example, had great difficulty running a telephone interview survey in Asia because of difficulty accessing each household. In addition to a shortage of phones, residents didn't let the survey takers into their homes and were noncooperative and dishonest in answering the questions.

As shown by Japan's experience, a relatively undeveloped level of marketing research creates new opportunities. Companies in Asia should look for ways to improve their insight into their markets by:

Importing Marketing Research Techniques

Marketing research techniques that have been successful in other parts of the world may offer insight into other Asian markets. While marketing research has been recognized in Japan, there are still opportunities to use it to gain an edge over competitors. Introduction of these techniques into other Asian markets may offer even greater opportunities for gaining competitive advantages.

Identifying the Information Needed

Examine how marketing information can help the company to change the competitive playing field. How could information about potential customers offer your firm increased opportunities to succeed in the market? How can you go about obtaining that information? By starting with the information you need, you can develop creative ways of obtaining that information, despite limitation of infrastructure or culture.

Understanding the Value of Information

Companies that gather information about customers should take advantage of all opportunities. They can analyze the data to identify new options, pool it with information from other firms, or use it to extend their own product or service lines. What information already collected can be used in new ways?

Adjusting For Cultural Differences

Just as surveys and focus groups need to be approached differently in Japan, cultural differences will affect marketing research in other markets. By paying attention to these differences and modifying approaches accordingly, companies can develop approaches that are customized for that particular market.

Recognizing That Issues of Privacy May Be More Important

While personal relationships have always been valued, database relationships (such as Ritz Carlton's system of tracking customer preferences across hotels) are viewed with suspicion by many Japanese consumers. As seen in the development of the Internet, there is perhaps and even greater concern for privacy in Japan than in the West. Companies need to proceed with caution lest positive relationship-building activities have a negative impact on customers.

Not Relying Blindly On Advertising Agencies

Many advertising agencies in Japan are still building their capabilities for marketing research. Companies that commission marketing research need to have experienced staff in-house who understand the customer and are capable of helping design and filter information from an outside firm. Many firms also develop capabilities to conduct marketing research in-house. In the process, advertising agencies will come up with many seemingly good ideas that will not work. There needs to be someone on staff with the skill and seniority to tell a powerful agency when they are wrong.

Decisions are Based on Multiple Data Sources

Japanese firms like to see the total picture. Even as more marketing research techniques are used, companies rarely rely exclusively on this research. It is one piece of evidence that is weighed by the product team and incorporated into the decision.

Using the Power of the Internet

As Japan has moved online, there are increasing opportunities to use the Internet for marketing research. While the initial small sample made it difficult to develop unbiased studies, the broadening of the online population makes such research possible. The Internet offers a way to conduct studies very quickly and efficiently.

As markets become more complex and diverse, the value of information continues to increase. Although some companies will succeed based on good intuition for a short time, in the long run, solid marketing information will be the basis of establishing and growing businesses in Japan and throughout Asia.

Points of Leverage

- To what extent do your decisions rely upon staff understanding of "typical" Japanese? Are these insights still valid?

- How can you use more sophisticated marketing research to understand your markets?

- Do you need to modify your research techniques to deal with issues such as reticent focus groups and middle-of-the-road responses to surveys?

- Given the growing heterogeneity of the Japanese market and competition for segments, do you need to increase the resources devoted to marketing research? In what areas?

- To what extent have you used Internet-based marketing research?

- Have you focused on quantification of qualitative data?

- Have you designed your marketing research as an integral part of your decision-support system, with links to databases and modeling approaches?

- Is your marketing research function structured so that your market knowledge is accumulated with each new research study? Is there a built-in mechanism for learning and updating the knowledge?

Conclusion:

Leveraging the Future

Despite the current economic crisis in Japan—and in some cases, because of it—there are tremendous opportunities in Japan. Some of these opportunities have always been there, like a pearl in an oyster—difficult to penetrate because of a hard shell of regulations, traditions, and structures. Other opportunities are emerging from shifts in consumer values and related changes in the business environment in Japan.

Success in Japan requires more advanced skills and a deeper understanding of marketing than ever before. Business relationships are less important. Powerful corporations are less important. It is the ability of the company to connect to the market that is now one of the most powerful advantages.

• The common sense of five years ago no longer applies today. A little outdated knowledge about the Japanese market can be a dangerous thing. Advisors who emphasize the differences in Japan may be basing their insight on outdated wisdom. Aspects of "culture" may actually be due to structure—and that structure is changing. Challenge all assumptions about the Japanese market, because it is quite often these inaccurate beliefs that are the greatest limit on discovering opportunities in Japan.

• Recognize where global marketing concepts, methods, and insight can be imported. The modernization of Japan presents many opportunities to apply Western marketing approaches. Comparative advertising, retail shopping malls, and marketing research have all been successfully imported to Japan. Some approaches that have been successful in the West, have yet to be tried in Japan, and this creates opportunities to import business models and best practices from other parts of the world.

• Know where the analogies to Western markets end. Success requires a deeper understanding of the Japanese market itself. It is becoming more modern, but certainly not Western. Even with the ubiquity of Coca-Cola, McDonald's, BMW, Estée Lauder, HMV, The Gap, and other Western brands, there is no danger of mistaking Tokyo for New York. The differences are very plain, in the attitudes of consumers and in behaviors. Japan is changing, but it is still Japan. One must never lose sight of that.

• Japan and Asia will keep moving forward. The new consumer can be expected to become even newer. Japanese teenagers toting around cellular phones and laptops are already plotting to further transform the Japanese market. Perhaps some of these shifts will not be so dramatic as the shift from a producer-driven to a consumer-driven market, but they will create a very different atmosphere in the future. As they listen to Japanese pop music on their Walkmen, don't expect these Japanese youth to merely follow global trends. They will create a future market that will continue to be distinctly Japanese. At the same time, the current influx of foreign companies will continue to accelerate the changes in the market and remove the last crumbling artifacts of the old systems. The lessons of the Japanese market will continue to evolve and change.

Changes in Global Marketing Practice

The changes in Japanese marketing needs to be seen in the context of transformations in the practice of marketing worldwide. Driven by advances in information technology and the technology for customization and relationships, shifting organizational forms, increasing globalization, changes in consumer behavior and other

forces, the concepts, methods and practice of marketing is changing. Some of these shifts are summarized in the following table:

Shifting Realities of Marketing Strategy

	Old Model	New Model
Relationship with customers	Passive consumer	Co-producer
Customer needs	Articulated	Unarticulated
Segmentation	Mass market	Customized segments of one
Product and service offerings	Line extensions and modifications; R&D drives new product development	Customer-driven customization of products and services; marketing interactions drive new product development
Pricing	Fixed prices and discounting	New value-based pricing models and emergence of consumer-determined pricing
Communication	Advertising and PR	Integrated, interactive, customized marketing communication, education, and entertainment
Distribution	Traditional retailing and Direct marketing to segments	Direct (electronic) distribution and rise of third-party logistics services
Strategic intent	Market participation	Leadership and innovation in target segment
Supply chain	Inventory	Integrated global supply chain including global delivery; just-in-time (JIT)
Geographic scope	Domestic and International	Global
Competitive advantage	Marketing power	Marketing finesse

Source: J. Wind, "The Challenge of Customer-Driven Customization."

As with any change, these are both creative and destructive. As you shape your marketing strategy in Japan, ask yourself:

- How do these changes create new opportunities?

- What capabilities are needed to be the first to capitalize on these opportunities?

- How do these changes undermine my current approaches to marketing in Japan?

Climbing Mount Fuji a Second Time

As Asian economies regain their footing and begin a somewhat slower and more deliberate path of development, experience in Japan will become more valuable. While the Japanese model will not be imitated in its entirety—just as Japan never imitated the West—there will be borrowings and influences. This will make an understanding of the Japanese market even more imperative to understanding and succeeding in other emerging markets in Asia.

There is an old Japanese saying: "He who has never climbed Mount Fuji is a fool; he who would climb it twice is also a fool. (*Fuji-ni noboranu baka; nido noboru baka.*)" Certainly the companies who have never ascended the Japanese market because of the difficulty of the terrain may be foolish to remain on the sidelines. On the other hand, it may be necessary for those who painstaking climbed Mount Fuji a first time, learning their hard lessons in the old Japanese market, to make the climb once again. So much has changed. As the success stories in this book have shown, scaling Mount Fuji a second time is well worth the effort—for the learning involved in the process, the direct rewards reaped in Japan, and the perspectives on Asia gained from the summit.

Points of Leverage

- Do you have a process that will allow you to continuously understand the changes in the Japanese environment?

- Do you have structures and processes to support continuous experimentation with different approaches, so over time you are truly a learning organization and can increase your understanding of successful strategies Japan?

- Do you continuously evaluate how your insight from Japan can be utilized in Asia and in the rest of the world?

Notes

Chapter One

1. Ono, Y. "Tiffany Glitters, Even in Gloomy Japan," *Wall Street Journal*, July 21, 1998, B-1.

2. Strom, S. "Recession in Japan? Not for Luxury-Goods Firms," *New York Times*, Oct. 29, 1998.

3. *Nikkei*, Nov. 24, 1998.

4. "McDonald's Japan: Rise in Revenue/Profit for Five Successive Periods," *Nikkei*, Mar. 9, 1999.

5. "Attitude Survey of Foreign Corporations Toward Direct Investments in Japan," JETRO, Oct. 1998.

6. MITI, "31st Survey of Trends in Foreign Capital Enterprises," Sept. 1997.

7. Japanese External Trade Organization (JETRO), Dec. 10, 1998.

8. "Foreign Capital Companies Turning Toward Japan," *Asahi Shimbun*, Aug. 9, 1997.

9. *Asahi Shinbun*, Evening Edition, Oct. 11, 1997.

10. *Distribution Almanac*, 1996.

11. *Nihon Keizai Shimbun*, Jan. 1, 1999, 25.

12. *Nihon Keizai Shimbun*, Dec. 16, 1998.

13. Personal interview by Hotaka Katahira with Mario Massetti, director of Gucci, in May 1996; *Nikkei Shimbun*, Apr. 22, 1996.

14. *Comparative International Statistics*, 1995, BOJ, Economic Planning Agency, in *Japan 1996: An International Comparison* (Keizai Koho Center, 1996).

15. Bremner, B. "Two Japans," *Business Week*, Jan. 27, 1997, 27.

16. Montgomery, D. B. "Understanding the Japanese as Customers, Competitors, and Collaborators," *Japan and the World Economy* 3(1991), 61–91.

17. JETRO Investment White Paper, 1999.

18. *Human Studies*, Mar. 1997, 23–28.

19. Nikkei Ryutsu Shimbun, Nov. 1998.

20. *Distribution Almanac*, 1996.

21. "Japan is Dialing 1 800 BUY AMERICA," *Business Week*, June 12, 1995, 54.

22. Based in part upon a discussion of myths and realities published in column by George Fields, "Japanese Shopper Power," *The Asian Wall Street Journal*, Aug. 10, 1994, 5.

23. Shirouzi, N. "P&G's Joy Surprises in Japan's Mature Market," *The Asian Wall Street Journal*, Dec. 11, 1997, 1.

24. Shirouzi, N. "P&G's Joy Surprises in Japan's Mature Market," *The Asian Wall Street Journal*, Dec. 11, 1997, 1.

25. *Nihon Keizai Shinbun*.

26. *Nikkei Market Share Index*, 1997.

27. *Nikkei Ryutsu Sinbun*, Aug. 1996.

28. Miyashita, C. "Japanese DM Crime, Cultural Gaffes, and Other News," *DM News International*, Feb. 16, 1998, 19.

29. Armacost, M. *Friends or Rivals?* (New York: Columbia University Press, 1996), 238.

30. JETRO Investment White Paper, 1999, survey of 705 companies, response rate of 21.5%.

31. "Uncorking the Genie," Ogilvy & Mather, May 1997.

32. Bartholet, J. "That's Godzilla at Bat," *Newsweek (Japan/Korea)*, July 15, 1996, 9.

Chapter Two

1. Shirouzu, N. "Flouting 'Rules' Sells GE Fridges in Japan," *The Wall Street Journal*, Oct. 31, 1995, B-1.

2. Shirouzu, N. "Flouting 'Rules' Sells GE Fridges in Japan," *The Wall Street Journal*, Oct. 31, 1995, B-1.

3. Shirouzu, N. "Flouting 'Rules' Sells GE Fridges in Japan," *The Wall Street Journal*, Oct. 31, 1995, B-1.

4. Interview with Hotaka Katahira, Aug. 1998.

5. William, M. "The Outlook: Japan's Shoppers Bring a New Era to Economy," *The Wall Street Journal*, June 20, 1994, A-1.

6. Dentsu Institute of Human Studies, 1996.

7. Japanese Life Insurance Culture Center Study, 1996.

8. Economic Planning Agency, survey of approximately 2,000 registered companies, excluding financial institutions (response rate: 60%), Mar. 1998.

9. Ono, Y. "Japan Warms to McDonald's Doting Dad Ads," *The Wall Street Journal*, May 8, 1997, B-1.

10. Japanese Ministry of Education, National Traits Survey, 1996.

11. Japanese Life Insurance Culture Center Study, 1996.

12. Lee, L. "Ads in Asia Show Men Doing Housework," *The Wall Street Journal*, Aug. 14, 1998, B-6.

13. Video Research Ltd, HomeScan Panel Data; Oct. 1993 to Sept. 1994.

14. Katahira, H. "Advertising and Brand Building in Japan," University of Tokyo, July 1998.

15. "Survey of 7,000 White Collar Workers Between 20 Years and 49 Years," Recruit Research.

16. *Asahi Shinbun*, June 6, 1998.

17. *Nihon Keizai Shinbun Survey*, May 4, 1998.

18. Pollack, A. "Can the Pen Really Be Mightier Than the Germ?" *The New York Times*, July 27, 1995.

19. Japanese Life Insurance Culture Center Study.

20. Nikkei Industry Consumption Institute.

21. Asahi Shinbun/Lew Harris Survey, *Asahi Shinbun*, Jan. 1, 1998.

22. Prime Minister's Office, in *Japan Almanac 1996* and Japan Travel Bureau.

23. Courtis, K. S. "Japan and Global Capital Flows," *Deutche Morgan Grenfell Global Strategy Research*, Sept. 20, 1996.

24. "Changing Japan: Whispering Reform," *The Economist*, Jan. 11, 1997, 21.

25. ICAO *Digest of Statistics, Financial and Traffic, 1996* and annual reports of the three Japanese airlines (1996). The Japanese average was Y4.6 per kilometer, while U.S. airlines ranged between 1.5 for USAir to 1.2 for United Airlines.

26. Ohmae, K. "Letter From Japan," *Harvard Business Review*, May–June 1995, 154.

27. *The Economist—Survey: Tomorrow's Japan*, July 13, 1996, 12.

28. Reported by George Fields.

29. "The Deregimentation Job at Home," *The Economist—Survey: Tomorrow's Japan*, July 13, 1996, 10.

30. Tyson, L. D. "Managing Trade by Rules and Outcomes," *Who's Bashing Whom: Trade Conflicts in High Technology Industries*. Washington, D.C.: Institute for International Economics, 1992, 118.

31. Sapsford, J. "Quake-Hobbled Kobe Shows How Land Law Can Paralyze Japan," *The Wall Street Journal*, Dec. 12, 1996, A-1.

32. "Structural Changes in Japan's Distribution System." Report, Japan Economic Institute, Washington, D.C.: JEI, Nov. 1989.

33. "Structural Changes in Japan's Distribution System." Report, Japan Economic Institute, Washington, D.C.: JEI, Nov. 1989.

34. *Nikkei*, Apr. 3, 1999, reporting on MITI survey, 1997.

35. MITI.

36. Kano, C. and A. Taylor III. "The Cult of the Astro Van," *Fortune*, Aug. 18, 1997, 44.

37. Berger, "Investment, Infrastructure, and Image: The Key to Success in Japan's Auto Market," *JAMA Forum* 14.2 (Oct. 1995).

Chapter Three

1. Japanese External Trade Organization (JETRO), Dec. 10, 1998.

2. "More Foreign Affiliates Entering Japan," *Focus Japan*, Mar. 1997.

3. Higuchi, T. "How To Succeed in Vietnam," *Japan Productivity Center*, Nov. 25, 1998.

4. Abeglenn, J. *The Great East Asian Markets*, Japanese document, Tokyo: TBS Britannica, 1994, 284–86.

5. Huntington, S. P. *The Clash of Civilizations and the Remaking of World Order*. New York: Simon & Schuster, 1996.

6. Naisbitt, J. *Megatrends Asia: Eight Asian Megatrends That Are Reshaping Our World*. New York: Simon and Schuster, 1996.

7. Pyle, K. B. *The Japanese Question: Power and Purpose in a New Era*. Washington, D.C.: The AEI Press, 1992, 132.

8. Pyle, K. B. *The Japanese Question: Power and Purpose in a New Era*. Washington, D.C.: The AEI Press, 1992, 135–136.

9. Pyle, K. B. *The Japanese Question: Power and Purpose in a New Era*. Washington, D.C.: The AEI Press, 1992, 137.

10. Mohamad, M. and S. Ishihara. *The Voice of Asia*. Tokyo: Kodansha International, 1995, 17.

11. Mohamad, M. and S. Ishihara. *The Voice of Asia*. Tokyo: Kodansha International, 1995, 32.

12. Picken, S. D. B. "Japan's Tilt Towards Asia: Questions for Americans," A lecture to the Japan-America Society of Greater Philadelphia, The Cosmopolitan Club, April 1, 1997.

13. Mohamad, M. and S. Ishihara. *The Voice of Asia*. Tokyo: Kodansha International, 1995, 87.

14. Mohamad, M. and S. Ishihara. *The Voice of Asia*. Tokyo: Kodansha International, 1995, 88.

15. *Nikkei Shinbun*, Apr. 8, 1998.

16. Mohamad, M. and S. Ishihara. *The Voice of Asia*. Tokyo: Kodansha International, 1995, 146.

17. Mohamad, M. and S. Ishihara. *The Voice of Asia*. Tokyo: Kodansha International, 1995, 88.

18. Koseki, K. "Marketing Strategies As Adopted by Ajinomoto in Southeast Asia," *Marketing Strategies*, 309–312.

19. "Uncorking the Genie," Ogilvy & Mather report, 1997.

20. "Report on the First 'Comparative Analysis of Global Values,' Tokyo and Five Other Asian Cities: Diversity and Common Ground," Dentsu Institute for Human Studies, June 1997.

21. From a presentation by Michio Kamoshida, "Modern Asianness: Homecare Workshop in Japan," *Nippon Lever*, Sept. 3, 1996.

22. Hsiao, H. M. "Discovering East Asian Middle Classes: Formation, Differentiation, and Politics," in *Discovery of the Middle Classes in East Asia*. Taiwan: Institute of Ethnology, Academia Sinca, 1993, 4.

23. Hsiao, H. M. "Discovering East Asian Middle Classes: Formation, Differentiation, and Politics," in *Discovery of the Middle Classes in East Asia*. Taiwan: Institute of Ethnology, Academia Sinca, 1993, 13.

24. From a presentation by Michio Kamoshida of Nippon Lever based on research by CRAM International, 1996

25. *Asahi Shinbun*, Evening Edition, Oct. 18, 1997.

26. *Asahi Shinbun*, Evening Edition, Oct. 18, 1997.

27. "Korean Retailers Take Stock," AC *Nielsen Insights Asia Pacific*, Feb. 1999, p. 3.

28. Hirsh, M. and E. K. Henry. "The Unraveling of Japan Inc.," *Foreign Affairs* 76: 2, 12.

29. "JETRO White Paper on Investments, 1999."

30. Bank for International Settlements, Dec. 31, 1997.

31. "JETRO White Paper on Investments, 1999."

32. Mohamad, M. and S. Ishihara. *The Voice of Asia*. Tokyo: Kodansha International, 1995, 17.

33. Schlender, B. R. "Matsushita Shows How To Go Global," *Fortune*, July 11, 1994, 160.

34. Honda Corporate Profile.

35. *Honda in Thailand 1996*, Honda Motor Company.

36. *Asian Business*, Aug. 1995, 42.

37. Bloom, J. "Japan's National Approach to Business Intelligence," Notes from the Fifth International Conference on Japanese Information in Science, Technology & Commerce, July 30–Aug. 1, 1997, Washington, D.C., 8.

38. Based on interview by H. Katahira with Mr Takiguchi, CEO of HVN and Mr Iuchi, director of sales of HVN.

39. See for example Nonaka, I. and H. Takeuchi. *The Knowledge-Creating Company*. New York: Oxford University Press, 1995.

40. "The Right Person," *Gaishi*, Oct. 1995, 35.

41. "JETRO White Paper on Investments, 1999."

Chapter Four

1. Miyashita, C. "Lands' End Expands, Williams-Sonoma Pulls the Plug," *DM News International*, May 11, 1998, 30.

2. MITI, September 1997, reported by JETRO.

3. "Japan Entries Accelerating With the Tail Winds of Deregulation," *Nihon Keizai Shimbun*, Nov. 12, 1997.

4. "Japan 'Toys R Us' Tops Toy Retailing But Faces Competition," *Nikkei Shinbun*, Mar. 27, 1997.

5. "Japan Entries Accelerating With the Tail Winds of Deregulation," *Nihon Keizai Shimbun*, Nov. 12, 1997.

6. "Further Stormy Seas of International Competition," *Nihon Keizai Shimbun*, Nov. 12, 1997.

7. "Japan Entries Accelerating With the Tail Winds of Deregulation," *Nihon Keizai Shimbun*, Nov. 12, 1997.

8. "Japan Entries Accelerating With the Tail Winds of Deregulation," *Nihon Keizai Shimbun*, Nov. 12, 1997.

9. *Asahi Shinbun*, Evening Edition, Oct. 11, 1997.

10. "Further Stormy Seas of International Competition," *Nihon Keizai Shimbun*, Nov. 12, 1997.

11. *Asahi Shinbun*, Evening Edition, Oct. 11, 1997.

12. *Asahi Shinbun*, Evening Edition, Oct. 11, 1997.

13. *Nikkei Ryutsu Shinbun*, Sept. 3, 1998.

14. "Doing Business in Japan Still Difficult," *Gaishi*, Aug. 1997, 53.

15. *Focus Japan*, JETRO, 1998.

16. "Doing Business in Japan Still Difficult," *Gaishi*, Aug. 1997, 53.

17. "Survey of foreign-affiliated companies regarding direct investment in Japan," Oct. 1995, JETRO.

18. Sapsford, J. "Tokyo Déjà Vu: Foreigners Buy Up Real Estate," *Wall Street Journal*, May 19, 1998, p. A-1.

19. "Miyashita, C. "Competing in Japan's Catalog Market," *Target Marketing*, Apr. 1998, 30.

20. "Nestlé Japan's Marketing Muscle," *Gaishi*, Oct. 1995, 48–49.

21. Fields, G. *From Bonsai to Levis*. New York: Macmillan, 1983.

22. Shirouzu, N. "Snapple in Japan: How a Splash Dried Up," *Wall Street Journal*, Apr. 15, 1996, B-1.

23. Kishi, N. and D. Russell. *Successful Gaijin in Japan* NTC Business Books: Lincolnwood, Ill., 1996, 26.

24. *Nihon Keizai Shinbun*, Sept. 7, 1997.

25. Spindle, B. "In a Matter of Months, Merrill Sets Itself Up as a Force in Japan," *Wall Street Journal*, Apr. 8, 1998, A-1.

26. *Nihon Kerizai Shinbun*, June 1, 1998.

27. *Nihon Kerizai Shinbun*, June 1, 1998.

28. "How Well Did They Know the Japanese Playing Field? Case Study of Evacuated Gaishi and Their Problems," *Gaishi*, Nov.–Dec. 1996.

29. "Companies That Had (and Still Have) What It Takes to Succeed in Japan," *Gaishi*, Oct. 1995, 22.

30. Uchimura, K. "Reebok: In Step With the Market," *Journal of Japanese Trade & Industry* 2 (1989), 44–46.

31. Ono, Y. "Tiffany Glitters, Even in Gloomy Japan," *Wall Street Journal*, July 21, 1998, B-1.

32. "Taking Charge," *Gaishi*, Oct. 1995, 46–47.

33. Kristof, N. "'Wonchu' Wows the Girl in Japan," *International Herald Tribune*, Oct. 23, 1997.

34. *Nihon Keizai Shimbun*, Mar. 20, 1999, 3.

35. Jones, K. K. and W. E. Shill. "Japan: Allying for Advantage," in *Collaborating to Compete: Using Strategic Alliances and Acquisitions in the Global Marketplace*. New York: John Wiley & Sons, 1993, 122.

36. Jones, K. K. and W. E. Shill. "Japan: Allying for Advantage," in *Collaborating to Compete: Using Strategic Alliances and Acquisitions in the Global Marketplace*. New York: John Wiley & Sons, 1993, 130.

Chapter Five

1. Stalk, G. Jr. and A. M. Webber. "Japan's Dark Side of Time," *Harvard Business Review*, July–Aug. 1993, 99.

2. McCreery, J. L. "The Japanese Consumer Whom We Are Talking About," *ACCJ Journal*, Feb. 1998.

3. Katahira, H. and S. Yagi. "Marketing Information Revolution." Cambridge: Harvard University Press, Jan. 1992.

4. Johansson, J. and I. Nonaka. *Relentless: The Japanese Way of Marketing*. New York: Harper Business, 1996.

5. Personal communication from Professor Quian Xiaojun of Tsinghua University to one of the authors, Mar. 25, 1999.

6. *Japan Almanac 1996*.

7. Asano, K. "Japan's Distribution System Information Network," *The Japanese Distribution System: Opportunities & Obstacles, Structures & Practices*. Chicago: Probus Publishing, .

8. "Doing Business in Japan Still Difficult," *Gaishi*, Aug. 1997, 53.

9. *The Weekly Toyo Keizai*. Special Edition on Foreign Capital Enterprises, June 3, 1998.

Chapter Six

1. "Japan's Beer Wars," *The Economist*, Feb. 28, 1998, 68.

2. Yamaki, T. *Kokoku Kokusai Hikaku to Gurobaru Senryaku*. International Comparison of Advertising and Global Strategies. Tokyo: Sanno Daigaku Shuppan-bu, 1990.

3. Ries, A. and J. Trout. *Positioning: The Battle For Your Mind.* New York: Warner Books, 1993.

4. Katahira, H., M. Mizuno, and J. Wind. "New Product Successes in the Japanese Consumer Goods Market." Working Paper: SEI Center for Advanced Studies in Management. The Wharton School, Apr. 1993.

5. Keizai, T. Jan. 14, 1995.

6. Nikkei newspaper, Nov. 14, 1995.

7. Berger, "Investment, Infrastructure, and Image: The Key to Success in Japan's Auto Market," JAMA *Forum,* 14.2 (Oct. 1998).

8. Shirouzu, N. "Selling U.S. Goods in Japan is a Snap: Let 'George' Do It," *The Wall Street Journal,* July 28, 1997, A-1.

Chapter Seven

1. Shirouzu, N. "For Coca-Cola in Japan, Things Go Better With Milk," *Wall Street Journal,* Jan. 20, 1997, B-1

2. Nikkei POS Data Service, based on sale value per 1,000 customers.

3. Shirousu, N. "Local Retailer Challenge U.S. Chains," *Wall Street Journal,* Dec. 30, 1998, B-1.

4. Katahira, H., M. Mizuno, and J. Wind. "New Product Successes in the Japanese Consumer Goods Market." Working Paper: SEI Center for Advanced Studies in Management, The Wharton School, Apr. 1993.

5. Tanaka, H. "Branding in Japan," in *Brand Equity and Advertising,* David A. Aaker and Alexander L. Biel (eds.) Hillsdale, N.Y.: Lawrence Erlbaum Assoc., 1993.

6. Alpert, F., M. Kamins, J. Graham, T. Sakano, and N. Onzo. "Pioneer Brand Advantage in Japan and the United States." Working Paper Report No. 96–101, Marketing Science Institute, Mar. 1996.

7. Takeuchi, H. and I. Nonaka. "The New New Product Development Game," *Harvard Business Review,* Jan.–Feb. 1986, 137–146.

8. Katahira, H. Adapted from "Japanese Markets and Marketing." *Nihon Keizai Shinbun,* Nov.–Dec. 1992.

9. Kotler and Hamilton. *A Guide to Japan's Patent System*. Department of Commerce, Office of Technology Policy, Asia-Pacific Technology Program, Nov. 1996.

10. *Asahi Shimbun Japan Almanac 1996*, 246.

11. "R&D Scoreboard: What's the World in the Làb? Collaborate," *Business Week*, June 27, 1994, 44.

12. Murakami, T. "Intellectual Asset Creation and Characteristics of Japan's Market Economy," Nomura Research Institute, Conference on Market Economies, Jan. 21–22, Tokyo, 1993.

13. Murakami, T. "Intellectual Asset Creation and Characteristics of Japan's Market Economy," Nomura Research Institute, Conference on Market Economies, Jan. 21–22, Tokyo, 1993, 137.

14. Stalk, G. Jr. and A. M. Webber. "Japan's Dark Side of Time," *Harvard Business Review*, July–Aug. 1993, 92–102.

15. "Marketing in Japan: Taking Aim." *The Economist*, Apr. 24, 1993, 74.

16. "Marketing in Japan: Taking Aim." *The Economist*, Apr. 24, 1993, 74.

17. Tatsuno, S. *Created in Japan: From Imitators to World Class Innovators*. New York: Ballinger, 1990.

18. Montgomery, D. B. "Understanding the Japanese as Customers, Competitors, and Collaborators," *Japan and the World Economy* 3 (1991), 61–91.

19. Montgomery, D. B. "Understanding the Japanese as Customers, Competitors, and Collaborators," *Japan and the World Economy* 3 (1991), 61–91.

Chapter Eight

1. Miller, K. L. "Japan's New Credo: Average Can Be Good Enough," *Business Week*, May 3, 1993, 124.

2. *Nikkei Business*, July 13, 1998, 10.

3. *Nikkei*, Nov. 24, 1998.

4. *Nikkei*, June 21, 1998.

5. Sazanami, Y., S. Urata, and H. Kawai. *Measuring the Costs of Protection in Japan*. Tokyo: Institute for International Economics, 1995.

6. Simon, H. "Market Entry in Japan." Working Paper 16, The Marketing Science Group of Germany, 1986.

7. Economic Planning Agency, Survey, Nov. 1998.

8. Montgomery, D. "Understanding the Japanese as Customers, Competitors, and Collaborators," *Japan and the World Economy* 3 (1991), 74.

9. Fields, G. "The Japanese Market Culture," *Japan Times*, 1988.

10. Prime Minister's Office, from George Fields article, "The Price is Right (Or Getting There)".

11. Noguchi, T. Presentation to the 9th Strategic Marketing Software Study Group, Hotel Ukua, June 14, 1994, translated by George Fields.

12. Noguchi, T. Presentation to the 9th Strategic Marketing Software Study Group, Hotel Ukua, June 14, 1994, translated by George Fields.

13. Miller, K. L. "Japan's New Credo: Average Can Be Good Enough," *Business Week*, May 3, 1993, 124.

14. Shill, W. E., T. Guild, and Y. Yamaguchi. "Cracking Japanese Markets," *McKinsey Quarterly* 3 (1995), 34.

15. Ono, Y. "Once Proud Japanese Discover Outlet Malls," *Wall Street Journal*, Dec. 30, 1998, B-1.

16. "Chilly Autumn Winds Blowing on Discounters," *Nihon Keizai Shinbun*, Sept. 27, 1997.

17. Montgomery, D. "Understanding the Japanese as Customers, Competitors, and Collaborators," *Japan and the World Economy* 3 (1991), 74.

18. Noguchi, T. Presentation to the 9th Strategic Marketing Software Study Group, Hotel Ukua, June 14, 1994, translated by George Fields.

19. Furukawa, I. "The Pricing Decisions of Japanese Firms: An Empirical Perspective," Discussion Paper 93-05, Osaka University, Tokyo, 1994.

20. Morimoto, K. " 'Contac' Multi-Symptom Cold Medicine: New Product Success in Japan," *Dentsu Japanese Marketing*, 69–72.

Chapter Nine

1. Ogilvy, D. *Ogilvy on Advertising*. New York: Vintage Books, 1983, 188.

2. Kishii, T. "Message vs. Mood—A Look at Some of the Differences Between Japanese and Western Television Commercials," Dentsu Japan Marketing/Advertising, 1988, 51–53.

3. Fields, G. "Japanese Advertising Today and Yesterday in the Global Market." *Japan Economic Journal*, Dec. 9, 1989.

4. Fields, G. "The Foreigner in Japanese Advertising—A New Phase?" *Tokyo Business Today*, Dec. 1991, 37.

5. Blair, M. "Could There Be a Big Bang in Japanese Advertising," Ogilvy & Mather Asia Pacific, Dec. 1998.

6. Blair, M. "Could There Be a Big Bang in Japanese Advertising?" Ogilvy & Mather, Dec. 1998.

7. Nihon Keizai Shimbun, March 8, 1999, 15.

8. Nihon Keisai Shimbun, March 11, 1999, 15.

9. Nihon Keizai Shimbun, January 1, 1999, 13.

10. Maykuth, A. "Diamond Cartel is Besieged," *Philadelphia Inquirer*, Oct. 14, 1996, A-1.

Chapter Ten

1. Survey conducted by Inpress and the Japan Internet Association with Access Media International, Feb. 1998.

2. *Nikkei Sangyo Shimbun*, Jan. 26, 1999, 3.

3. "Online Shopping Plateaus in Japan," *AsiaBizTech*, Feb. 3, 1999. Based on a survey of 8,812 users between Nov. 18 and Dec. 2, 1998.

4. "Japanese E-commerce Worth US$695 Million in 1997," *Internetnews.com*, Dec. 14, 1998.

5. Nikkei Ryutsu Shinbun, Apr. 6, 1999.

6. "Japanese Online Ad Revenue Up 50 Percent," *AsiaBizTech*, Nov. 27, 1998.

7. "Investigating the Net's Audience Rating," *Nikkei*, Sept. 10, 1998.

8. "Japan's Postal Ministry Ties Up with Firms on Net Shop," *Reuters*, Jan. 3, 1999.

9. Satoh, F. "The Current State and Potential of Internet." Presentation to the Japan Productivity Center for Socio-Economic Development, Mar. 1999.

10. "Number of Japanese Women Online Surges," *AsiaBizTech*, Jan. 13, 1999.

11. "Specialized Internet Service for Women Gaining Popularity," *Nikkei*, Mar. 20, 1999.

12. Nikkei Ryutsu Shinbun, Apr. 6, 1999.

13. Swisher, K. "At Home To Offer Internet Access in Japan in Sumitomo Venture," *Wall Street Journal*, Apr. 7, 1999.

14. Kunii, I. M. "Honk If You Bought Your Car Online," *Business Week Online*, Feb. 8, 1999.

15. Granoff, P. Presentation at the Wharton Impact Conference on Electronic Commerce, The Wharton School, May 9, 1996.

16. Boone, R. "Japanese Internet/E-Commerce Growth Blocked by Government, Cultural Traits," *Internetnews.com*, Nov. 16, 1998.

17. "Pitch the Tent, Then Fire Up the Laptop," *Nikkei Weekly*, Sept. 14, 1998.

18. Angeline, B. "Socio-Technical Considerations in Japan's Transition to a Networked Society," Fifth International Conference on Japanese Information in Science, Technology & Commerce, July 30–Aug. 1, 1997, Washington, D.C., 115.

19. Boone, R. "Sales Booming for Young Japanese-based Online Business," *Internetnews.com*, Oct. 12, 1998.

20. "Online Shopping Plateaus in Japan," *AsiaBizTech*, Feb. 3, 1999.

21. De Bellis, J. *Asahi Evening News*, "A Coy Start to Internet Chat in Japan."

22. NUA Internet Surveys and Paul Budde Communications, Dec. 18, 1999.

23. Erickson, J. "The World on a Wire," *Asiaweek*, Apr. 17, 1998, 46–55.

24. Whaling, C. "The Market for Electronic Commerce in Asia: CHINA—The New Frontier," Fifth International Conference on Japanese Information in Science, Technology & Commerce, July 30–Aug. 1, 1997, Washington, D.C., 54.

25. "Officials Say 1.5 Million Online in China," *San Jose Mercury News*, Jan. 15, 1999.

26. "3.5 Million Online in Taiwan by the Millennium," *AsiaBizTech*, Jan. 15, 1999.

27. "Taiwan To See Online Advertising Boom," Report by YamWeb Co., *AsiaBizTech*, Nov. 20, 1998.

28. "Ecommerce Takes Off in Korea," *AsiaBizTech*, Oct. 21, 1998.

29. 1997 Asian Target Markets Survey (ATMS).

30. Whaling, C. "The Market for Electronic Commerce in Asia: CHINA—The New Frontier," Fifth International Conference on Japanese Information in Science, Technology & Commerce, July 30–Aug. 1, 1997, Washington, D.C., 53.

31. "Japan and China Form Joint Net Think Tank," *Internetnews.com*, Dec. 4, 1998.

32. "Singapore—Asia's Top Surfers," *ACNielsen Insights Asia Pacific*, Feb. 1999.

Chapter Eleven

1. Thornton, E. "Revolution in Japanese Retailing," *Fortune*, Feb. 7, 1994, 143.

2. Interview with Evan Denhardt of Hanna Andersson, Jan. 28, 1999.

3. Fields, G. *Tokyo Business Today*, Aug. 1991.

4. *Nihon Keizai Shinbun*, July 4, 1998.

5. *International Herald Tribune*, July 4, 1995.

6. *Nikkei Ryutsu Shimbun*, Feb. 25, 1999, 1.

7. Nomura, Y. "The Vending Machine: Japan's Ultimate Convenience Store," *Kansai Forum*, 1994, 22–26.

8. Shirouzu, N. "For Coca-Cola in Japan, Things Go Better With Milk," *Wall Street Journal*, Jan. 20, 1997, B-1.

9. Japanese Franchise Chain Association, 1997.

10. *Nikkei Business*, 672 (Jan. 11, 1993), quoted in Itoh, M. "The Structure and Function of the Distribution System: The Japanese Case," Conference on Market Economy, Jan. 21–22, 1993, 83.

11. "Keiretsu Supplier System Changing," *Focus Japan* 23.11 (Nov. 1996), 3.

12. Shill, W. E., T. Guild, and Y. Yamaguchi. "Cracking Japanese Markets," *McKinsey Quarterly*, 1995 (3), 35.

13. "It Requires Courage, Money and Patience: An Interview with Rainer Jahn," *The JAMA Forum*, 14:1, Oct. 1995.

Chapter Twelve

1. Ono, Y. "Will Good Housekeeping Translate Into Japanese?" *Wall Street Journal*, Dec. 30, 1997, B-1.

2. Kishi, N. and D. Russell. *Successful Gaijin in Japan*. Lincolnwood, Ill.: NTC Business Books, 1996, 315–333.

3. *Nihon Keizai Shimbun*, Mar. 31, 1998, 11.

4. "Eddie Bauer Japan—Expertise Combined Trading House Mobility a la U.S.," *Nihon Ryutsu Shinbun*, Apr. 7, 1998.

5. Ryutsu Shinbun, Nov. 1, 1994.

6. *Tokyo Shimbun*, July 12, 1996, reprinted in *Japan Times*, July 13, 1996, 18.

7. Okimoto, D. I. *Between MITI and the Market: Japanese Industrial Policy for High Technology*. Stanford, CA: Stanford University Press, 1989, 14–15.

8. Japan Credit Industry Association, 1993.

Chapter Thirteen

1. Miller, K. L. "Listening to Shoppers' Voices," *Business Week/Reinventing America 1992*, 69.

2. Koyama, S. "The Impact of Just-In-Time Distribution On Marketing Information Strategies,"

3. Johansson, J. K. and I. Nonaka. "Market Research—The Japanese Way." *Harvard Business Review*, May–June 1987, 16–22.

4. Johansson, J. K. and I. Nonaka. "Market Research—The Japanese Way." *Harvard Business Review*, May–June 1987, 16–22.

5. Asano, K. "Japan's Distribution System Information Network," *The Japanese Distribution System: Opportunities & Obstacles, Structures & Practices*, edited by M. R. Czinkota and M. Kotabe. Chicago: Probus Publishing, 1993.

Index

A

advertising: "big bang," 221–22; celebrities featured in, 212; comparative, 132–33, 219–20; cultural differences in, 207–17; diverse approaches in, 222–24; entry opportunities in, 226; expenditures on, 198; failure to pre-test, 277–78; families featured in, 214, 215; generation gap featured in, 214–16; global campaigns, 226; growth of, 136, 222–23; harmony with nature reflected in, 209; humor used in, 217, 219; images used in, 207–15; in Japan and Asia, 224–26; increased spending on, 222–23; individualism featured in, 214–16; Internet, 232, 244; length of, 216, 226; long-running campaigns, 216; marketing, 21; message, 204–7, 217–19, 225; mood, 204–7, 217–19, 225; new rules of, 203–27; new products, 212; online, 232, 244; preferred to sales promotions, 197; seasons featured in, 209; seniors featured in, 214; structural differences in,

216; tailoring, 225; values reflected in, 38, 40–42; Western approaches applied to, 225–26; word of mouth, 216–17. *See also* advertising agencies; advertising industry

advertising agencies: differences with clients, 221–22, 287; domestic mergers of, 222; foreign investment in, 221–22; foreign, 110; foreign, opportunities for, 21

advertising industry: concentration of, 220–21; in Japan, 219–24

Afternoon Tea, 94

AIG, 21

Ajinomoto, 118, 155–56, 175–78, 225, 257, 281–82

All Nippon Airways (ANA), 269–70

Allergen, 99

alliance strategies, 115–20

AMC, 111

America Online (AOL), 239

American Malls International (AMI), 60

Amway, 94

Aoyama Shoji, 183–84